Communications in Computer and Information Science

2175

Editorial Board Members

Joaquim Filipe ⓘ, *Polytechnic Institute of Setúbal, Setúbal, Portugal*
Ashish Ghosh ⓘ, *Indian Statistical Institute, Kolkata, India*
Lizhu Zhou, *Tsinghua University, Beijing, China*

Rationale

The CCIS series is devoted to the publication of proceedings of computer science conferences. Its aim is to efficiently disseminate original research results in informatics in printed and electronic form. While the focus is on publication of peer-reviewed full papers presenting mature work, inclusion of reviewed short papers reporting on work in progress is welcome, too. Besides globally relevant meetings with internationally representative program committees guaranteeing a strict peer-reviewing and paper selection process, conferences run by societies or of high regional or national relevance are also considered for publication.

Topics

The topical scope of CCIS spans the entire spectrum of informatics ranging from foundational topics in the theory of computing to information and communications science and technology and a broad variety of interdisciplinary application fields.

Information for Volume Editors and Authors

Publication in CCIS is free of charge. No royalties are paid, however, we offer registered conference participants temporary free access to the online version of the conference proceedings on SpringerLink (http://link.springer.com) by means of an http referrer from the conference website and/or a number of complimentary printed copies, as specified in the official acceptance email of the event.

CCIS proceedings can be published in time for distribution at conferences or as post-proceedings, and delivered in the form of printed books and/or electronically as USBs and/or e-content licenses for accessing proceedings at SpringerLink. Furthermore, CCIS proceedings are included in the CCIS electronic book series hosted in the SpringerLink digital library at http://link.springer.com/bookseries/7899. Conferences publishing in CCIS are allowed to use Online Conference Service (OCS) for managing the whole proceedings lifecycle (from submission and reviewing to preparing for publication) free of charge.

Publication process

The language of publication is exclusively English. Authors publishing in CCIS have to sign the Springer CCIS copyright transfer form, however, they are free to use their material published in CCIS for substantially changed, more elaborate subsequent publications elsewhere. For the preparation of the camera-ready papers/files, authors have to strictly adhere to the Springer CCIS Authors' Instructions and are strongly encouraged to use the CCIS LaTeX style files or templates.

Abstracting/Indexing

CCIS is abstracted/indexed in DBLP, Google Scholar, EI-Compendex, Mathematical Reviews, SCImago, Scopus. CCIS volumes are also submitted for the inclusion in ISI Proceedings.

How to start

To start the evaluation of your proposal for inclusion in the CCIS series, please send an e-mail to ccis@springer.com.

Jianping Wang · Bin Xiao · Xuanzhe Liu
Editors

Service Science

CCF 17th International Conference, ICSS 2024
Hong Kong, China, May 11–12, 2024
Revised Selected Papers

Editors
Jianping Wang
City University of Hong Kong
Kowloon, Hong Kong

Bin Xiao
The Hong Kong Polytechnic University
Kowloon, Hong Kong

Xuanzhe Liu
Peking University
Beijing, China

ISSN 1865-0929　　　　　　　ISSN 1865-0937 (electronic)
Communications in Computer and Information Science
ISBN 978-981-97-5759-6　　　ISBN 978-981-97-5760-2 (eBook)
https://doi.org/10.1007/978-981-97-5760-2

© The Editor(s) (if applicable) and The Author(s), under exclusive license
to Springer Nature Singapore Pte Ltd. 2024

This work is subject to copyright. All rights are solely and exclusively licensed by the Publisher, whether the whole or part of the material is concerned, specifically the rights of translation, reprinting, reuse of illustrations, recitation, broadcasting, reproduction on microfilms or in any other physical way, and transmission or information storage and retrieval, electronic adaptation, computer software, or by similar or dissimilar methodology now known or hereafter developed.
The use of general descriptive names, registered names, trademarks, service marks, etc. in this publication does not imply, even in the absence of a specific statement, that such names are exempt from the relevant protective laws and regulations and therefore free for general use.
The publisher, the authors and the editors are safe to assume that the advice and information in this book are believed to be true and accurate at the date of publication. Neither the publisher nor the authors or the editors give a warranty, expressed or implied, with respect to the material contained herein or for any errors or omissions that may have been made. The publisher remains neutral with regard to jurisdictional claims in published maps and institutional affiliations.

This Springer imprint is published by the registered company Springer Nature Singapore Pte Ltd.
The registered company address is: 152 Beach Road, #21-01/04 Gateway East, Singapore 189721, Singapore

If disposing of this product, please recycle the paper.

Preface

This volume contains the papers from the CCF 17th International Conference on Service Science (CCF ICSS 2024). The conference was hosted by Hong Kong Polytechnic University. CCF ICSS is an annual academic event directed by the Technical Committee of Services Computing, China Computer Federation, China. It is also one of the top events of the service science community in China. ICSS features a unique mix of academic, industrial, and cross-discipline topics, and provides a platform for the presentation and exchange of research results and practical experiences as well as educational development in serviceology. ICSS aims to bridge the perspectives of researchers and the needs of practitioners.

This conference attracted 21 paper submissions. After the hard work of the Program Committee, 14 papers were accepted to appear in the conference proceedings, with an acceptance rate of 66.7%. The paper review process followed a single-blind principle. All submitted papers were first reviewed by the committee to confirm whether they met the requirements such as word count and page limit. Only qualified papers entered the subsequent review process. Each paper was reviewed by 3–4 reviewers, and all reviewers needed to reach a consensus and provide a final review score. Finally, papers were accepted in order of review score from highest to lowest. The accepted papers cover a wide range of areas related to service science and service computing.

We would like to thank all the Program Committee members, 108 coming from 71 institutes, for their hard work in completing the review tasks. Their diverse expertise in each individual research area has helped us to create an exciting program for the conference. Their comments and advice helped the authors to improve the quality of their papers and gain deeper insights. Great thanks should also go to the authors and participants for their tremendous support in making the conference a success. We also thank Springer for their trust and for publishing the proceedings of CCF ICSS 2024.

May 2024

Jianping Wang
Bin Xiao
Xuanzhe Liu

Organization

Steering Committee

Rong Chang	IBM Research Watson, USA
Xiucheng Fan	Fudan University, China
Yushun Fan	Tsinghua University, China
Zhiyong Feng	Tianjin University, China
Yanbo Han	North China University of Technology, China
Keqing He	Wuhan University, China
Ying Huang	Lenovo Group/Peking University, China
Changjun Jiang	Tongji University, China
Hai Jin	Huazhong University of Science and Technology, China
Zhi Jin	Peking University, China
Bing Li	Wuhan University, China
James Spohrer	IBM Global University Programs, USA
Sen Su	Beijing University of Posts and Telecommunications, China
Jun Wei	Chinese Academy of Sciences, China
Zhaohui Wu	Zhejiang University, China
Zhonghai Wu	Peking University, China
Xiaofei Xu	Harbin Institute of Technology, China
Jianwei Yin	Zhejiang University, China
Liang-Jie Zhang	Kingdee Research, China
Jie Zhou	Tsinghua University, China

Honorary Chairs

Xiaofei Xu	Harbin Institute of Technology, China
Jianwei Yin	Zhejiang University, China

General Chairs

Song Guo	Hong Kong University of Science and Technology, China
Zhongjie Wang	Harbin Institute of Technology, China

Program Chairs

Jianping Wang — City University of Hong Kong, China
Bin Xiao — Hong Kong Polytechnic University, China
Xuanzhe Liu — Peking University, China

Organization Chairs

Shiqi Wang — City University of Hong Kong, China
Yutao Ma — Central China Normal University, China
Yingjie Wang — Yantai University, China
Ying Liu — Northeastern University, China
Yang Mo — Hunan University, China

Panel Chairs

Shuiguang Deng — Zhejiang University, China
Huawei Huang — Sun Yat-sen University, China
Bo Han — Hong Kong Baptist University, China

Publicity Chairs

Shangguang Wang — Beijing University of Post and Telecommunications, China
Ping Li — Hong Kong Polytechnic University, China
Nanxi Chen — Shanghai Institute of Microsystem and Information Technology, CAS, China
Haoran Tan — Hunan University, China
Zhicheng Cai — Nanjing University of Science and Technology, China

Publication Chairs

Hongning Dai — Hong Kong Baptist University, China
Zhiying Tu — Harbin Institute of Technology, China
Zhi Yan — Hunan University, China

Technical Program Committee

Ao Zhou	Beijing University of Posts and Telecommunications, China
Baihong Jin	University of California, Berkeley, USA
Bing Li	Wuhan University, China
Bo Yang	Beijing Forestry University, China
Bo Zhang	China University of Mining and Technology, China
Buqing Cao	Hunan University of Science and Technology, China
Chunyan Sang	Chongqing University of Posts and Telecommunications, China
Cong Liu	Shandong University of Technology, China
Deyu Lin	Nanchang University, China
Fei Dai	Yunnan University, China
Guiling Wang	North China University of Technology, China
Guobing Zou	Shanghai University, China
Hang Liu	National University of Singapore, Singapore
Hongji Yang	Bath Spa University, UK
Incheon Paik	University of Aizu, Japan
Jiachi Chen	Monash University, Australia
Jialei Liu	Anyang Normal University, China
Jianmao Xiao	Tianjin University, China
Jie Zhang	Hong Kong Polytechnic University, China
Jifeng Xuan	Wuhan University, China
Jing Fan	Zhejiang University of Technology, China
Jing Li	Hong Kong Polytechnic University, China
Jing Li	Shandong University of Technology, China
Jingcai Guo	Hong Kong Polytechnic University, China
Jinwen Liang	Hong Kong Polytechnic University, China
Jiuyun Xu	China University of Petroleum (East China), China
Jun Jiang	National University of Singapore, Singapore
Junna Zhang	Henan Normal University, China
Kai Ma	Yanshan University, China
Kaizhou Gao	Macau Institute of Systems Engineering, China
Kan Hu	Agency for Science, Technology and Research (A*STAR), Singapore
Keman Huang	Renmin University of China, China
Lei Song	King Mongkut's University of Technology Ladkrabang, Thailand

Li Kuang	Central South University, China
Liang Xu	Swiss Federal Institute of Technology Lausanne, Switzerland
Lianlian Jiang	Agency for Science, Technology and Research (A*STAR), Singapore
Lianyong Qi	China University of Petroleum, China
Lingyan Zhang	Central South University, China
Lizhen Cui	Shangdong University, China
Lu Bai	Agency for Science, Technology and Research (A*STAR), Singapore
Madhuri Siddula	North Carolina A&T State University, USA
Maojiao Ye	Nanyang Technological University, Singapore
Min Gao	Chongqing University, China
Ming Jin	Virginia Tech, USA
Mingwei Zhang	Northeastern University, China
Neng Zhang	Sun Yat-sen University, China
Ning Li	Harbin Institute of Technology, China
Panpan Qi	National University of Singapore, Singapore
Pengcheng Zhang	Hohai University, China
Qian He	Guilin University of Electronic Technology, China
Qiang He	Swinburne University of Technology, Australia
Quan Chen	Guangdong University of Technology, China
Quanwang Wu	Chongqing University, China
Ran Zhang	Nanyang Technological University, Singapore
Ruibing Jin	Agency for Science, Technology and Research (A*STAR) Singapore
Ruoxi Jia	Virginia Tech, USA
S. Kannadhasan	Cheran College of Engineering, India
Samantha Kumara	Sabaragamuawa University of Sri Lanka, Sri Lanka
Shan Gao	Hong Kong Polytechnic University, China
Shen Li	National University of Singapore, Singapore
Shenglin Zhang	Nankai University, China
Shi Dong	Zhoukou Normal University, China
Shizhan Chen	Tianjin University, China
Ting He	Huaqiao University, China
Tong Mo	Peking University, China
Wei Song	Nanjing University of Science and Technology, China
Wei Zhang	University of Adelaide, Australia
Weifeng Pan	Zhejiang Gongshang University, China
Wenchao Xu	Hong Kong Polytechnic University, China

Xianzhi Wang	University of Technology Sydney, Australia
Xiao Ma	Beijing University of Posts and Telecommunications, China
Xiao Xue	Tianjin University, China
Xiaolong Xu	Nanjing University of Information Science and Technology, China
Xiaoping Li	Southeast University, China
Xiaoyi Pang	Hong Kong University of Science and Technology, China
Xingjian Lu	East China University of Science and Technology, China
Xiuqin Xu	National University of Singapore, Singapore
Xuyang Teng	Hangzhou Dianzi University, China
Yan Hong	Soochow University, China
Yan Huang	Kennesaw State University, USA
Yanchun Sun	Peking University, China
Yanmei Zhang	Central University of Finance and Economics, China
Yifang Yin	Agency for Science, Technology and Research (A*STAR), Singapore
Yilong Yang	Beihang University, China
Ying Liu	Northeastern University, China
Ying Zhang	Northwestern Polytechnical University, China
Yingjie Wang	Yantai University, China
Yipeng Pang	Nanyang Technological University, Singapore
Yong Xie	Qinghai University, China
Yuanlong Cao	Jiangxi Normal University, China
Yucong Duan	Hunan University, China
Yueshen Xu	Xidian University, China
Yunni Xia	Chongqing University, China
Yutao Ma	Central China Normal University, China
Yuxin Su	Sun Yat-sen University, China
Yuxun Zhou	University of California, Berkeley, USA
Yuyu Yin	Hangzhou Dianzi University, China
Yuze Huang	Chongqing Jiaotong University, China
Zhenghua Chen	Nanyang Technological University, Singapore
Zhenjiang Dong	Nanjing University of Posts and Telecommunications, China
Zhi Feng	Nanyang Technological University, Singapore
Zhicheng Cai	Nanjing University of Science and Technology, China
Zhiying Tu	Harbin Institute of Technology, China
Zhuofeng Zhao	North China University of Technology, China

Zhuojun Duan   James Madison University, USA
Zibing Zheng   Sun Yat-sen University, China
Zichuan Liu   Nanyang Technological University, Singapore
Zigui Jiang   Sun Yat-sen University, China

Contents

Cloud Service and Edge Service

FIPO: Software-Defined Packet Scheduling Primitive for Time-Sensitive Networking 3
   Shang Liu, Shuai Gao, Jia Chen, Xu Huang, Dongsheng Qian, and Chenxi Liao

Multi-stage Pricing Mechanism in Duopoly Computation Markets 14
   Pengyang Chen, Quyuan Wang, Jiadi Liu, Ying Wang, and Zhiwei Guo

Electricity Cost Minimization for Workflows Scheduling in Geo-Distributed Data Centers 30
   He Zhang, Yueyou Zhang, Shuang Wang, and Jixiang Lu

DRT: A Deterministic Computing and Network Resources Tradeoff Mechanism for Holographic-Type Communication 46
   Xu Huang, Jia Chen, Deyun Gao, Jingjing Liu, Chenxi Liao, Dongsheng Qian, and Shang Liu

Knowledge-Inspired Service

The State of Charge Predication of Lithium-Ion Battery Using Contrastive Learning 63
   Yifeng Xiong, Ting He, Yingzhe Mao, Wenlong Zhu, and Yongxin Liao

A Feature Dataset of Microservices-Based Systems 73
   Weipan Yang, Bingyu Song, Yongchao Xing, Yiming Lyu, Huihui Cui, Zhihao Liang, and Zhiying Tu

Crawling and Exploring RESTful Web APIs from RapidAPI 88
   Wen Li, Hongshuai Ren, Yamei Nie, Zihao Liu, Guosheng Kang, Jianxun Liu, and Zhenlian Peng

Trustworthy Services

A Trustworthy Service Transaction Framework for Privacy Protection 107
   Ziyu Li, Tong Mo, Weiping Li, and Zhiying Tu

Towards Efficient Backdoor Attacks Against Federated Self-supervised
Learning as a Service Through Intra-Union Aggregation 122
    *Shuchi Wu, Chuan Ma, Kang Wei, Ming Ding, Jiyun Yang,
and Yuwen Qian*

AMFiD: Attention Mechanism Based Deep Forgery Face Image Detection
for Fintech Regulation 136
    *Shijing Hu, Hengqi Guo, Jing Liu, Mingyu Gu, Zhihui Lu, Jirui Yang,
Yuan Deng, and Qiang Duan*

Service Application

Reservoir Flood Prediction Service Based on Seq2seq Model 153
    Lincong Liu, Shijun Liu, and Li Pan

Optimization Algorithm for Emission Reduction Schemes Based
on Carbon Footprint Prediction 174
    Hongliang Sun, Feifei Wang, Meng Wang, Jinlan Liu, and Qiao Guan

CCRisk: Automated Risk Detection on Heterogeneous Consortium Chains
for Supply Chain Finance 188
    *Junxiong Lin, Ruijun Deng, Mingyu Gu, Jing Liu, Zhihui Lu,
Yubing Bao, Sheng Mao, and Qiang Duan*

Wiki2GH: A Recommendation Service to Link Software Engineering
Knowledge to Practical Development 203
    Yuqi Zhou, Yanchun Sun, Jiawei Wu, Jiaqi Zhang, and Gang Huang

Author Index 221

Cloud Service and Edge Service

FIPO: Software-Defined Packet Scheduling Primitive for Time-Sensitive Networking

Shang Liu[1], Shuai Gao[1], Jia Chen[1,2(✉)], Xu Huang[1], Dongsheng Qian[1], and Chenxi Liao[1]

[1] National Engineering Research Center for Advanced Network Technologies, School of Electronic and Information Engineering, Beijing Jiaotong University, Beijing 100044, China
chenjia@bjtu.edu.cn
[2] Peng Cheng Laboratory, Shenzhen 518055, China

Abstract. Software-Defined Networking (SDN) improves the flexibility of the network by separating the data plane and the control plane, bringing revolutionary changes to the network architecture. However, with the development of metaverse as well as holographic technology, applications require the network to provide different levels of deterministic transmission guarantees including data rate, delay, and jitter. In addition, these deterministic requirements may also change over time. This demands the network to have diverse deterministic transmission capabilities on the one hand, and to flexibly and quickly switch deterministic transmission mechanisms according to the application requirements on the other hand. In this paper, we propose a new software-defined packet scheduling primitive, First-In-Pick-Out (FIPO). FIPO integrates SDN with Time-Sensitive Networking (TSN) to achieve programmable deterministic transmission. FIPO can express existing TSN scheduling algorithms, and is flexible enough to support future algorithms. Furthermore, based on FIPO we design a software-defined packet scheduling prototype system, which can support flexible switching of diverse deterministic transmission mechanisms. The experimental results show that the prototype system is able to correctly express diverse deterministic scheduling algorithms and quickly respond to changes in network requirements, reducing configuration time by 60% compared to NETCONF.

Keywords: Programmable Data Plane · Programmable Scheduling · Software-Defined Networking · Time-Sensitive Networking

1 Introduction

Traditional network devices have greatly undermined the development of the networking field because they utilize specialized hardware that creates a tight coupling between the control plane and data plane [1]. Software-Defined Networking (SDN) technology separates the control plane from the device, forming a centralized controller that operates a general set of processing primitives within the switch. The controller constructs processing primitives in the data plane into pipeline through a unified interface to express complex network functions, providing dynamic configurability for the network.

However, SDN lacks programmable capabilities in traffic management and consequently cannot provide dynamically configurable deterministic packet scheduling [2]. This leads to limited applications of SDN in many fields, such as in metaverse and holographic communications where dynamic end-to-end delay guarantees are required. In distance instruction, the delay requirement for the instructor to correct a trainee's movement is 1–10 ms; the delay requirement for the trainee to observe a movement demonstration is 1–100 ms; less than 2 ms are required for remote machine operation and less than 50 ms delay is required for remote machine monitoring [3]. Moreover, for the same use case, the delay requirements may vary with the state of the interaction. Therefore, how to fulfill dynamically configurable deterministic transmission in SDN has become an important research direction.

To ensure quality of service for time-sensitive applications, the IEEE 802.1 TSN Task Force proposed Time-Sensitive Networking (TSN) and developed a series of related packet scheduling algorithms. Credit Based Shaper (CBS) [4], Time-Aware Shaping (TAS) [5], and Cyclic Queuing and Forwarding (CQF) [6], etc. are few named here as examples. On the combination of TSN and SDN, Nayak et al. proposed Time-Sensitive Software-Defined Networks (TSSDN) [7], which implements the use of SDN controllers for scheduling time-sensitive flows. Hackel et al. evaluated the feasibility and benefits of combining SDN with TSN in in-vehicular communication [8]. Xue et al. implemented cross-domain deterministic interconnection of multiple networks by scheduling time-sensitive flows through SDN controller [9]. Gerhard et al. proposed the concept and architecture of Software-Defined Flow Reservation (SDFR) [10], which realizes the configuration of time-sensitive flows over the OpenFlow protocol. However, the above TSSDN-based research approach focuses on configuring and scheduling time-sensitive flows using SDN controller. At the data plane, non-TSN devices coexist with TSN devices. This leads to the fact that non-TSN devices could become a bottleneck in improving the quality of deterministic transmission services in the network. For example, it is unable to schedule flow for CBS standards in non-TSN devices and fails to support diverse deterministic mechanisms. Therefore, existing work mainly considers the implementation of a limited number of deterministic transmission algorithms, and cannot fulfill diverse deterministic transmission mechanisms. In addition, existing work mainly uses NETCONF protocol to configure time-sensitive flows, which has a large configuration delay.

This paper strives to fulfill diverse deterministic transport mechanisms in SDN as well as fast configuration capabilities for time-sensitive flows. The main contribution of this paper is to propose the First-In-Pick-Out (FIPO) software-defined packet scheduling primitive and system architecture. FIPO allocates an eligible time property to each packet, and controls the packet to leave the queue at the proper time slot through the eligible time, thus expressing diverse deterministic scheduling algorithms. Based on FIPO, we design a software-defined packet scheduling prototype system, which provides a unified configuration of the data plane and can respond quickly to the changes in network requirements. Finally, this paper implements the FIPO primitive on the Behavior Model Version 2 (BMV2) software switch to experimentally verification the software-defined packet scheduling prototype system. Experimental results show that the prototype system can correctly express diverse deterministic transmission mechanisms and has a faster configuration time than NETCONF.

2 Related Works

In this section, we introduce the TSN standard on packet scheduling algorithms, and the related work in the field of programable packet scheduling.

2.1 TSN Standards on Packet Scheduling

Flows in time-sensitive networks can be categorized into three types: time-triggered flow (TT), audio/video bridged flow (AVB) and best-effort flow (BE). TT flow is periodic and urgent flow with the highest priority and strict time limits. AVB flow refers to flow that requires guaranteed bandwidth and delay, such as a voice call. The best-effort flow has a minimum delay requirement and can be discarded if necessary.

For different flows in time-sensitive network, the IEEE 802.1 TSN Task Force has standardized several packet scheduling algorithms. To solve the problem of transmission service quality guarantee for audio and video flow, Credit Based Shaper (CBS) has been proposed. CBS allocates the transmission bandwidth of data flows by accumulating credits. The credit increases at idle velocity (v_{idle}) while the packet waiting in the queue and decreases at send velocity (v_{send}) while the packet being sent. To transmission of periodic time-sensitive flow, Time-Aware Shaping (TAS) has been proposed. The TAS allocates time slots for each TT flow to generate a global Gate Control List (GCL) [11]. GCL guarantees that each time slot can only be used by one TT flow, so there is no need for queuing within the time slot, which can effectively reduce delay. However, TAS requires all terminals and network devices to adopt 802.1AS for network-wide clock synchronization [12]. To solve the problem of complex TAS configuration, Cyclic Queuing and Forwarding (CQF) was proposed. CQF schedules the flows at a fine-grained queue level, allowing multiple the flows to be transmitted in the same time slot, thus improving network bandwidth utilization.

2.2 Programmable Packet Scheduling

In the data plane, packet scheduling can easily become a bottleneck limiting the programmability of SDN. Most packet scheduling algorithms are tightly coupled with hardware structures, e.g., in the TSN standard, expressing different scheduling algorithms requires different hardware structures to support them. Thus, the specialized hardware architecture hinders the flexible application of packet scheduling algorithms. Programmable packet scheduling abstracts scheduling algorithms into the order and timing in which packets are scheduled, and expresses diverse scheduling algorithms on the same hardware through scheduling primitives. Scheduling primitives decouple scheduling algorithms from hardware, including Push-In-First-Out (PIFO), Push-In-Extract-Out (PIEO), and Push-In-Pick-Out (PIPO), etc. PIFO sets a customized rank for each packet and decides the order in which the packets should be scheduled based on the rank, to express most of the non-work conserving algorithms [13]. PIEO adds predicates to PIFO, which can further determine the time slot for packet out, and has more expressive power than PIFO [14]. PIPO is optimized for the TSN based on PIEO to reduce the overhead of the scheduling primitive implementation [15]. In this paper, we propose FIPO primitives for SDN that can express diverse deterministic scheduling algorithms.

3 A Software-Defined Packet Scheduling Prototype System Based on FIPO

3.1 Prototype System Architecture

This section introduces the architecture design of the software-defined packet scheduling prototype system based on the FIPO.

The prototype system consists of the control plane and the data plane. The control plane is made up of the TSN controller and the SDN controller. The data plane is composed of FIPO-enabled P4 devices. The prototype system has a fully centralized configuration model, where the TSN controller works as a Centralized User Configuration (CUC) entity and the SDN controller works as a Centralized Network Configuration (CNC) entity. The architecture of the software-defined packet scheduling prototype system based on FIPO is shown in Fig. 1.

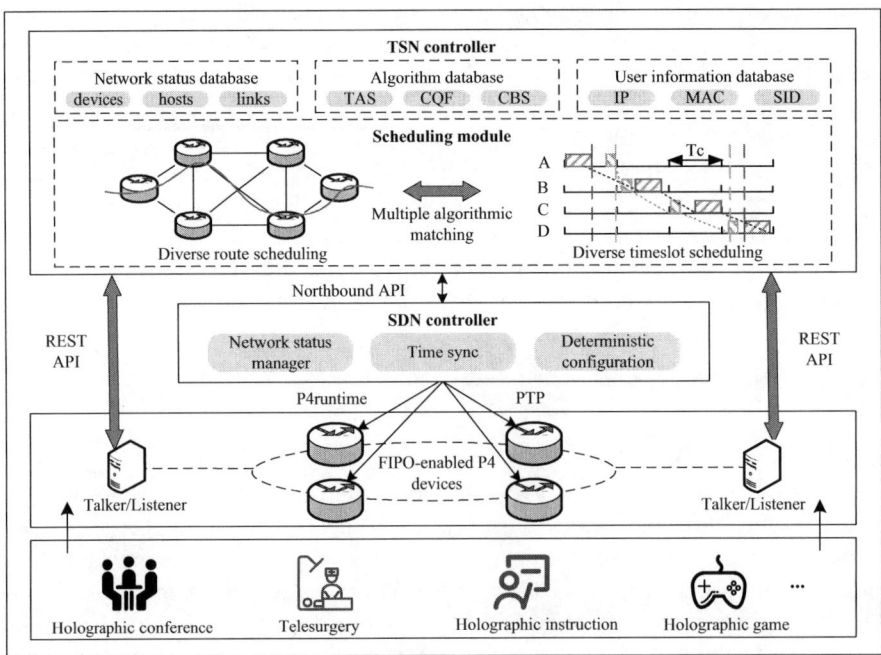

Fig. 1. Software-defined packet scheduling prototype system architecture based on FIPO.

The TSN controller includes a user information database, a network state database, an algorithm database, and a scheduling module. The user information database receives and stores the network service requirements in JSON format from users via REST API. The network state database obtains network state information through the northbound API of the SDN controller. The algorithm database includes the diverse routing and deterministic transmission algorithms, such as TAS, CQF, CBS, etc. The scheduling module matches the appropriate scheduling algorithms in the algorithm database according to the type of user requirements and the network state, implementing flexible online scheduling of routing paths and deterministic transmissions. The TSN controller sends the deterministic transmission scheduling result in JSON format to the SDN controller via the northbound API.

The SDN controller includes a network state manager, a time synchronization module, and a deterministic configuration module. The network status manager is responsible for perceiving and managing information about hosts, P4 devices, and links within the network. The manager perceives the IP and MAC addresses and the activity of hosts within the network by sending ARP protocol requests, and utilizes the P4RUNTIME southbound protocol to perceive and manage information about P4 devices, including device port details, device activity, and device flow table information. LLDP information is sent to P4 devices to perceive information about links within the network. Ultimately, manager completes the perception of the entire network status information. The time synchronization module uses the SDN controller as the primary clock to ensure network-wide time synchronization using Precision Time Protocol (PTP). The deterministic configuration module receives the deterministic transmission scheduling-result from the TSN controller through the northbound API, and translates the scheduling-result into the flow table to be distributed to the P4 devices in the network.

FIPO-enabled P4 devices include pipeline and traffic manager. The pipeline is characterized by the packet parsing, flow table matching, and other features normally found in P4 devices. Traffic manager uses a multi-priority FIPO queue. Packet with deterministic transmission requirement is allocated eligible time and priority in the pipeline according to the flow table. The order and time of packet dequeuing are determined in the traffic manager based on the eligible time and priority, so diverse deterministic scheduling algorithms can be expressed.

3.2 Prototype System Configuration.

This section presents a workflow for completing an end-to-end deterministic transmission service in the prototype system. The interaction workflow involves the TSN controller, the SDN controller, the P4 device, and the talker/listener. The workflow is shown in Fig. 2.

(1) The network state manager of the SDN controller perceives the talker/listener in the network by sending proxy ARP protocol messages. It manages P4 device information by running the P4RUNTIME protocol and obtains network topology information by sending LLDP messages, thus acquiring a comprehensive view of the entire network. The time synchronization module uses PTP to synchronize the time of the P4 device and the TSN controller, and also sends time synchronization requests

to the talker/listener. Based on the result of the request, it determines whether to establish time synchronization for talker/listener.
(2) The talker/listener sends the network service requirement to the TSN controller through the REST API.
(3) When the TSN controller receives a service requirement, it generates a unique service identification (SID) and stores the IP address, delay requirement, bandwidth requirement, etc. in the user information database. The network state database obtains the network state through the SDN controller northbound API. The scheduling module matches appropriate scheduling algorithms in the algorithm database based on service requirements and current network state. The scheduling algorithm integrates route path planning with deterministic transmission. If the scheduling is successful, the TSN controller sends the scheduling result through the SDN controller northbound API. If scheduling fails, the TSN controller returns the result to the talker/listener.
(4) The deterministic configuration module of the SDN controller converts the scheduling result into the flow tables, sends them to the P4 device through the P4RUNTIME protocol, and returns the configuration result.
(5) If the configuration is successful, the talker/listener starts data transmission of the time-sensitive flows. During the system operation, when failure or change occurs in network topology, P4 device will send the fault information to the SDN controller. The SDN controller, in turn, sends reconfiguration requests to the TSN controller to reconfigure user services.

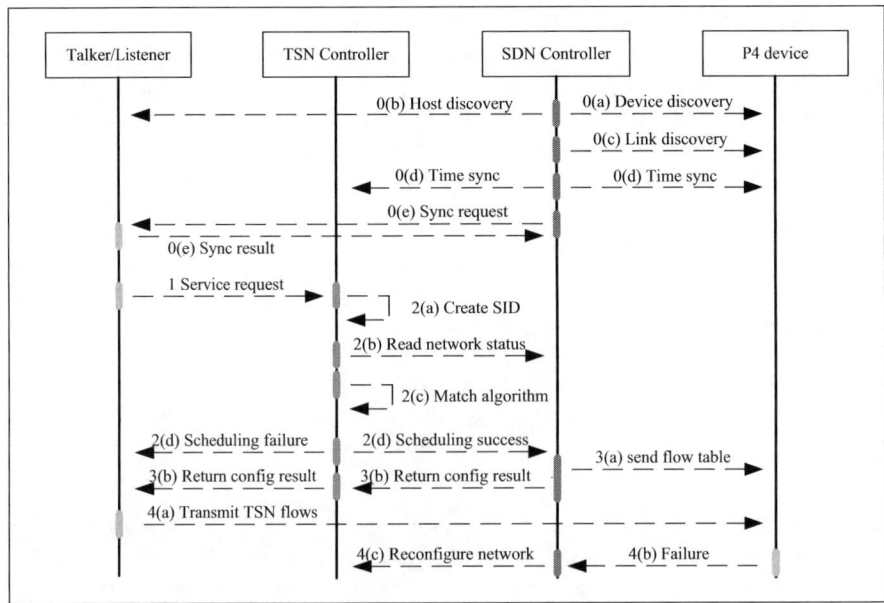

Fig. 2. The workflows of system configuration.

3.3 First-In-Pick-Out

In this section, the implementation of the FIPO primitive in the P4 device is presented.

The FIPO primitive allocates an eligible time property to each packet and queues them in First-In-First-Out (FIFO) order. The eligible time needs to be checked before the packet leaves the queue. If the eligible time is less than the current time, the packet can leave the queue, otherwise it will be blocked. In order to achieve this abstraction, the P4 device needs to be equipped with time synchronization, eligible time property, and support for checking the eligible time in the traffic manager. The architecture of a P4 device supporting the FIPO primitive is shown in Fig. 3. The time synchronization module updates the current time based on the time synchronization frame from the SDN controller. Packet is allocated the eligible time property and priority property at the ingress. Packets enter different priority queues in the traffic manager based on priority property. The traffic manager polls range from the highest priority queue to the lowest priority queue. The comparator will check the eligible time. If the queue is not empty and the packet's eligible time is less than the current time, an out-queue operation is performed and polling starts again from the highest priority queue. At this time, the packet can leave the queue within the promised time slot. If the queue is empty or the eligible time is more than the current time, polling continues. At this time, the time slot promised by the packet has not yet arrived. FIPO uses timestamps to represent time. By default, all packets are allocated a value of 0 for the eligible time property, so the FIPO primitive behaves in the initial state as FIFO.

The FIPO primitive incrementally adds comparator and time synchronization without impacting the original architecture of the P4 pipeline. In terms of complexity, FIPO can be executed in as few clock cycles as possible to keep up with increasing link speeds. In terms of scalability, FIPO supports flexible and programmable operations that can express most packet scheduling algorithms by configuring packet priority and eligible time property. The FIPO allows packets to be quickly checked for eligible time upon leaving the queue, with minimal impact on packet processing delay. However, FIPO requires setting up the comparator and eligible time, which raises the hardware overhead.

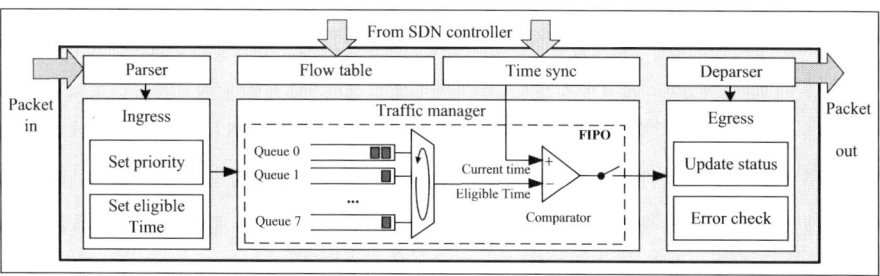

Fig. 3. FIPO-enabled P4 device architecture.

3.4 The Expressiveness of FIPO

In this section, the TAS, CQF, and CBS algorithms are expressed using FIPO-enabled P4 devices.

The key to expressing the TAS scheduling algorithm is to ensure that the packet is sent in the correct time slot. Therefore, it is necessary to set the correct eligible time and the highest priority for the packet. The TSN controller generates a GCL based on user requirement and network status. The SDN controller stores the GCL in the registers of the P4 device. At the P4 device ingress, set the highest priority and corresponding eligible time for the TT flow packet. In the FIPO queue, if the packet's eligible time is less than the current time, the packet can leave the queue in the correct time slot. At the egress of the P4 device, the state of the GCL needs to be updated in order to set the appropriate eligible time for the upcoming next packet. If the TT flow fails to leave the queue at the correct time slot, an incorrect message needs to be sent to the SDN controller. The use of FIPO-enabled P4 devices to express the TAS scheduling algorithm brings the following benefits: 1) Flexibility, which supports incremental updating of the GCL by the SDN controller. 2) Scalability, which supports the use of the TAS algorithm in conjunction with other scheduling algorithms. 3) Stability, which allows the SDN controller to quickly reschedule the TT flow when there are errors in the network.

Expressing the CQF scheduling algorithm requires packets entering the queue to definitely be sent in the next cycle. The SDN controller initializes the cycle length and the start time of the first cycle in the P4 device. For packets entering the P4 device, their eligible time will be assigned as the start time of the next cycle and enter the highest priority queue. At the egress, the algorithm checks the packet. If the packet is not egressing at the correct cycle, an incorrect message will be sent to the SDN controller.

In order to express the CBS scheduling algorithm, it is necessary to ensure that packets can be sent only when credit is nonnegative. At the ingress of the P4 device, the time that each packet has to wait in the queue is calculated and set to the eligible time. And according to the TSN controller scheduling result, the appropriate priority is allocated to the CBS flow. Ideally, no other prioritized traffic will preempt the port, and the packet will be out of the queue at the eligible time. If the preemption time exceeds the eligible time, the credit will be more than zero and the packet will be out of the queue as soon as the preemption is over. After one or more successive leaving the queue, the leaving time of the packet will converge to the ideal state again.

FIPO primitive expand the programmability and expression capabilities of P4 devices, allowing P4 devices to express more types of deterministic transmission algorithms. Multiple types of TT flow and BE flow can be supported for simultaneous transmission in the P4 device. And under the scheduling of the TSN controller, the deterministic transmission mechanism at the data plane can be flexibly scheduled according to the needs of different scenarios.

4 Prototype System Evaluation

This section first describes the implementation of a software-defined packet scheduling prototype system. Then, it verifies the diverse deterministic transmission capabilities and the rapid configuration response of the prototype system. Although, we only use TAS,

CQF and CBS as test cases, the prototype system can express a wider kind of scheduling algorithms.

The prototype system topology is shown in Fig. 4. The system uses ONOS as the SDN controller and uses the JAVA Spring framework to implement the TSN controller. Running the P4 software switch BMv2 on six general-purpose servers constitutes the data plane. Use P4RUNTIME as the southbound API to ONOS and Rest API as the northbound API to ONOS. All devices in the prototype system topology use PTP for time synchronization.

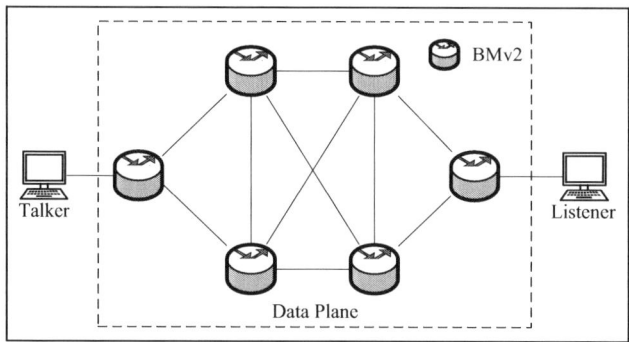

Fig. 4. Test topology.

In the prototype system, TSN scheduling algorithm is implemented for the flow between Talker and Listener. In a scheduling algorithm implementation, first the Talker submits a scheduling request to the TSN controller. Then the TSN controller runs the scheduling algorithm according to the Talker's requirements and the current network state, and the ONOS controller deploys the scheduling commands to the BMv2 switches in the network. Finally, the TSN controller responds the scheduling result to the Talker to complete a TSN scheduling. To accurately test the different types of time-sensitive flow from Talker to Listener in the prototype system topology, in-band telemetry is used to collect test data. Limited by the performance of the BMv2 software switch, the time accuracy of the test results is 0.1 ms.

The end-to-end delay of scheduling TT flows using the FIPO-TAS method and the FIPO-CQF method is tested in the prototype system and compared with the end-to-end delay of BE flows. The end-to-end delay of the TT flows is shown in Fig. 5(a), with 500 times of test data. In the test, the FIPO-TAS route is set up with a total of four hops and a time slot of 1.5 ms per hop, the average transmission delay of 5.99 ms and the maximum delay jitter of 0.4 ms. The FIPO-CQF route is set up with a total of four hops and a cycle of 5 ms, the average transmission delay is 19.51 ms and the maximum delay jitter is 8.6 ms. From the test results, it can be seen that the prototype system has diverse deterministic transmission capabilities, and it can set up end-to-end deterministic guarantees for different service levels according to user requirements.

The occupied bandwidth of AVB flows which are scheduled with FIPO-CBS algorithm is shown in Fig. 5(b). Set the link velocity to 200 KB/s in the test. The idle velocity (v_{idle}) is set to 30 KB/s, 40 KB/s, 50 KB/s, and 100 KB/s via the ONOS controller. Set the sending velocity (v_{send}) to 170 KB/s, 160 KB/s, 150 KB/s and 100 KB/s respectively. From the test results, it can be seen that the bandwidth of data flow can be flexibly scheduled online according to the flow table configuration of the ONOS controller, which proves that the prototype system has the ability of flexible deterministic transmission configuration.

The time of TSN algorithms configured using the ONOS controller is shown in Fig. 5(c). The test results show that the configuration completion time using P4RUNTIME as the unified interface in the prototype system is about 5 ms, while the configuration completion time using NETCONF is about 20 ms. The prototype system reduces the configuration time by 60% compared to other NETCONF-based deterministic transmission systems. This result demonstrates that the software-defined packet scheduling prototype system has fast configuration response capability. With fast configuration, the prototype system enables globally optimal resource scheduling in real time.

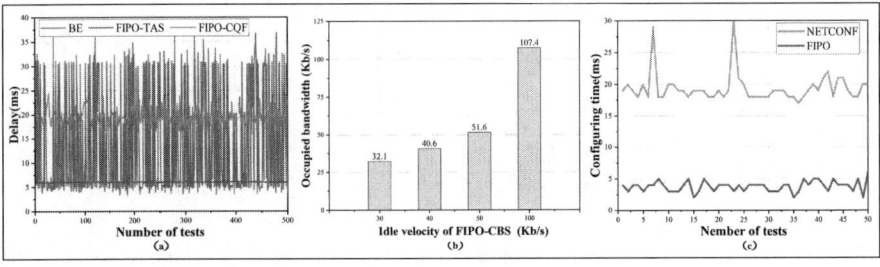

Fig. 5. Measurement results: a) TT flows end-to-end delay; b) AVB flows occupied bandwidth; c) Deterministic configuring time.

5 Conclusion

In this paper, we propose FIPO, a software-defined packet scheduling primitive, which can provide diverse deterministic transmission mechanisms as well as fast configuration response capabilities for networks. The FIPO can express diverse TSN scheduling algorithms without changing the hardware structure. Moreover, the software-defined packet scheduling prototype system based on FIPO has fast and flexible scheduling capability. However, limited by the performance of the P4 software switch BMv2, the time accuracy of the prototype system is only 0.1 ms. In future work, we will explore new hardware architectures to further improve the performance and accuracy of the P4 programmable switching device.

Acknowledgments. This work is supported by the National Key R&D Program of China 2023YFB2904400, the Major Key Project of PCL under grant No. PCL2023A06, Fundamental Research Funds for the Central Universities under grant no. 2023JBGP003, Nature and Science Foundation of China under grant no. 62394321, 62072030, 92167204.

References

1. Kreutz, D., Ramos, F.M.V., Esteves Verissimo, P., Esteve Rothenberg, C., Azodolmolky, S., Uhlig, S.: Software-defined networking: a comprehensive survey. In: Proceedings of the IEEE, vol. 103, no. 1, pp. 14–76 (Jan. 2015)
2. Bifulco, R., Retvari, G.: A Survey on the programmable data plane: abstractions, architectures, and open problems. In: 2018 IEEE 19th International Conference on High Performance Switching and Routing (HPSR), Bucharest, Romania, pp. 1–7. IEEE (Jun. 2018)
3. Shen, X., et al.: Toward immersive communications in 6G. Front. Comput. Sci. **4**, 1068478 (2023)
4. IEEE Standard for local and metropolitan area networks - virtual bridged local area networks amendment 12: forwarding and queuing enhancements for time-sensitive streams. In: IEEE Std 802.1Qav-2009 (Amendment to IEEE Std 802.1Q-2005), vol., no., pp.C1–72 (5 Jan. 2010)
5. IEEE Standard for local and metropolitan area networks -- bridges and bridged networks - amendment 25: enhancements for scheduled traffic. In: IEEE Std 802.1Qbv-2015 (Amendment to IEEE Std 802.1Q-2014 as amended by IEEE Std 802.1Qca-2015, IEEE Std 802.1Qcd-2015, and IEEE Std 802.1Q-2014/Cor 1–2015), vol., no., pp.1–57 (18 March 2016)
6. IEEE Standard for Local and metropolitan area networks--Bridges and Bridged Networks--Amendment 29: Cyclic Queuing and Forwarding. In: IEEE 802.1Qch-2017 (Amendment to IEEE Std 802.1Q-2014 as amended by IEEE Std 802.1Qca-2015, IEEE Std 802.1Qcd(TM)-2015, IEEE Std 802.1Q-2014/Cor 1–2015, IEEE Std 802.1Qbv-2015, IEEE Std 802.1Qbu-2016, IEEE Std 802.1Qbz-2016, and IEEE Std 802.1Qci-2017), vol., no., pp.1–30 (28 June 2017)
7. Nayak, N.G., Dürr, F., Rothermel, K.: Time-sensitive Software-defined Network (TSSDN) for real-time applications. In: Proceedings of the 24th International Conference on Real-Time Networks and Systems, Brest France: ACM, Oct. 2016, pp. 193–202
8. Hackel, T., Meyer, P., Korf, F., Schmidt, T.C.: Software-defined networks supporting time-sensitive in-vehicular communication. In: 2019 IEEE 89th Vehicular Technology Conference (VTC2019-Spring), Kuala Lumpur, Malaysia, pp. 1–5. IEEE (Apr. 2019)
9. Xue, J., Shou, G., Li, H., Liu, Y.: Enabling deterministic communications for end-to-end connectivity with software-defined time-sensitive networking. IEEE Netw. **36**(2), 34–40 (2022)
10. Gerhard, T., Kobzan, T., Blocher, I., Hendel, M.: Software-defined flow reservation: configuring IEEE 802.1Q time-sensitive networks by the use of software-defined networking. In: 2019 24th IEEE International Conference on Emerging Technologies and Factory Automation (ETFA), Zaragoza, Spain, pp. 216–223. IEEE (Sep. 2019)
11. Serna Oliver, R., Craciunas, S.S., Steiner, W.: IEEE 802.1QBV gate control list synthesis using array theory encoding. In: 2018 IEEE Real-Time and Embedded Technology and Applications Symposium (RTAS), Porto, pp. 13–24. IEEE (Apr. 2018)
12. IEEE Standard for local and metropolitan area networks--timing and synchronization for time-sensitive applications. In: IEEE STD 802.1AS-2020 (Revision of IEEE Std 802.1AS-2011), vol., no., pp.1–421 (19 June 2020)
13. Sivaraman, A., et al.: Programmable packet scheduling at line rate. In: Proceedings of the 2016 ACM SIGCOMM Conference, Florianopolis Brazil: ACM, pp. 44–57 (Aug. 2016)
14. Shrivastav, V.: Fast, scalable, and programmable packet scheduler in hardware. In: Proceedings of the ACM Special Interest Group on Data Communication, Beijing China: ACM, pp. 367–379 (Aug. 2019)
15. Zhang, C., et al.: PIPO: Efficient programmable scheduling for time sensitive networking. In: 2021 IEEE 29th International Conference on Network Protocols (ICNP), Dallas, TX, USA, pp. 1–11. IEEE (Nov. 2021)

Multi-stage Pricing Mechanism in Duopoly Computation Markets

Pengyang Chen[1], Quyuan Wang[1](✉), Jiadi Liu[1], Ying Wang[2], and Zhiwei Guo[1]

[1] Chongqing Key Laboratory of Intelligent Perception and BlockChain Technology, Chongqing Technology and Business University, Chongqing 400067, China
{qywang,liujiadi,zwguo}@ctbu.edu.cn

[2] College of Computer and Information Science, College of Software, Southwest University, Chongqing 400710, China
waying95@swu.edu.cn

Abstract. A new generation of computing paradigms has been proposed to facilitate people's daily lives, and there is a lot of literature on resource allocation in these paradigms to enhance the user experience. It is also essential to investigate how to incentive users to participate in these computing paradigms to share their surplus resources. In this paper, we formulate multi-stage profit-maximizing optimization problems in duopoly computation market considering consumer value, provider reputation, Bandwagon Effect, and consumer heterogeneity from an economic perspective. In the pre-sale phase we propose the Demand Priority Pricing Algorithm (DPPA) algorithm to help providers find optimal pre-sale prices. For the formal sales phase, we design the Community Proportion Prediction Algorithm (CPPA) to predict key parameters and the Incremental Priority Pricing Algorithm (IPPA) to help providers choose pricing schemes. Finally, experimental results show that our model describes market laws well and our algorithms assist providers in finding profit-maximizing pricing schemes for fair and stable markets.

Keywords: Multi-stage price · Bandwagon Effect · Duopoly computation market

1 Introduction

In the era of computational intelligence, computing paradigms such as Edge Computing (EC), Federated Learning (FL), and the Internet of Everything

---

This work is supported by the National Natural Science Foundation of China (No.62106029), the Natural Science Foundation of Chongqing (No. CSTB2023NSCQ-MSX0533), the Science and Technology Research Program of Chongqing Municipal Education Commission Grant (Nos.KJQN202200801, KJQN202200817), the Educational Reform Project of Chongqing Technology and Business University (Nos. 2023066, 2023068), and the High Talent Research Start-up Project of Chongqing Technology and Business University (Nos.2256001, 2256002).

© The Author(s), under exclusive license to Springer Nature Singapore Pte Ltd. 2024
J. Wang et al. (Eds.): ICSS 2024, CCIS 2175, pp. 14–29, 2024.
https://doi.org/10.1007/978-981-97-5760-2_2

(IoE) have significantly improved computing performance and facilitated daily life [2,9]. A great deal of work has been done to improve service performance from a resource allocation and optimization perspective with significant results [4,6,21,22]. However, from an economic market perspective, if the provision and solicitation of services are viewed as transactional behaviors, much of the work assumes that service providers are voluntary and non-competitive, which is contrary to the laws of real life.

Service providers expect to make a profit from their services, and the market is competitive because of consumer choice. Price becomes the bridge between providers and consumers. In other words, the pricing mechanism plays a crucial role in the trading behavior of buyers and sellers. Reasonable pricing can attract consumers to enhance competitiveness while generating significant revenues. Much of the literature develops a discussion of pricing models, but there is some work that ignores market characteristics such as dynamics and continuity [7,8,18].

In order to improve product quality and to help sellers with pricing through sales data, many newborn products and services will accomplish these goals by creating a pre-sale stage [13,20]. In the pre-sale stage, sellers often attract consumers to buy products at a relatively low price, and optimize product services by collecting consumer feedback. At the same time, these users are called original users, and have a higher chance of continuing to support the product during the formal sales stage. We introduce this sales paradigm into computing services to show the dynamics of the market through changes in provider reputation and consumer valuation at different stages, and to help providers develop optimal pricing strategies to maximize profit. At the same time, we explore the impact of accumulated subscribers and pre-sale pricing on the pricing in the formal sales stage to explore the continuity of the market.

In a well-designed duopoly computation market, with a goal of maximizing profits, service providers need to decide how to price their services at different stages. Additionally, the pricing mechanism also requires motivating more providers to join in computation market for better performance improvement. To summarize, our contributions are summarized as follows.

- We formulate the profits maximization problem for services providers at different stages while considering service providers' reputation, consumers' valuation, the Bandwagon Effect. In order to mimic consumers' consumption behaviors in certain specific scenarios, we also introduce the standardized Logistic Function to portray the consumer choice probability.
- We design Demand Priority Pricing Algorithm (DPPA) to achieve optimal prices of providers, where the most popular provider in the pre-selection phase has a first-move advantage. To overcome the difficulty of global information unawareness, we utilize multi-layer neural network models to help consumers predict the proportion of consumers in the same community. Finally, we design the price adjustment strategies for the formal sales phase to help providers maximize profits.

– Extensive experiments are conducted to evaluate performance. We compare profits, market demand, and optimal pricing at different stages for providers with different reputation. We also explore the impact of pre-sale pricing on formal sales pricing for the same provider. The experimental results show that the model we constructed can reflect the laws of the market, and the pricing algorithm we designed can maximize the provider's profit while satisfying the consumer's demand, and at the same time the algorithm can effectively guarantee the market fairness and stability.

The rest of the paper is organized as follows. Section 2 introduces related research, and Sect. 3 elucidates our system model. Then, Sect. 4 details the optimization problem and the price adjustment strategies are proposed. After that, the validation results are presented in Sect. 5. Finally, Sect. 6 concludes this paper.

2 Related Works

In related research, some research has begun to explore the application of multi-stage pricing strategies in markets.The authors analyze the dynamics of multi-stage market mechanisms for Physical Transmission Rights in [15]. Ma et al. shed light on seller-buyer interactions, emphasizing seller reputations and pricing competition [14]. In [19], they propose a pricing mechanism for multi-stage electricity markets that incentive efficient dispatch under uncertainty.

Meanwhile there are other scholars who have turned their attention to the impact of network effects on computational markets. Dou et al. explore the dynamic competition between platform-based products with two-sided network effects, highlighting the complex interplay between these products [5]. Moreover, Bondi develops a dynamic model elucidating consumer behaviors in response to product reviews [3], while Li et al. study pro-social motivations, such as altruism, collectivism, and egalitarianism [12]. However, it is worth noting that there are few studies on the "Bandwagon Effect" in the existing literature.

In duopoly markets, Jiao et al. propose a decentralized dynamic cooperation mechanism between two e-hailing platforms, aiming to mitigate market fragmentation and optimize pricing [10]. And Bany et al. discuss the profit maximization problem within a duopoly model of competing service providers using Antlion Optimization, offering valuable insights into the dynamics of duopoly markets [1]. In [16], the author examine the competition between mobile operators in a duopoly market from a game theory perspective.

In summary, the aforementioned research provides a foundational understanding of multi-stage pricing, network effects, and duopoly computing markets. Nevertheless, there remains a gap in characterizing consumer behavior in the purchasing process. By integrating economic principles, consumer behavior, and Bandwagon Effect, our research seeks to facilitate a comprehensive understanding of market dynamics and then design the effective pricing algorithms.

3 System Model

In this paper, we consider a duopoly computing market, where the intelligent computation service providers with different reputations price their services in multiple stages. In the intelligent computation market, computation services are treated as trading objects, service providers provide users with diverse resources such as storage space, computation capacity, data, and communication, and users pay for the purchased services. In the case of federated learning, for example, edge devices provide data and computation capacity to improve the accuracy of global training while protecting data privacy and task publishers pay for such services.

Like most nascent product services, we have categorized service provider pricing into the pre-sales stage and the formal sales stage, and the pricing scheme and demand data of itself and its competitors in the pre-sales stage will influence the pricing strategy in the formal sales stage. We denote the price during the pre-sale stage as p^p, and correspondingly denote the price of the formal sales stage as p^f.

To quantitatively analyze the providers' profit, we denote the standardized unit cost of providing computing services as c. To measure consumer satisfaction, we use valuation as the consumer demand for services, specifically, the valuation represents the consumer's expectation of the service or the maximum price that consumers are willing to pay for a product psychologically. Consumer expectations of service change at different stages of sale, during the pre-sale stage, consumer values the computing services as v^p, while during the formal sales stage, their valuation is represented by v^f.

We consider the reputation value of the service provider and the Bandwagon Effect to design the utility function of the consumer in order to analyze the movement of the market equilibrium, specifically the relationship between the service providers' price strategy and consumer choice.

3.1 The Trading Process

As the transaction proceeds, consumers tend to have a better understanding of the product during the formal sales stage compared to the pre-sale stage, and typically have lower expectations, as evidenced by a lower maximum price they are willing to pay. In other words, consumers will have a lower valuation in the formal sales stage generally. In this paper, we use value transfer coefficient α to represent the decay of consumer's value. The relationship between the valuations of the two stages is as follows:

$$v^f = \alpha v^p \quad (0 < \alpha \leq 1). \tag{1}$$

In addition, consumer value performance (expectations of services) varies for different providers. In this paper, we consider service providers with different reputation, which are related to their service quality, after-sales service, etc. In the specific duopoly scenario, we assume that A is the service provider with a high reputation, and the relationship between the reputation of the two providers is as follows:

$$v_B^p = \beta v_A^p \quad (0 < \beta \leq 1), \tag{2}$$

where β is the reputation decay factor, which reflects the reputation's relationship between the duopoly. In summary, Table 1 shows the value that consumers place on different providers at different stages of the trading process.

Table 1. Consumer valuation of services at different stages

	High reputation	Low reputation
Pre-sale	v^p	βv^p
Formal sales	αv^p	$\alpha \beta v^p$

3.2 Pre-sale Stage Utility

In a duopoly market, consumer's utility consists of two main components, one of which is referred to as acquisition utility (U_a), which is expressed as the difference between the consumer's expectations and the provider's price after the purchase of a service. Mathematically, the difference between the consumer's value and the provider's price, $v - p$. The other part of the utility benefits from comparisons, called comparative utility (U_c), specifically in the form of price differentials between providers, $p_A - p_B$.

For the consumer, the utility of the pre-sale stage is the sum of the above two parts. The following equation is the consumer's utility for provider A at pre-sale stage:

$$\begin{aligned} U_A^p &= U_{A,a}^p + U_{A,c}^p \\ &= v_A^p - p_A^p + p_B^p - p_A^p, \end{aligned} \tag{3}$$

where p_A^p and p_B^p represent the pre-sale prices of provider A and B, respectively. Similarly, the consumer's utility to provider B in the pre-sale stage is $U_B^p = v_B^p - p_B^p + p_A^p - p_B^p$. A rational consumer will choose the provider that makes total utility high.

3.3 Formal Sales Stage Utility

At the end of the pre-sale stage, consumers can observe the sales data of different providers in the pre-sale stage, which will influence their choices in the formal sale stage, and consumers will subconsciously tend to the provider with a good sales quantity, thus we consider the Bandwagon Effect in the purchase in conjunction with psychological theories.

The Bandwagon Effect, also known as the herd effect, describes the tendency of individuals to doubt and change their opinions and judgments when influenced by a group, and generally individuals tend to move in the direction of the majority of the group, i.e., follow the trend [11,12,17]. In the intelligent computation market, the Bandwagon Effect is portrayed as the tendency of consumers to imitate or follow the purchase behavior of neighbors when facing decision-making.

In order to highlight the heterogeneity of consumers, we designed a psychological threshold θ to characterize the sensitivity of consumers to follow their neighbors' behavior. When more than a certain percentage of a consumer's neighbors choose the same provider, the consumer also chooses this one provider, at which point the consumer is considered to be affected by the Bandwagon Effect, with the binary BE (Bandwagon Effect) variable δ set to 1, which is expressed as follows:

$$\delta = \begin{cases} 1, if \ \frac{n_{i,A}}{(n_{i,A}+n_{i,B})} \geq \theta \\ 0, otherwise \end{cases}, \tag{4}$$

where $n_{i,A}$ and $n_{i,B}$ represent the number of i's neighbors choosing A and B, respectively. Since it is specifically expressed as a ratio of numbers, the psychological threshold θ takes on a range $[0,1]$. We define the Bandwagon Effect utility for consumer i as follows:

$$U_{BE} = \delta_i g_i(n_{-i} + \delta_i), \tag{5}$$

where n_{-i} is the number of communities excluding i, and g_i is, in general, a non-decreasing function to represent the positive feedback from the Bandwagon Effect. When i makes a decision to follow the crowd, he enjoys the bonus from the increase in the number of people in the community $(g_i(n_{-i} + 1))$, and if i does not follow the crowd then his corresponding utility is 0. This function can be carved out based on specific scenarios and consumer characteristics, e.g. there are consumers who have greater marginal utility with respect to number of people.

The utility function in the formal sales stage consists of acquisition utility U_a, comparative utility U_c, and Bandwagon Effect utility U_{BE}:

$$\begin{aligned} U_A^f &= U_{A,a}^f + U_{A,c}^f + U_{A,BE}^f \\ &= v_A^f - p_A^f + p_B^p - p_A^p + \delta_{i,A} g_i(n_{-i,A} + \delta_{i,A}), \end{aligned} \tag{6}$$

where the corresponding valuations and prices are at the formal sales stage. Similarly, the consumer's utility to provider B in the formal sales stage is $U_B^f = v_B^f - p_B^f + p_A^p - p_B^p + \delta_{i,B} g_i(n_{-i,B} + \delta_{i,B})$.

4 Formulation and Solutions

In our designed duopoly intelligent computation market, the prerequisite for performing services is to ensure user experience, i.e., consumer utility should be greater than a set value. Secondly each service provider will pursue its own profit maximization. Service pricing directly affects consumer utility, which in turn influences the number of people purchasing the service and ultimately has an impact on the provider's profit.

In this case, service providers can develop different pricing strategies at different stages in order to maximize profits based on factors such as its own reputation, Bandwagon effects, market demand, and so on. In this section, we will formulate the profit maximization problem at different stages and design pricing strategies respectively, and then explore the linkages between pricing strategies at different stages.

4.1 Problem Formulation

For arbitrary consumers, their purchase decisions are related only to their own utility. The simplest carve-out in a duopoly market is to choose whichever provider brings the highest utility, which applies to perfectly rational consumers. However, the fact is that consumers do not necessarily perceive the utility gap and make uncertain choices when the difference between the two utilities offered is small.

When the utility difference is large, the user is more determined to choose a provider, and when the utility difference is small the user makes a choice with a probability. In particular, when the utility difference is 0, the user chooses a provider randomly. Therefore, we invoke the standardized Logistic Function to characterize the relationship between the user's choice probability and the utility difference, as follows:

$$L_{i,A}^p = \frac{1}{1+e^{-(U_{i,A}^p - U_{i,B}^p)}}, \qquad (7)$$

where $L_{i,A}^p$ is the probability that consumer i choose provider A at pre-sale stage. $U_{i,A}^p$ and $U_{i,B}^p$ are the utilities of consumer i at the pre-sale stage, respectively.

Intuitively, a provider's profit can be modeled as the amount sold times the difference between the service price and the unit cost. Here, the amount sold is the market demand, i.e. the number of consumers who chose this provider. We use the above probability to to define the market demand for a provider as the expected number of people who will choose him as follows:

$$D_j^p = \sum_i^{N_p} L_{i,j}^p \quad j \in \{A, B\}, \qquad (8)$$

where D_j^p is the market demand of provider j at pre-sale stage, and N_p is the total number of consumers at pre-sale stage. Then we denote the profit of provider j as follows:

$$P_j^p = D_j^p(p_j^p - c), \qquad (9)$$

where p_j^p is the price of service set by provider j at pre-sale stage. The objective function of the profit maximization problem considering the service price for each provider is inscribed as follow (take A as an example):

$$\textbf{OPT-1:} \quad \max_{p^p} P_A^p = D_A^p(p_A^p - c) \tag{10}$$

subject to $\forall i \in \mathcal{I}$:

$$\text{C1:} \quad U_{i,A}^p = v_{i,A}^p - p_A^p + p_B^p - p_A^p \geq \kappa_i,$$
$$\text{C2:} \quad p_A^p - c \geq 0,$$
$$\text{C3:} \quad 1 \geq L_{i,A}^p \geq 0.$$

In the optimization problem, $\mathcal{I}$ represents the set of available consumers, κ_i is the consumer's psychological expectation on utility. C1 indicates that for any consumer, if he chooses a provider the corresponding utility should be greater than or equals to consumer's psychological expectation on utility. This constraint protects consumers' rights while maximizing the profits of providers. C2 ensures that the provider's unit profit is non-negative. C3 is a natural setting on the probability of consumer choice.

Similar to the pre-sale stage, the provider profit maximization problem for the formal sales stage can be constructed by simply replacing the corresponding utilities, prices, and costs with the relevant expressions at the formal sales stage. However, it is worth noting that the valuation of the user changes at the formal sales stage, which may affect the user's choice, and more importantly, the cumulative number of users and the incorporation of the Bandwagon Effect make the design of the pricing mechanism more challenging.

4.2 Price Adjustment Strategies at Different Stages

In the pre-sale phase, the trading parties only need to make choices and price adjustments based on publicly available information in the market, especially in a duopoly market where the number of service providers is 2. Therefore, the problem is simplified and we propose a Demand Priority Pricing Algorithm (DPPA) for providers.

Algorithm 1 shows the main idea and steps of DPPA. The algorithm consists of two main phases, the warm-up phase (1–6) and the final adaptation phase (7–15). Consumers compare the utility brought by different providers based on the initial pricing and make an initial choice in warm-up phase. And then the providers are ranked according to the number of people selected, and the one with the most consumers is the most popular provider, who has the first-mover advantage. In the final adaptation phase, the most popular provider first adjusts the price based on a pre-defined step, the other provider calculates its own optimal price based on this price, and finally the most popular provider calculates the optimal price strategy based on the other's optimal price. The two prices

Algorithm 1. Demand Priority Pricing Algorithm (DPPA)

Require: Initial service price, reputation, valuation, price adjustment step
Output: Optimal service price p^p, profits P^p
1: **for** consumer i in $\mathcal{I}$ **do**
2:     Compare the utility according to the valuation and initial prices
3:     Computing the probability according to the utility
4:     Conduct provider selection and record the result
5: **end for**
6: Ranking the providers by the number of initial users
7: The Top-ranked provider adjust prices first:
8:     $NewPrice = Initialprice + PriceAdjustmentStep$
9:     Update price
10: Another provider makes a price adjustment:
11:     Computing the optimal price strategy according to the adjusted prices
12: The Top-ranked provider update the optimal price
13: Repeat 1 to 5
14: Computing the profits
15: **return** Optimal service price p^p and profits P^p respectively

---

obtained are the optimal price in the pre-sale stage, and the consumer then chooses the provider based on prices and calculates the profits.

In the formal sales phase, we introduce the Bandwagon Effect, where the utility derived is related to the number of neighbors choosing a particular provider, but in an incomplete information scenario, this is global information that is not available to consumer i. Therefore, before price adjustments are made in the formal sales phase, consumers should first make a prediction of the number of people in the same community.

In transactional behavior, the consumption behavior of neighbors is often not linearly related to a single parameter, but involves a nonlinear relationship between multiple parameters, such as service price, service quality, and sales volume in the pre-sale stage. Considering the excellent performance of neural networks in dealing with nonlinear relationships, as well as their strong fitting ability and flexibility, we help consumers predict the proportion of people choosing a certain community based on neural network models and design the Community Proportion Prediction Algorithm (CPPA).

Algorithm 2 shows the main idea and steps of CPPA. The CPPA algorithm consists of three main steps, model construction, pre-training and prediction. We predict neighbor selection behavior based on three characteristics: valuation, pre-sale pricing, and psychological expectation. The valuation reflects the consumer's expectations on the provider, which in part reflects the quality and functionality of the service and the provider's reputation. A good pre-sale pricing can not only attract a group of loyal customers during the pre-sale stage, they may also be more inclined to continue purchasing the product during the formal sale stage, without considering the products of other competitors. The psychological expec-

Algorithm 2. Community Proportion Prediction Algorithm (CPPA)

Require: The number of consumers N, pre-sale price p_A^p, pre-sale valuation v_A^p psychological expectation κ, trained neural network model.
Output: The community proportion $n_{i,A}/N$ and $n_{i,B}/N$
1: Define Neural Network Model:
2:     Add input and hidden layers (4 nodes, activation function: ReLU)
3:     Add output layer (1 node, activation function: Sigmoid)
4:     Compile Model (loss='mean squared error', optimizer='adam')
5: Call Neural Network Model
6: Train Neural Network model on training dataset
7: Obtain Trained Model
8: Define Prediction (data, trained model):
9:     Predict using trained model on p_A^p, v_A^p, and κ
10:    Return $n_{i,A}/N$ and $n_{i,B}/N$.
11: Call Prediction
---

tation κ reflects consumer preferences, purchasing power, purchasing habits, and other characteristics.

We used a dataset of size 10000 for model construction and pre-training, with each sample containing valuation coefficient, pre-sale price, psychological expectation, and neighbor selection results. And further handle outliers and missing values to ensure the quality of the data. The dataset is randomly divided into a training set and a testing set in an 8 : 2 ratio for model construction and model performance evaluation, respectively. Because valuation and pre-sale pricing have a more important impact on consumer trust and choice, we designed weights of 0.4 for each of them. Psychological expectation have relatively fewer decisive factors, so we set a weight of 0.2. We utilize the ReLU as the activation function of input and hidden layers and the Sigmoid as the activation function an output layer.

The biggest difference between the optimization problem in the formal sales stage and the pre-sale stage is the introduction of the Bandwagon Effect utility, when the consumers predict the proportion of community size they can calculate the Bandwagon Effect utility, and thus compare the utility at the formal sales stage to choose the provider, we improve the DPPA to obtain the optimal pricing scheme of the provider in this stage.

The basic idea of Algorithm 3 is same as DPPA. There are two main differences, first, due to the inclusion of the Bandwagon Effect utility so consumers call the CPPA algorithm to predict the community size before calculating the utility (Line 2). Second, in DPPA we utilize consumer demand as the basis for ranking providers, whereas in IPPA we use the incremental number of users between the two stages as the basis for ranking providers (Line 7), which provides more incentives for providers to improve the quality of service to attract consumers as the top-ranked providers still have a first-mover advantage.

5 Performance Simulation

In this section, we evaluated the rationality of the proposed model and the performance of the designed mechanisms. We consider a duopoly market with 100 customers and two computation service providers. We have standardized the setting of some common parameters. The reputation decay factor β among two providers is set to 0.8, and the value transfer coefficient α between the two stages is 0.8. The unit cost of the computation service is set to 0.2, and the psychological threshold θ about Bandwagon Effect is initialized to 0.6. During the simulation, consistent with the previous section, we set A to be the high reputation service provider.

Algorithm 3. Incremental Priority Pricing Algorithm (IPPA)

Require: The number of consumers N, pre-sale price, reputation, valuation, price adjustment step, psychological threshold θ, Bandwagon Effect function $g(\cdot)$
Output: Optimal service price p^f, profits P^f
1: **for** consumer i in $\mathcal{I}$ **do**
2:   Call the CPPA algorithm to obtain $n_{i,A}/N$ and $n_{i,B}/N$
3:   Computing the relevant utility
4:   Computing the probability according to the utility
5:   Conduct provider selection and record the result
6: **end for**
7: Ranking the providers by the increment of consumers
8: The Top-ranked provider adjust prices first:
9:     $NewPrice = Initialprice + PriceAdjustmentSteps$
10:    Update price
11: Another provider makes a price adjustment:
12:    Computing the optimal price strategy according to the adjusted prices
13: The Top-ranked provider update the optimal price
14: Repeat 1 to 6
15: Computing the profits
16: **return** Optimal service price p^f and profits P^f respectively

---

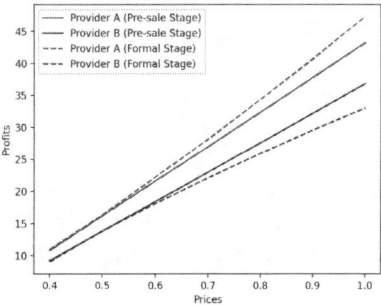

Fig. 1. Trends in profits with price at different stages

We first explored the trends in profit with pricing at different pricing stages for two service providers. Figure 1 highlights the first conclusion that Provider A's profits are always higher than Provider B's profits, regardless of the stage. This result is due to the fact that A is a high-reputation provider, which is also in line with expectations. Overall, within a certain range, all providers' profits at each stage rises with price. In addition, we find that the profit of A is higher and grow faster in the formal sales stage than in the pre-sale stage, which is because the high reputation makes A perform better in the pre-sale stage, and more and more consumers will choose A with the support of the Bandwagon Effect, which makes its formal sales stage more profitable. Correspondingly, B's profits in the formal stage are naturally reduced.

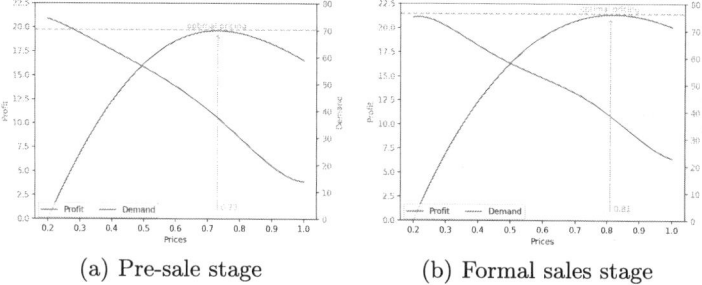

(a) Pre-sale stage   (b) Formal sales stage

Fig. 2. Trends in demand and profit of the high-reputation provider over price

Figure 2 reveals the change in profits, optimal price, and user demand for the high-reputation provider A when the prices of the low-reputation provider B are fixed. We fix the price of B's services at 0.5, and through simulation, it was found that the optimal price of A in the pre-sale stage is 0.73, and the optimal price in the formal sales stage is 0.81. A's optimal price and profits are higher in the formal sales stage than in the pre-sale stage, which is in accordance with the conclusions in Fig. 1. In terms of the overall trend, A's profit increases and then decreases with price, and user demand decreases with price. Before the optimal price, the profits from price increases outweighs the negative effect of subscriber loss. After the price peak, the decline in user demand intensified and its negative impact on profits dominated, leading to a decline in A's profits. Finally, we find that the optimal price of A at any stage is greater than 0.5, which allows higher quality services to sell for higher prices, contributing to market equity and stability.

The change in optimal price of A when the price of the low reputation provider B changes is shown in Fig. 3. The optimal price is the price that maximizes the provider's profit. Before the tipping point, consumers are willing to choose A even if A's price is higher than B's because A delivers a better service, and the idea that a higher price means a better service makes A more profitable. But as demand decay dominates (mentioned earlier), driven by market competition and consumer behavior, A chooses a lower price than B to maintain service

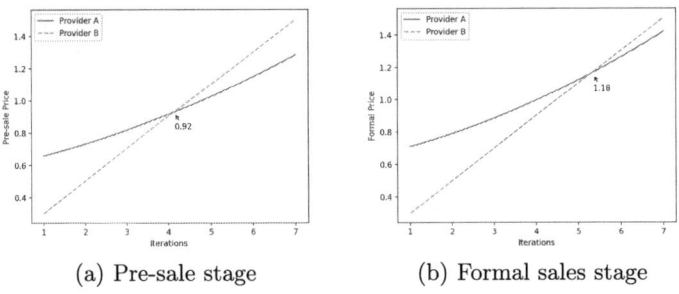

(a) Pre-sale stage (b) Formal sales stage

Fig. 3. The optimal price of the high reputation provider

attractiveness. Such a conclusion can help providers to apply appropriate pricing strategies to maximize profits in different market environments.

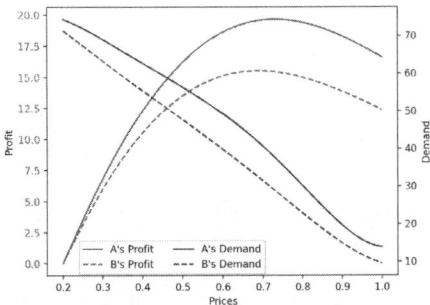

Fig. 4. Trends in demands with price at different stages

Figure 4 shows the trend in user demand with providers' price. The market demand and profits of high reputation providers are higher at the same prices. Low-reputation providers can achieve relatively high returns or even outperform high-reputation providers by setting the right prices.

Finally we explore the impact of pre-sale stage prices on prices and profits in the formal sales stage, the results are shown in Fig. 5. Once again, we fixed the low reputation provider's price at 0.5. In terms of the overall trend, as the price in the pre-sale stage increased, the price in the formal stage tended to decrease. Specifically, the A's formal stage price is no less than the pre-sale price until the pre-sale price was about 0.75. In this case, A attracts some consumers at a relatively reasonable price during the pre-sale stage, and can raise its price slightly during the formal stage to seek greater profits. Otherwise, the high pre-sale price of A will lose a large number of consumers, so that its formal sales stage price will have to be lower than the pre-sale price in order to make a relatively good profit.

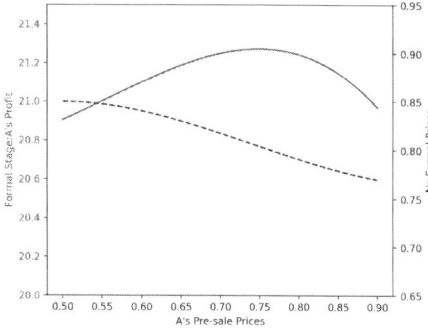

Fig. 5. The impact of pre-sale prices on the formal sale stage

From a profit perspective in Fig. 5, we can refer to the profit curve in Fig. 2(b) from right to left. When the pre-sale price is low, the formal sales price is relatively high, which will lose some consumers resulting in low profits. When the pre-sale price is high, the formal price is relatively low, there is no accumulation of the number of consumers in the pre-sale stage and the unit profit is small, the profit is also relatively low. If and only if the pre-sale price is optimal, it can attract a certain amount of consumers, and the formal price is also optimal to maintain the price attractiveness, but also to ensure that the unit profit is reasonable, so as to achieve the optimal profits.

In summary, through simulation experiments, we have verified that the model we designed can accurately describe the laws of the real market, and the pricing mechanism we proposed can help different service providers to seek the pricing scheme that maximizes the profit at different stages under the premise of guaranteeing the utility of users.

6 Conclusion

In order to incentive service providers to provide quality services to consumers in the intelligent computation market, we formulate two-stage profit-maximizing optimization problems for service providers to help them improve their competitiveness and gain higher profits by adjusting the pricing of their services, while guaranteeing the demand of consumers. In that problem we consider the impact of consumer value, provider reputation, Bandwagon Effect, and consumer heterogeneity on pricing strategies. In the pre-sale phase we propose the Demand Priority Pricing Algorithm (DPPA) algorithm to help providers find optimal prices. In order to overcome the difficulty of inaccessible of the global information in the formal sales phase, we first design Community Proportion Prediction Algorithm (CPPA) to predict the key parameters, and then propose Incremental Priority Pricing Algorithm (IPPA) to help providers choose pricing schemes. The experimental results prove that the model we constructed is able to describe the laws of the market, and the designed algorithm is able to help providers find profit-maximizing pricing schemes while ensuring fair and stable markets. However, this paper is only a discussion of the duopoly market, and our next work will discuss more provider competition, as well as do further research and exploration targeting provider reputation alerts, collapses, and reconstruction.

References

1. Bany Salameh, H., Samara, M.Q., Elrefae, G.A., Al-Ajlouni, A.: Profit-maximization spectrum sharing in opportunistic duopoly market under dynamic spectrum pricing and QoS constraints. Clust. Comput. **27**(2), 1491–1502 (2024)
2. Beltrán, E.T.M., et al.: Decentralized federated learning: Fundamentals, state of the art, frameworks, trends, and challenges. IEEE Commun. Surv. Tutorials. **25**(4), 2983–3013 (2024)
3. Bondi, T.: Alone, Together: A Model of Social (Mis) Learning from Consumer Reviews (2023). SSRN 4453685
4. Chai, F., Zhang, Q., Yao, H., Xin, X., Gao, R., Guizani, M.: Joint multi-task offloading and resource allocation for mobile edge computing systems in satellite IoT. IEEE Trans. Veh. Technol. **72**, 7783–7795 (2023)
5. Dou, G., Wei, K., Ma, L., Lin, X.: Dynamic competition and market structure for platform-based products: roles of product quality and indirect network effect. Int. Trans. Oper. Res. **31**, 3245–3279 (2024)
6. Fan, W., Su, Y., Liu, J., Li, S., Huang, W., Wu, F., Liu, Y.: Joint task offloading and resource allocation for vehicular edge computing based on V2I and V2V modes. IEEE Trans. Intell. Transp. Syst. **24**(4), 4277–4292 (2023)
7. Gupta, R., Gupta, J.: Federated learning using game strategies: state-of-the-art and future trends. Comput. Netw. **225**, 109650 (2023)
8. He, W., Yao, H., Mai, T., Wang, F., Guizani, M.: Three-stage stackelberg game enabled clustered federated learning in heterogeneous UAV swarms. IEEE Trans. Veh. Technol. **72**, 9366–9380 (2023)
9. Hua, H., Li, Y., Wang, T., Dong, N., Li, W., Cao, J.: Edge computing with artificial intelligence: a machine learning perspective. ACM Comput. Surv. **55**(9), 1–35 (2023)
10. Jiao, G., Ramezani, M.: A real-time cooperation mechanism in duopoly e-hailing markets. Trans. Res. Part C: Emerging Technol. **162**, 104598 (2024)
11. Leibenstein, H.: Bandwagon, snob, and Veblen effects in the theory of consumers' demand. Q. J. Econ. **64**(2), 183–207 (1950)
12. Li, J., Deng, X., Cheng, Y., Pan, Y., Xia, X., Yang, Z., Xie, J.: Altruism, collectivism and egalitarianism: on a variety of prosocial behaviors in binary networked public goods games. In: Proceedings of the 2023 International Conference on Autonomous Agents and Multiagent Systems, pp. 609–624 (2023)
13. Lu, D., Wang, P.: Dynamic pricing for new experience products in pre-sale mode with social learning. J. Retail. Consum. Serv. **76**, 103569 (2024)
14. Ma, Q., Huang, J., Başar, T., Liu, J., Chen, X.: Reputation and pricing dynamics in online markets. IEEE/ACM Trans. Netw. **29**(4), 1745–1759 (2021)
15. de Belloy de Saint-Lienard, E., Marecek, J., Kungurtsev, V.: The effects of transmission-rights pricing on multi-stage electricity markets. arXiv e-prints arXiv:2401.15772 (2024)
16. Soltani, R., Ashrafi, M., Esfahani, M.M.S., Farvaresh, H.: Competitive pricing of complementary telecommunication services with subscriber churn in a duopoly. Expert Syst. Appl. **237**, 121447 (2024)

17. Sun, T., Gong, S., Fan, G.Q., Xu, G.: Competitive influence maximization with uncertain competitor sources and the bandwagon effect in social networks. Asia-Pacific J. Oper. Res. 2350034 (2023)
18. Wang, Q., Guo, S., Liu, J., Pan, C., Yang, L.: Profit maximization incentive mechanism for resource providers in mobile edge computing. IEEE Trans. Serv. Comput. **15**(1), 138–149 (2019)
19. Werner, L., Christianson, N., Zocca, A., Wierman, A., Low, S.: Pricing uncertainty in stochastic multi-stage electricity markets. In: 2023 62nd IEEE Conference on Decision and Control (CDC), pp. 1580–1587. IEEE (2023)
20. Xu, J., Deng, L., Hu, X., Wang, Q., Zhang, Y.: Joint optimization of multistage pricing and seat allocation for high-speed railways integrating pre-sale period division. IEEE Trans. Intell. Transp. Syst. **25**(5), 4398–4412 (2024)
21. Zhang, J., Liu, Y., Qin, X., Xu, X., Zhang, P.: Adaptive resource allocation for blockchain-based federated learning in internet of things. IEEE Internet Things J. **10**(12), 10621–10635 (2023)
22. Zhou, X., Liu, C., Zhao, J.: Resource allocation of federated learning for the metaverse with mobile augmented reality. IEEE Trans. Wireless Commun. (2023)

Electricity Cost Minimization for Workflows Scheduling in Geo-Distributed Data Centers

He Zhang[1,3], Yueyou Zhang[1], Shuang Wang[1,2(✉)], and Jixiang Lu[3]

[1] The School of Computer Science and Engineering, Southeast University, Dhaka, Bangladesh
shuangwang@seu.edu.cn
[2] Key Laboratory of New Generation Artificial Intelligence Technology and Its Interdisciplinary Applications (Southeast University), Ministry of Education, Nanjing, China
[3] NARI Research Institute, NARI Technology Co., Ltd., Nanjing, Jiangsu, China
lujixiang@sgepri.sgcc.com.cn

Abstract. Geo-distributed data centers (GDCs) located around the world serve massive workflow applications, incurring high electricity cost. Since electricity prices of GDCs vary according to both geographical locations and time periods, different scheduling schemes result in varied electricity costs. How to reduce electricity costs while satisfying deadline constraints of workflows is critical for efficient operation of GDCs due to geographical and temporal variations in electricity prices. To solve the problem, a Frequency and Electricity Cost aware Multiple Workflows Scheduling algorithm (FECMWS) is proposed based on the Dynamic Voltage and Frequency Scaling (DVFS) technique, aiming at minimizing the electricity costs of all workflows while satisfying the deadline constraints. This algorithm first constructs the scheduling sequence of workflow tasks through three stages, including workflow sequencing, deadline partition and task sequencing. To approach the global optimum of scheduling objective, the algorithm adopts two graph embedding models and a policy network to solve the Markov Decision Process (MDP) of task resource allocation, assigning VMs to each task in the sequence. Experiments are conducted based on a large number of randomly generated scientific workflow instances and the results are analyzed using multi-factor analysis of variance (ANOVA). The FECMWS is calibrated and then compared to existed methods. The results demonstrate the effectiveness of the proposal.

Keywords: Multiple workflows scheduling · Geo-distributed data centers · Electricity cost optimization · Dynamic voltage and frequency scaling

1 Introduction

With the deepening advancement of global digital transformation, Geo-distributed Data Centers, as information technology infrastructures, are used worldwide. These data centers are located in different geographical locations, accessing and transmitting data through the network, providing efficient and reliable services for global users, supporting application scenarios in various fields including big data analysis, scientific computing, financial risk management, etc. The advantage of geo-distributed data centers is that they provide higher fault tolerance and availability, while adjusting services according to the needs of users in different regions. For example, Alibaba Cloud provides a hybrid cloud multi-data center big data geo-distributed computing service[1].

Many applications deployed in geo-distributed data centers are represented as Directed Acyclic Graphs (DAGs), submitted to servers in the form of workflows. For instance, in the field of scientific computing, Montage [1] is an astronomical image mosaic application, its workflow involves multiple image processing and data analysis tasks. CyberShake [2] is a computational application for earthquake simulation, and its workflow involves multiple earthquake data analysis and simulation tasks. These applications need to handle a large amount of data and complex computational processes in reality, thus posing higher requirements for the task scheduling strategies of data centers. To solve the problem, service providers of geo-distributed data centers need to ensure that each application can be completed before the deadline as required by the Service Level Agreement (SLA). These deadline constraints are crucial for ensuring customer satisfaction and maintaining the reputation of the service provider. In addition, service providers need to make full use of the resources in geo-distributed data centers, including computing and networks, etc., while ensuring application performance to reduce operational costs as much as possible [3].

However, a large number of servers deployed in geo-distributed data centers generate a huge amount of energy consumption when executing these applications. According to statistics, the energy consumption of data centers accounts for about 2–5% of global energy consumption which increases year by year [4]. This energy consumption leads to expensive electricity costs. Therefore, how to reduce electricity costs meanwhile meeting application performance requirements has become a key issue in the operation of geo-distributed data centers. As electricity prices vary with geographical location and time, the electricity cost incurred when an application is scheduled to be executed at different times in different data centers is also different [5]. For example, electricity prices in some areas are lower at night and on weekends, while other areas have preferential policies at specific times. Therefore, service providers need to adjust the scheduling strategy of workflow tasks flexibly according to the characteristics of electricity prices at different data centers, in order to reduce the overall electricity cost.

In this paper, from the perspective of service providers, we consider the workflows with deadline constraints, heterogeneity of servers and diversity of electricity prices in geo-distributed data centers, to minimize the electricity cost. The main contributions of this paper are summarized as following:

1. The problem of scheduling multiple workflows to minimize electricity cost in geo-distributed data centers is studied formally. The architecture of multiple

---

[1] https://help.aliyun.com/document_detail/402337.html.

workflows scheduling system in geo-distributed data centers is proposed. The mathematical model of the studied problem is established.
2. A frequency and electricity cost aware multiple workflows scheduling algorithm (FECMWS) is proposed. This algorithm, comprising four stages: workflow sequencing, deadline partition, task sequencing, and resource allocation. During the resource allocation stage, tasks in the sequence are allocated specific data centers, virtual machines and VF levels. Utilizing the Proximal Policy Optimization (PPO) based policy network, the algorithm addresses the Markov decision process (MDP) of task resource allocation, thereby globally optimizing the overall electricity cost.
3. Experiments are conducted based on a large number of randomly generated scientific workflow instances, and the results are analyzed using the Analysis of Variance (ANOVA) method. The proposed FECMWS is calibrated and then compared to existed algorithms, thereby demonstrating its effectiveness.

The remainder of this paper is organized as follows. The related research is reviewed and compared in Sect. 2. The mathematical model is defined for the workflow scheduling problem in GDCs in Sect. 3. In Sect. 4, we demonstrate the components of ECMWS algorithm to minimize the electircity cost. The experimental results with real-world datasets are analyzed and reported in Sect. 5. Finally, the conclusion is summarized in Sect. 6 with several highlighting remarks.

2 Related Work

Scheduling workflow tasks in distributed environments to optimize objectives is a well-known NP-hard problem [6]. While energy-efficient task scheduling in data centers has been extensively studied, there is limited research on minimizing electricity costs for multi-workflows across multiple geographically dispersed data centers with varying electricity prices.

DVFS (Dynamic Voltage and Frequency Scaling) technology is widely used for energy-efficient workflow scheduling. Kumar et al. [7] proposed a DVFS-based algorithm to minimize idle time slots, improve resource utilization, and reduce energy consumption while meeting SLA constraints. Stavrinides et al. [8] designed an energy-saving scheduling algorithm using Per-Core DVFS technology for real-time workflows. Garg et al. [9] introduced a reliable and energy-saving workflow scheduling algorithm that considers both reliability and energy consumption. Zhou et al. [10] proposed a scheduling algorithm that combines DVFS with slack time utilization to enhance system reliability. Garg et al. [11] developed an energy-efficient workflow scheduling method for heterogeneous computing systems. These studies demonstrate the benefits of DVFS in achieving energy efficiency and improving resource utilization in workflow scheduling. However, few of them considered the cross-domain data center deployment scenario, which is widely applied around the world nowadays.

In the field of task scheduling in distributed environments, several studies have proposed innovative methods. Attiya et al. [12] introduced a hybrid swarm intelligence approach for IoT task scheduling, combining Manta Ray Foraging Optimization (MRFO) with the Salp Swarm Algorithm (SSA) to enhance local search capability and reduce convergence time. Rizvi et al. [13] focused on fair scheduling for scientific workflows under budget constraints, aiming to minimize makespan while ensuring cost efficiency through a multi-objective approach. Samia et al. [14] addressed the energy consumption and makespan optimization problem in fog-cloud environments using a two-stage scheduling algorithm called Energy Makespan Optimization (EMO), which dynamically assigns tasks to fog and cloud resources based on their computational requirements. Furthermore, Rodriguez et al. [15] presented EPSM, a dynamic scheduling algorithm for multi-tenant Workflow as a Service (WaaS) environments, considering deadline constraints and optimizing resource utilization by incorporating factors such as supply delay, performance fluctuations, and periodic pricing models. These studies contribute to the advancement of task scheduling techniques, improving workflow efficiency and resource allocation in distributed systems.

In this paper, we focus on energy-saving task scheduling to reduce electricity costs and efficient scheduling of multiple workflows to minimize their cumulative electricity costs. Unlike the previous studies discussed, which primarily focused on specific aspects such as fairness, IoT, or fog-cloud environments, our research specifically addresses the challenges posed by multi-workflow scheduling. This scenario introduces additional complexities, as the scheduling decisions need to consider factors that impact energy consumption and electricity costs during task execution across multiple workflows. By considering these factors and optimizing the scheduling process, we aim to achieve significant energy savings and cost reductions for the execution of multiple workflows.

3 Problem Description

To describe the problem, a total of N workflow applications $\mathbb{G} = \{G_1, G_2, ..., G_N\}$ are randomly submitted to the system. Each application $G_w \in \mathbb{G}$ has a submission time T_w^{submit} and a user-specified deadline d_w, and includes n_w tasks $\{v_1^w, v_2^w, ..., v_{n_w}^w\}$. Let $T_{w,i}^B$ be the start time of v_i^w, and $T_{w,i}^F$ be the finish time of v_i^w. Each task v_i^w can only start executing after all its predecessor tasks $v_{i'}^w \in PR_i^w$ have finished, hence there is a constraint:

$$T_{w,i}^B \geq \max_{i' \in PR_i^w} \{T_{w,i'}^F\} \tag{1}$$

Workflow tasks are scheduled for execution on virtual machines. This paper uses the binary decision variable $x_{w,i;k,j,l}$ to represent whether an arbitrary task v_i^w is scheduled for execution on the virtual machine $\mathcal{V}_{j,l}^k$. Since a task can only be executed by one virtual machine, for each task v_i^w, there is a constraint:

$$\sum_{k=1}^{M} \sum_{j=1}^{\mu_k} \sum_{l=1}^{\omega_j^k} x_{w,i;k,j,l} = 1 \tag{2}$$

where M represents the total number of data centers, μ_k represents the number of servers in data center D_k, and ω_j^k indicates the number of virtual machines on server H_j^k.

A virtual machine can only execute one task at a time, so for each virtual machine $\mathcal{V}_{j,l}^k$, any two tasks assigned to it, v_i^w and $v_{dti}^{w'}$, should have non-overlapping execution times which satisfies:

$$x_{w,i;k,j,l} \cdot x_{w',i';k,j,l} \cdot (-T_{w,i}^B T_{w',i'}^B - T_{w',i'}^F T_{w,i}^F) \geq 0 \tag{3}$$

The completion time of a task, $T_{w,i}^F$, is determined by the start time, $T_{w,i}^B$, and the execution time of the task v_i^w on the virtual machine, $T_{w,i}^D$, which includes the maximum transmission time required to transfer data from the predecessor task to the current task and the time, $T_{w,i}^{work}$, to complete the workload $W_{w,i}$:

$$T_{w,i}^F = T_{w,i}^B + T_{w,i}^D \tag{4}$$

$$T_{w,i}^D = T_{w,i}^{work} + \max_{v_{i'}^w \in PR_i^w} \{T_{w,i',i}^{trans}\} \tag{5}$$

$$T_{w,i}^{work} = \sum_{k=1}^{M} \sum_{j=1}^{\mu_k} \sum_{l=1}^{\omega_j^k} x_{w,i;k,j,l} \times \frac{W_{w,i}}{\xi_{k,j,l}} \tag{6}$$

Here, the workload $W_{w,i}$ is measured in Million of Instructions (MI), and the processing frequency of the virtual machine $\xi_{k,j,l}$ is in MIPS (MI Per Second). The time for each predecessor task $v_{i',i}^w \in PR_i^w$ to transmit data to v_i^w is $T_{w,i',i}^{trans}$.

In order to calculate $T_{w,i',i}^{trans}$, it is also necessary to determine the network bandwidth for data transmission based on the location relationship of the tasks $v_{i'}^w$ and v_i^w assigned to the virtual machines. Therefore, this paper introduces a ternary auxiliary variable e: for two tasks v_i^w and $v_{i'}^w$ in the same workflow, when their assigned virtual machines are on the same physical machine, the value of $e_{i',i}$ is 0; when the two virtual machines are on different physical machines in the same data center, the value of $e_{i',i}$ is 1; when the two virtual machines are in different data centers, the value of $e_{i',i}$ is 2. According to the problem assumption, this paper sets the transmission bandwidth between virtual machines on different servers in the same data center to be B_{in}, and the transmission bandwidth between virtual machines in different data centers to be B_{out}. Hence, $T_{w,i',i}^{trans}$ is calculated as follows:

$$T^{trans}_{w,i',i} = \frac{e_{i',i} S_{w,i',i}}{2(e_{i',i}-1)B_{out} + (2-e_{i',i})B_{in}} \quad (7)$$

$$e_{i',i} = e^D_{i',i} + \frac{1}{2} e^S_{i',i} \quad (8)$$

$$e^D_{i',i} = \sum_{k=1}^{M} \left(\sum_{j=1}^{\mu_k} \sum_{l=1}^{\omega^k_j} x_{w,i;k,j,l} \oplus \sum_{j'=1}^{\mu_k} \sum_{l'=1}^{\omega^k_{j'}} x_{w,i';k,j',l'} \right) \quad (9)$$

$$e^S_{i',i} = \sum_{k=1}^{M} \sum_{j=1}^{\mu_k} \left(\sum_{l=1}^{\omega^k_j} x_{w,i;k,j,l} \oplus \sum_{l'=1}^{\omega^k_j} x_{w,i';k,j,l'} \right) \quad (10)$$

where $S_{w,i',i}$ represents the data volume to be transferred from $v^w_{i'}$ to v^w_i.

On the user level, this problem needs to ensure that each workflow application G_w is completed before the deadline d_w, i.e., the finish time of the latest completed workflow task does not exceed d_w:

$$\max_{i \in \{1,\ldots,n_w\}} \{T^F_{w,i}\} \leq d_w \quad (11)$$

The optimization objective of this problem is to minimize the electricity cost of executing all workflow tasks, which is closely related to the electricity price $p_k(t)$ of the data center, the execution time $T^D_{w,i}$ of the task on the virtual machine, and the power $P_{k,j,l}$ of the virtual machine. The mathematical model of the problem being studied is established as following:

$$\min Z = \sum_{w=1}^{N} \sum_{i=1}^{n_w} C_{w,i} \quad (12)$$

$$C_{w,i} = \sum_{k=1}^{M} \sum_{j=1}^{\mu_k} \sum_{l=1}^{\omega^k_j} \int_{T^B_{w,i}}^{T^F_{w,i}} x_{w,i;k,j,l} \times P_{k,j,l} \times p_k(t) dt \quad (13)$$

$$\min_{i=1,\ldots,n_w} \{T^B_{w,i}\} \geq T^{submit}_w \quad (14)$$

$$\max_{i=1,\ldots,n_w} \{T^F_{w,i}\} \leq d_w \quad (15)$$

4 Proposed Algorithm

To optimize resource allocation in multi-workflow scheduling, we propose the Frequency and Electricity Cost aware Multiple Workflows Scheduling algorithm (FECMWS). By adjusting the VF levels of high-performance virtual machines, FECMWS lowers electricity costs while meeting deadline constraints. It consists of four stages: workflow sequencing, deadline partitioning, task sequencing, and resource allocation. FECMWS effectively reduces costs by selecting appropriate data centers, virtual machines, and VF levels for each task. The algorithm framework is shown in Algorithm 1.

Algorithm 1: FECMWS

Input: System termination time T^{term}; Scheduling interval τ
Output: Total electricity cost Z
begin
$\quad Z \leftarrow 0, t \leftarrow 0$;
$\quad$ Estimate the performance parameters of the virtual machine ;
$\quad$ **while** $t < T^{term}$ **do**
$\quad\quad t' \leftarrow \min{t + \tau, T^{term}}$;
$\quad\quad \mathbb{G} \leftarrow$ workflows submitted to the system from t to t' ;
$\quad\quad$ **if** $\mathbb{G} \neq \emptyset$ **then**
$\quad\quad\quad$ Estimate the time parameters of workflow tasks ;
$\quad\quad\quad$ Workflow Sequencing;
$\quad\quad\quad$ **for** $w = 1$ **to** N' **do**
$\quad\quad\quad\quad$ Deadline Partition;
$\quad\quad\quad\quad$ Task Sequencing;
$\quad\quad\quad\quad$ **for** $i = 1$ **to** n_w **do**
$\quad\quad\quad\quad\quad$ Recourse Allocation;
$\quad\quad\quad\quad\quad$ Calculate the electricity cost $C_{w,i}$ by Eq.(13) ;
$\quad\quad\quad\quad\quad Z \leftarrow Z + C_{w,i}$;
$\quad\quad\quad\quad$ **end**
$\quad\quad\quad$ **end**
$\quad\quad$ **end**
$\quad\quad t \leftarrow t'$;
$\quad$ **end**
$\quad$ **return** Z ;
end

4.1 Parameter Estimation

The data transfer time of tasks $\hat{T}_{w,i}^{trans}$ is estimated using the average data transfer bandwidth $\overline{B}$ which is between virtual machines:

$$\hat{T}_{w,i}^{trans} = \max_{v^w i' \in PR_i^w} \{\hat{T}_{w,i',i}^{trans}\} \tag{16}$$

$$\hat{T}_{w,i',i}^{trans} = \frac{S_{i',i}^w}{\overline{B}} \tag{17}$$

Here, $\hat{T}_{w,i',i}^{trans}$ denotes the data transfer time between task v_i^w and its direct predecessor task $v^w i'$.

In order to more comprehensively reflect the average processing capability of the virtual machine, we use the average processing frequency of all virtual machines at all VF levels as the average processing frequency of the virtual machine:

$$\overline{\xi} = \frac{\sum_{k=1}^{M} \sum_{j=1}^{\mu_k} \sum_{l=1}^{\omega_j^k} \sum_{f=1}^{F} \xi_{k,j,l}(f)}{\overline{\omega} \times F} \tag{18}$$

Therefore, based on the average processing frequency $\overline{\xi}$ of the virtual machine, the execution time $\overline{T}_{w,i}^{work}$ of a given task v_i^w is estimated:

$$\overline{T}_{w,i}^{work} = \frac{W_{w,i}}{\overline{\xi}} \qquad (19)$$

Then, combined with the task data transmission time $\hat{T}_{w,i}^{trans}$, we can get the earliest start time $\overline{T}_{w,i}^{EST}$ and the earliest completion time $\overline{T}_{w,i}^{EFT}$ of the task:

$$\overline{T}_{w,i}^{EFT} = \overline{T}_{w,i}^{EST} + \overline{T}_{w,i}^{work} + \hat{T}_{w,i}^{trans} \qquad (20)$$

$$\overline{T}_{w,i}^{EST} = \begin{cases} \lceil \frac{T_w^{submit}}{\tau} \rceil \times \tau, & \text{if } PR_i^w = \emptyset \\ \max_{v_{i'}^w \in PR_i^w} \{\overline{T}_{w,i'}^{EFT}\}, & \text{otherwise} \end{cases} \qquad (21)$$

In addition, three virtual machine performance indicators based on the lowest VF level (i.e., the highest processing frequency), the highest VF level (lowest processing frequency), and the average VF level (average processing frequency) of a single virtual machine are also estimated:

$$\overline{\xi}_{slow} = \frac{\sum_{k=1}^{M} \sum_{j=1}^{\mu_k} \sum_{l=1}^{\omega_j^k} \xi_{k,j,l}(F)}{\overline{\omega}} \qquad (22)$$

$$\overline{\xi}_{fast} = \frac{\sum_{k=1}^{M} \sum_{j=1}^{\mu_k} \sum_{l=1}^{\omega_j^k} \xi_{k,j,l}(1)}{\overline{\omega}} \qquad (23)$$

$$\overline{\xi}_{avg} = \frac{\sum_{k=1}^{M} \sum_{j=1}^{\mu_k} \sum_{l=1}^{\omega_j^k} \frac{1}{F} \sum_{f=1}^{F} \xi_{k,j,l}(f)}{\overline{\omega}} \qquad (24)$$

The time complexity of parameter estimation performed by FECMWS, is $O(F \times \overline{\omega} + \overline{\omega}^2 + \sum_{w=1}^{N} n_w^2)$.

4.2 Workflow Sequencing

In workflow sequencing, we calculate the workload factor $WL(G_w)$ and frequency-aware slack time factor $FST(G_w)$ for each workflow G_w. It also calculates the resource contention $Contention_w$ and resource contention factor $CT(G_w)$. Based on these factors, the rank Rk_w is calculated for each workflow and generates a scheduling sequence in ascending order of rank. To simplify parameter calibration, a constraint is added to narrow down the parameter space.

$$\alpha_1 + \alpha_2 + \alpha_3 = 1 \qquad (25)$$

For each workflow $G_w \in \mathbb{G}$, the calculation methods of the three factors are introduced as follows:

1. The frequency-aware slack time factor $FST(G_w)$ is defined as follows:

$$FST(G_w) = \frac{d_w - \overline{T}_w^{EFT}}{\max_{w'=1,\ldots,N'}\{d_{w'} - \overline{T}_{w'}^{EFT}\}} \tag{26}$$

2. The workload factor $WL(G_w)$ is defined as the normalized value of the sum of all task workloads W_w in the workflow:

$$WL(G_w) = \frac{W_w}{\max_{w'=1,\ldots,N'}\{W_{w'}\}} \tag{27}$$

$$W_w = \sum_{i=1}^{n_w} W_{w,i} \tag{28}$$

3. The resource contention factor $CT(G_w)$ is defined as the normalized value of the workflow resource contention $Contention_w$:

$$CT(G_w) = \frac{Contention_w}{\max_{w'=1,\ldots,N'}\{Contention_w\}} \tag{29}$$

Here, $Contention_w$ represents the maximum number of virtual machines that the workflow may occupy simultaneously during execution. Prioritizing workflow applications with higher $Contention_w$ may result in more violations of deadlines for other applications in the same batch. The calculation process of this indicator is as follows: Firstly, the execution time interval from the earliest start time $\hat{T}_{w,i}^{EST}$ to the earliest finish time $\hat{T}_{w,i}^{EFT}$ of each task in the workflow is added to the queue $Interval$, then $Interval$ is reordered in ascending order of $\hat{T}_{w,i}^{EST}$, and finally, for each task, the number of overlapping time intervals $curContention$ with all other tasks that start later is calculated, with the maximum value taken as $Contention_w$.

For a given total of T batches of workflows to be scheduled and the number of workflows in each batch $\{N_1, \ldots, N_T\}$, the total time complexity of workflow sequencing is $O(\sum_{w=1}^{N} n_w \log n_w + \sum_{t=1}^{T} N_t \log N_t)$.

4.3 Deadline Partition and Task Sequencing

In deadline partition, we propose a way to calculate the task ranks based on the configuration of the VF levels of the virtual machines: Considering that each task is assigned different VF levels uniformly at random when executed on a virtual machine, the average task completion rank is calculated by the estimated average processing frequency of the virtual machine $\overline{\xi}_{avg}$ as follows:

$$Rk_{w,i}^{avg} = \max_{v_j^w \in SU_i^w}\{Rk_{w,j}^{avg} + \hat{T}_{w,i,j}^{trans}\} + \overline{T}_{w,i}^{avg} \tag{30}$$

$$\overline{T}_{w,i}^{avg} = \frac{W_{w,i}}{\overline{\xi}_{avg}} \tag{31}$$

Since the calculation of the task ranks requires traversing each edge in the workflow DAG, and the calculation of the task sub-deadlines requires traversing each task in the workflow, for a total of N workflows submitted to the system, the total time complexity of deadline partition is $O(\sum_{i=1}^{N} n_w^2)$.

Then, we propose the rank of the task sub-deadline division:

$$d_{w,i} = d_w \times \frac{Rk_{w,0}^{avg} - Rk_{w,i}^{avg} + \overline{T}_{w,i}^{avg}}{Rk_{w,0}^{avg}} \qquad (32)$$

$$Rk_{w,0}^{avg} = \max_{\substack{1 \leq i \leq n_w \\ PR_i^w = \emptyset}} \{Rk_{w,i}^{avg}\} \qquad (33)$$

In task sequencing, we sort the tasks based on their average completion rank. To accomplish this, we use the average completion rank $(Rk_{w,i}^{avg})$ calculated from Eq. (30), and subsequently arrange them in descending order. This method ensures that tasks with higher average completion ranks are prioritized. Since only sorting operations are required, the total time complexity of this algorithm is $O(\sum_{w=1}^{N} n_w \log n_w)$.

4.4 Resource Allocation

In the resource allocation phase, we train a frequency and electricity cost-aware policy network using the PPO algorithm. This network selects the appropriate data center and virtual machine for each task in the scheduling sequence based on the real-time system state. It also sets the optimal VF level to achieve global optimization using DVFS technology.

The task graph is a Directed Acyclic Graph (DAG): Nodes represent workflow tasks, with features including task workload, deadline, index of the virtual machine allocated to the task, and the VF level to be set when the virtual machine executes the task; directed edges between nodes represent the partial order relation between tasks, and edge weights represent the amount of data transferred between tasks. And the resource graph is a weighted undirected graph, where nodes represent resource entities (such as virtual machines, servers, or data centers). To avoid the risk of overfitting due to the increased model complexity, we introduces a random dropout mechanism [16]. It reduces the model's dependence on individual neurons by randomly turning off neurons (excluding them from forward and backward propagation calculations) during training.

The task graph embedding model under variable virtual machine frequency and power adopts a two-layer GCN (Graph Convolutional Networks) structure. The output of each layer of the GCN goes through dropout. Similarly, the resource graph embedding model also adopts a three-layer GCN structure. The output of each layer of the GCN also goes through dropout. We use the mean pooling technique to generate the corresponding task graph embedding vectors. The resource graph embedding vector is formed by concatenating the embedding vectors of all data center nodes and server nodes.

We trains a policy network based on the Actor-Critic framework and PPO algorithm. At each time step t of M', it outputs the optimal resource allocation action A'_t based on the real-time system state S'_t. To select the most suitable data center D_k from M data centers, and to choose the most suitable virtual machine from the ω^k virtual machines of the data center and set the optimal VF level, the Actor network outputs a probability vector representing the optional action distribution. This vector is formed by concatenating the sub-action probability vectors for selecting the data center, virtual machine, and VF level. Sampling from the three vectors yields the selected data center (index), virtual machine (index), and VF level.

For resource allocation policies, the Actor and Critic networks proposed in this section have more feedforward layers. The output dimensions of each layer of the State Encoder are $D'_{encoder}(1), D'_{encoder}(2), D'_{encoder}(3)$ respectively. Then, the Actor network and Critic network each output a dimension D'_{action} action and a dimension 1 value function to estimate values through 2 feedforward layers, respectively, with the output dimensions of each layer being $D'_{actor}(1), D'_{actor}(2) = D'_{action}, D'_{critic}(1), D'_{critic}(2) = 1$ respectively. The input dimensions of the Actor and Critic networks, D'_{state}, are still fixed as the sum of the dimensions of the task graph embedding vector, resource graph embedding vector, electricity price vector, and algorithm parameter vector:

$$D'_{state} = D'_{task} + D'_{vm} + D_{price} + D'_{params} \tag{34}$$

5 Performance Evaluation

5.1 Experiment Settings

The geo-distributed data center system consists of four data centers, located in California, USA, Toronto, Ontario, Canada, London, UK, and Munich, Germany. The electricity prices of each data center at different times are set, based on the real data from the literature [17]. Table 1 shows the configuration of servers and virtual machines.

We use the Relative Percentage Deviation (RPD) to evaluate the performance of the algorithm. RPD is calculated as shown in Eq. (35):

$$RPD(\%) = \frac{Z - Z^*}{Z^*} \times 100\% \tag{35}$$

where Z represents the objective function value generated when the algorithm under consideration schedules workflow instances, i.e., the electricity cost calculated according to Eq. (12). Z^* represents the minimum electricity cost generated by all algorithms when executing the corresponding workflow instances.

We test different parameters of workflow sequencing factor weights. Figure 1 displays the RPD values of the FECMWS algorithm under the optimal three combinations. The algorithm performance differences among the three combinations are not significant, but $(\alpha'_1, \alpha'_2, \alpha'_3) = (0.3, 0.2, 0.5)$ is slightly better than the other two combinations, so we set the three factor weights of the workflow sequencing to be $0.3, 0.2, 0.5$ respectively.

Table 1. Servers and VMs Configuration

Type	VM1	VM2	VM3	VM4	VM5	S1	S2	S3	S4	S5
MIPS/Core	520	600	440	440	560	400	280	520	440	480
GHz/Core	2.6	3.0	2.2	2.2	2.8	2.0	1.4	2.6	2.2	2.4
Cores#	1	1	1	1	1	4	8	4	8	4
VF Level 1 - MIPS	520	600	440	440	560	–	–	–	–	–
VF Level 1 - Power (W)	85	140	110	75	105	–	–	–	–	–
VF Level 2 - MIPS	500	580	420	420	520	–	–	–	–	–
VF Level 2 - Power (W)	65	110	85	55	80	–	–	–	–	–
VF Level 3 - MIPS	460	540	380	380	480	–	–	–	–	–
VF Level 3 - Power (W)	55	90	70	45	60	–	–	–	–	–
VF Level 4 - MIPS	400	480	340	340	440	–	–	–	–	–
VF Level 4 - Power (W)	45	70	55	35	50	–	–	–	–	–
VF Level 5 - MIPS	360	420	300	300	380	–	–	–	–	–
VF Level 5 - Power (W)	35	50	40	25	40	–	–	–	–	–

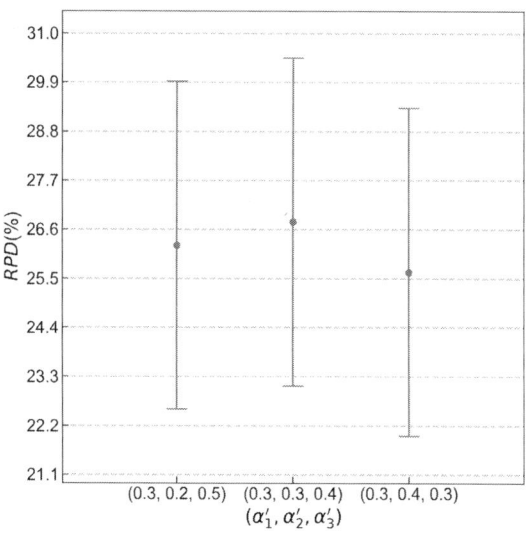

Fig. 1. Performance comparison of different FCWSsorting factor weight combinations under 95% Tukey HSD confidence interval

All the experiments in the computer equipped with an Intel Core i5-13600 KF processor, an NVIDIA GeForce RTX 3090 graphics card, and 64 GB DDR4-3600 MHz memory. This paper extends the CloudSim Plus platform to support multi-workflow scheduling for minimizing electricity cost across data centers.

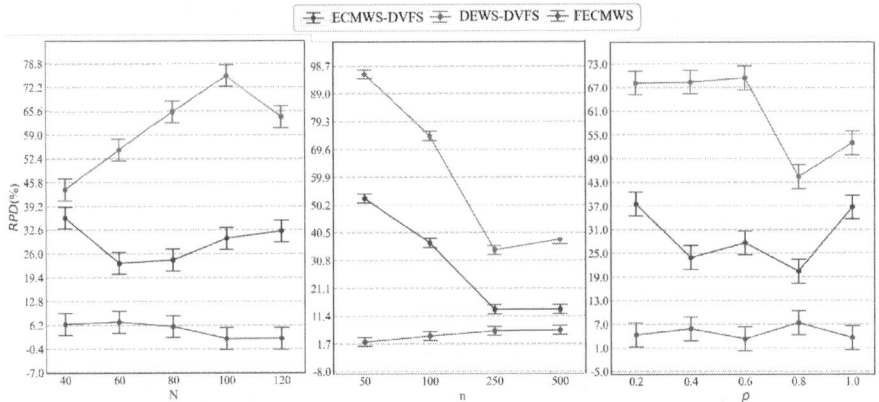

Fig. 2. Average RPD of Genome workflow instances

5.2 Algorithm Comparison

Two commonly used scientific workflow instances are selected from related research: Montage, and Genome. The ECWSD algorithm [18] and the DEWS algorithm [19] are selected as the benchmark algorithms. The former is a static scheduling algorithm for the multiple workflows electricity cost optimization problem, while the latter only considers a single workflow.

Figure 2 presents the average RPD of the electricity cost for the three algorithms under different numbers of Genome workflow instances. The FECMWS algorithm is always significantly better than the other two baseline algorithms as the number of workflows (N) increases, and it is not very sensitive to the number of workflows. In addition, as the number of tasks (n) increases, the FECMWS algorithm is always significantly better than the other two algorithms, and it is not very sensitive to the number of tasks. Also, as ρ which represents tightness of workflow application deadlines increases and the workflow deadline constraint becomes looser, the FECMWS algorithm is always significantly better than the other two algorithms, and it is not very sensitive to the setting of the workflow deadline constraint level.

Figure 3 shows the average RPD of the electricity cost for the three algorithms under different numbers of Montage workflow instances. As the number of workflows increases, the FECMWS algorithm is always significantly better than the other two baseline algorithms, and it is not very sensitive to the number of workflows. Also, as the number of tasks increases, the FECMWS algorithm is always superior to the other two algorithms. However, when $n = 500$, due to the high resource utilization of the system, the optimization space for electricity cost under the deadline constraint is small, so the performance gap between this algorithm and the other two algorithms drastically reduces. In addition, as ρ increases and the workflow deadline constraint becomes looser, the performance of all algorithms generally improves, and the FECMWS algorithm is always

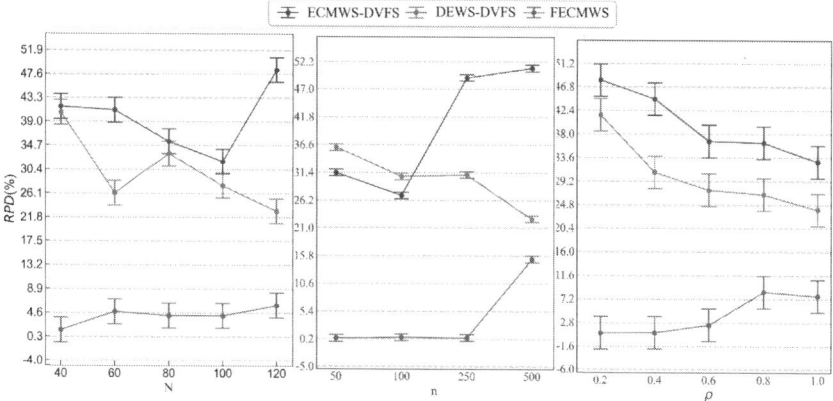

Fig. 3. Average RPD of Montage workflow instances

Table 2. Runtime efficiency comparison for Genome

	ECWSD	DEWS	FECMWS
Genome RPD	32.407%	61.462%	5.790%
Genome CPU Time	163.458	89.746	182.893
Montage RPD	38.848%	30.044%	3.468%
Montage CPU time	171.086	97.085	196.220

significantly better than the other two algorithms. However, the looser deadline constraint also allows the other two algorithms to exploit the task's slack time more, set a higher VF level, and therefore, the performance gap between the proposed algorithm and the other two algorithms is gradually decreasing.

Table 2 shows the effectiveness and execution efficiency of the three algorithms. For Genome and Montage workflows, the FECMWS algorithm performs best in terms of electricity cost. Its algorithm execution time is longer, but it is also within an acceptable range for engineering implementation.

6 Conclusion

This paper focused on the problem of minimizing electricity costs in the scheduling of multiple workflows in geo-distributed data centers. To address this problem, we proposed the FECMWS algorithm based on the Dynamic Voltage and Frequency Scaling (DVFS) technique. Experimental evaluations were conducted using randomly generated scientific workflow instances. The results demonstrated the effectiveness of the FECMWS algorithm in comparison to existing methods. However, there are still areas for further exploration. Specifically, future research should consider multi-dimensional task resource requirements, incorporate heterogeneity in network communication resources, and develop adaptive scheduling techniques to handle dynamic workflow arrivals and varying resource demands.

Acknowledgments. This work is supported by the National Key Research and Development Program (No. 2022YFF0902800), Natural Science Foundation of Jiangsu Province (No. BK20220803), and National Natural Science Foundation of China (No. 62302095).

References

1. Jacob, J.C., Katz, D.S., Kesselman, C., Nitzberg, B., Pordes, R., Sundquist, E.: Montage: a grid portal and software toolkit for building science gateways. Concurrency Comput. Pract. Experience **20**(2), 125–135 (2008)
2. Graves, R.W., Pitarka, A., Day, S.M., Minster, J.B., Jordan, T.H.: CyberShake: a physics-based seismic hazard model for southern California. Pure Appl. Geophys. **168**(3–4), 367–381 (2011)
3. Wang, Y., Li, J., Zhang, X., Wang, X.: Multi-objective optimization for cross-domain data center service scheduling. J. Parallel Distrib. Comput. **129**, 1–11 (2019)
4. Agency, I.E.: Global energy review 2022. Tech. Rep, World Energy Outlook (2022)
5. Wang, X., Zhu, X., Zhang, X., Li, B.: Electricity cost optimization for data centers. IEEE Trans. Parallel Distrib. Syst. **25**(12), 3159–3169 (2014)
6. Zhang, X., Liang, Y., Zhang, J., Liang, Y., Zhang, J.: A two-stage multi-population genetic algorithm with adaptive crossover operator for workflow scheduling in heterogeneous distributed computing environments. In: 2021 IEEE International Conference on Systems, Man and Cybernetics (SMC), pp. 1–8. IEEE (2021)
7. Kumar, N., Vidyarthi, D.P.: A green SLA constrained scheduling algorithm for parallel/scientific applications in heterogeneous cluster systems. Sustain. Comput. Inform. Syst. **22**, 107–119 (2019)
8. Stavrinides, G.L., Karatza, H.D.: Energy-aware scheduling of real-time workflow applications in clouds utilizing DVFS and approximate computations. In: 2018 IEEE 6th International Conference on Future Internet of Things and Cloud (FiCloud), pp. 33–40. IEEE (2018)
9. Garg, R., Mittal, M., Son, L.H.: Reliability and energy efficient workflow scheduling in cloud environment. Clust. Comput. **22**(4), 1283–1297 (2019)
10. Zhou, J., Sun, J., Zhang, M., Ma, Y.: Dependable scheduling for real-time workflows on cyber–physical cloud systems. IEEE Trans. Industr. Inf. **17**(11), 7820–7829 (2020)
11. Garg, N., Singh, D., Goraya, M.S.: Energy and resource efficient workflow scheduling in a virtualized cloud environment. Clust. Comput. **24**, 767–797 (2021)
12. Attiya, I., Abd Elaziz, M., Abualigah, L., Nguyen, T.N., Abd El-Latif, A.A.: An improved hybrid swarm intelligence for scheduling IoT application tasks in the cloud. IEEE Trans. Ind. Inform. **18**(9), 6264–6272 (2022)
13. Rizvi, N., Ramesh, D.: Fair budget constrained workflow scheduling approach for heterogeneous clouds. Clust. Comput. **23**, 3185–3201 (2020)
14. Ijaz, Samia, Munir, Ehsan Ullah, Ahmad, Saima Gulzar, Rafique, M. Mustafa., Rana, Omer F..: Energy-makespan optimization of workflow scheduling in fog–cloud computing. Computing **103**(9), 2033–2059 (2021). https://doi.org/10.1007/s00607-021-00930-0

15. Rodriguez, M.A., Buyya, R.: Scheduling dynamic workloads in multi-tenant scientific workflow as a service platforms. Futur. Gener. Comput. Syst. **79**, 739–750 (2018)
16. Ji, S., Xu, W., Yang, M., Yu, K.: 3D convolutional neural networks for human action recognition. IEEE Trans. Pattern Anal. Mach. Intell. **35**(1), 221–231 (2013)
17. Forestiero, A., Mastroianni, C., Meo, M., Papuzzo, G., Sheikhalishahi, M.: Hierarchical approach for efficient workload management in geo-distributed data centers. IEEE Trans. Green Commun. Netw. **1**(1), 97–111 (2017)
18. Li, X., Yu, W., Ruiz, R., Zhu, J.: Energy-aware cloud workflow applications scheduling with geo-distributed data. IEEE Trans. Serv. Comput. **15**(2), 891–903 (2022)
19. Hussain, M., Wei, L.-F., Rehman, A., Abbas, F., Hussain, A., Ali, M.: Deadline-constrained energy-aware workflow scheduling in geographically distributed cloud data centers. Futur. Gener. Comput. Syst. **132**, 211–222 (2022)

DRT: A Deterministic Computing and Network Resources Tradeoff Mechanism for Holographic-Type Communication

Xu Huang[1], Jia Chen[1,2](✉), Deyun Gao[1], Jingjing Liu[3], Chenxi Liao[1], Dongsheng Qian[1], and Shang Liu[1]

[1] National Engineering Research Center for Advanced Network Technologies, School of Electronic and Information Engineering, Beijing Jiaotong University, Beijing 100044, China
chenjia@bjtu.edu.cn
[2] Peng Cheng Laboratory, Shenzhen 518055, China
[3] China Mobile Group Liaoning Company Limited, Liaoning 110179, China

Abstract. With the emergence of the 6th Generation (6G) and the Metaverse, holographic-type communication (HTC) has become a crucial aspect of future communication. While the HTC system can deliver an immersive experience, it demands stringent real-time processing, substantial computing resources, and high bandwidth. However, current HTC systems struggle with ensuring ultra-low latency and finding a tradeoff between network and computing resources. In this paper, we introduce the Deterministic Computing and Network Resources Tradeoff mechanism (DRT). This mechanism ensures bounded MTP latency by implementing traffic shaping mechanisms and modeling computing latency. Additionally, we propose a routing and scheduling algorithm based on the constraints of DRT, which efficiently allocates network and computing resources, thereby minimizing MTP latency for users. Experimental results demonstrate that DRT ensures minimum MTP latency compared to other mechanisms, with the lowest recorded MTP latency at 34.78 ms, approximately three times lower than cases without DRT.

Keywords: Holographic-type Communication · Deterministic Networking · Time-Sensitive Network · Resource Management

1 Introduction

With the emergence of the Metaverse, Holographic-Type Communication (HTC) is positioned to shape the future of digital object representation and human interaction [1]. Holographic data records the amplitude and phase of optical wavefronts of objects, typically stored as point clouds or light fields [2], resulting in significantly larger data compared to 2-D images. In contrast to traditional media, the HTC system offers users an immersive 3-D experience by delivering 3-D models [2,3]. This process involves a series of algorithms for data processing, including registration, reconstruction, and rendering. Holographic data introduces higher network latency, while holographic processing incurs additional computation latency. The two latency contribute significantly to the Motion-to-Photon (MTP) latency in the HTC system. MTP latency describes the time between the movement of a tracked object and its corresponding movement rendered and depicted by computer-generated images on a graphical output screen. Elevated MTP latency may induce cybersickness and negatively impact the user experience. To mitigate cybersickness and provide low MTP latency, the current HTC system confronts two challenges.

The first challenge lies in finding a tradeoff between networking latency and computing latency to achieve the minimum Motion-to-Photon (MTP) latency. Article [4] proposes the reduction of network bandwidth and latency through the development of efficient compression techniques, even though this approach may increase computing latency. Meanwhile, Article [5] advocates for the use of the In-Network Computing (INC) paradigm instead of the edge computing paradigm. However, the INC paradigm is limited to deploying simple algorithms, such as compression and decompression. The authors in [6] leverage the power of ML and propose an AI-empowered point cloud streaming system for mobile edge networks. The AI system can reduce bandwidth consumption and alleviate the computational pressure by sensing the network bandwidth. However, the AI model will bring extra computing overhead.

The second challenge revolves around ensuring ultra-low transmission latency with massive holographic data. Current research primarily targets the transport and network layers to achieve this ultra-low latency transmission. In terms of transport layer protocols, UDP-based options, including The MPEG Dynamic Adaptive Streaming over HTTP (MPEG-DASH) [8,9], Quick UDP Internet Connections (QUIC) over HTTP/3 [10], and Web Real-Time Communications (WebRTC) [11], demonstrate the capability to provide low end-to-end latency [7]. At the network layer, the New IP proposes a novel data plane forwarding paradigm that leverages semantic communication and packet wash for the HTC system [12]. Network 2030 introduces three different time-related services, aiming to guarantee low latency by controlling data packet arrival times [13]. Despite these efforts, they currently fall short of providing bounded latency for the HTC system.

In addressing the first challenge, we conduct a comprehensive analysis of the entire processing pipeline of the HTC system, establishing a mathematical model that illustrates the relationship between computing latency and network latency. For the second challenge, we contend that Deterministic Networking (DetNet) and Time-Sensitive Networks (TSN) can provide zero congestion loss and bounded latency through the reservation of network resources [14,15]. Therefore, the main contributions of this paper are as follows.

– We propose the Deterministic Computing and Network Resources Tradeoff mechanism (DRT). For the computing part, we provide a detailed description

of the entire processing of the HTC system, including a simple modeling of the computing latency for each step. In the network part, we adopt the Cycle Queuing and Forwarding (CQF) mechanism within TSN to ensure bounded end-to-end latency and jitters. The DRT aims to balance the computing and network parts to minimize MTP latency.
- We design the routing and scheduling algorithm based on the DRT. The scheduling constraints are established, encompassing network resource constraints and computing resource constraints. The routing and scheduling algorithm, based on these constraints, aims to achieve the optimal result using the concept of heuristic algorithms.
- We have developed an HTC prototype based on DRT. In the data plane, we employ the Programmable Data Plane (PDP) to realize CQF and ensure deterministic forwarding. In the control plane, network resources and status are monitored by the SDN controller. In the application plane, we offer immersive holographic services to users.

Section 2 analyzes the computing latency and network latency in detail. Section 3 proposes the DRT mechanism. Section 4 designs the routing and scheduling algorithm. Section 5 presents the simulation results. Finally, Sect. 6 concludes the article.

2 The Latency Analysis of HTC System

2.1 Holographic Traffic Analysis

Before introducing the HTC system, it is crucial to analyze the attributes of holographic traffic, as outlined in Table 1. In this paper, holographic traffic is generated by RGBD cameras. These cameras capture frames at a rate of $FPS_{capture}$, where FPS denotes frames per second. The display terminal also has the characteristic of FPS, and satisfactory experiences are achieved only when the FPS exceeds 25fps. Notably, the FPS of display terminals not only depends on the FPS of capture cameras but also on the computing and network latency within the HTC system.

2.2 Computing Latency Analysis

The most basic computing process in the HTC system includes data registration, data compression, reconstruction, and rendering, as shown in Fig. 1. Based on the deployment location in the network, it can be simply divided into two parts: pre-computing and post-computing.

The pre-computing phase includes data registration and data compression, both of which impact the size and quality of the point cloud data. Data registration aims to find a transformation that aligns multiple sets of points from different coordinate systems into a common coordinate system. Consequently, this process increases data size and latency in the post-computing phase. We define α as the registration ratio, equal to DS_{reg}/DS_{raw}, and W_{reg} as the time

Table 1. The attributes of holographic traffic.

Symbol	Meaning	Examples or values
f	Holographic frame	f_1
F	Holographic frame set	$F = f_1, f_2 \ldots, f_N$
DS_{raw}	Data size of one frame	$5 \sim 10$ MB
DS_{reg}	Data size after registration	$10 \sim 20$ MB
DS_{comp}	Data size after compression	500 KB $\sim$ 2 MB
$FPS_{capture}$	The FPS of the capture	$5 \sim 60$ fps
$FPS_{display}$	The FPS of the display	$5 \sim 60$ fps
$f.priority$	The priority of frame	7
$f.period$	The period of frame	$1/FPS_{capture}$
$f.deadline$	The deadline of frame	$1/FPS_{display}$
$f.src$	The source of frame	node A
$f.dst$	The destination of frame	node B
$f.routing$	The routing path of frame	(src, node, dst)

factor of registration. The latency of data registration can be illustrated as Eq. (1).

$$L_{reg} = W_{reg} \times \alpha DS_{raw} \quad (1)$$

Data compression plays a crucial role in reducing data size, thereby alleviating bandwidth requirements at the cost of increased computing latency. Similar to data registration, we define β as the compression ratio, equal to DS_{comp}/DS_{reg}, and W_{comp} as the time factor of compression. The latency of data compression can be illustrated as Eq. (2).

$$L_{comp} = W_{comp} \times \beta DS_{reg} \quad (2)$$

The post-computing part comprises data decompression, data reconstruction, and rendering. Data decompression is the reverse process of data compression and is set to be lossless to preserve the reality of the data cloud. Therefore, the latency of decompression can be illustrated as Eq. (3).

$$L_{decom} = W_{decom} \times \beta \quad (3)$$

The algorithms for data reconstruction and rendering are indeed crucial challenges, but they are not the focus of this paper. Therefore, we simplify by setting the latency of reconstruction and rendering as a constant T, which is influenced by the registration ratio α, as shown in formula (4).

$$L_{cr} = \alpha \times T \quad (4)$$

In summary, the computing latency can be defined as formula (5).

$$L_{computing} = W_{reg} \times \alpha DS_{raw} + W_{comp} \times \beta DS_{reg} + W_{decom} \times \beta + \alpha \times T \quad (5)$$

2.3 Network Latency Analysis

The switch adopted CQF can be divided into the parser, queues, gate control, selection transmission, and deparser, as depicted in Fig. 2. The parser model processes the packet's header, directing packets into specified queues. The queue model comprises eight priority queues for buffering packets of different traffic types. Gate control supplements one gate at the end of each queue, permitting packet transmission only when the gate is open. The gate control adjusts its state based on the Gate Control List (GCL) generated by scheduling algorithms. The Selection Transmission module forwards packets from the highest priority queue with an open gate. The deparser encapsulates and transmits the packets.

The CQF mechanism employs two queues with the highest priority, operating as a ping-pong approach to forward holographic packets. When the odd queue sends packets, the even queue buffers incoming packets. In the subsequent time slot (we call it cycle), the even and odd queues exchange the roles of sending and buffering. CQF can ensure the bounded latency for holographic traffic by the even-odd queues. Within a single cycle, after sending holographic packets, the remaining queues sequentially transmit Time-Triggered flows, Audio/Video Bridging flows, and Best-effort flows.

In the network, latency can be divided into four parts: processing latency, queuing latency, sending latency, and propagation latency. Processing latency is associated with physical equipment such as the CPU in switches, typically small and negligible. Sending latency is determined by the data size, while propagation latency depends on the distance between two adjacent nodes. However, queuing latency is the only aspect that remains unclear.

Thanks to the CQF mechanism, we can calculate the maximum end-to-end latency and jitter in the network using formulas (6) and (7), where the cycle represents the time slot determined by the characteristics of holographic traffic, and the offset denotes the time shift for scheduling. Both will be introduced in the Sect. 4.

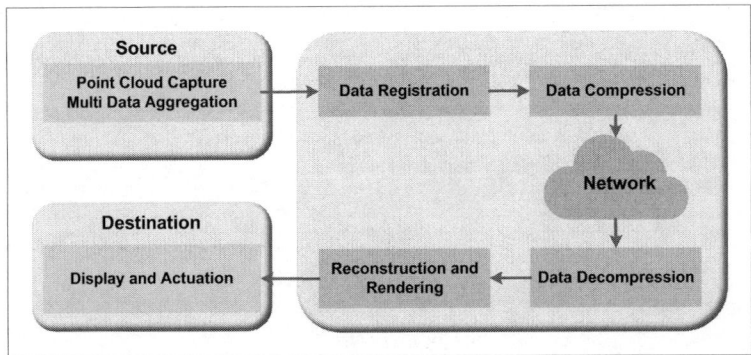

Fig. 1. The process of holographic-type communication.

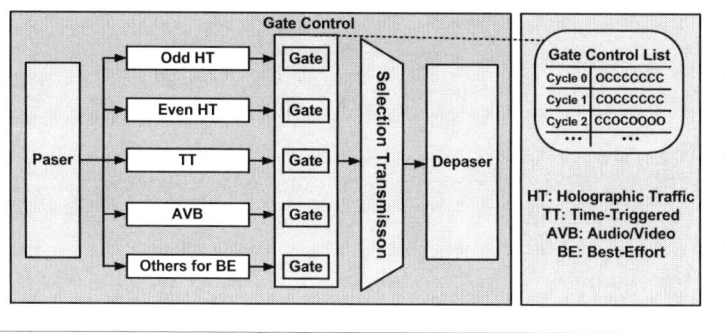

Fig. 2. The model of CQF mechanism.

$$L_{\text{network}} \leq \text{cycle} \times (\text{offset} + \text{hop\_count} + 1) \tag{6}$$

$$J_{\text{network}} \leq 2 \times \text{cycle} \tag{7}$$

3 The DRT Mechanism

3.1 Architecture of HTC System with DRT

The system architecture of HTC can be separated into the application plane, control plane, and data plane, as shown in Fig. 3. The application plane can generate the traffic model and holographic QoS based on the network, computing, and holographic business information. The control plane will adapt the scheduling policy to trade off the networking resources and computing resources. Then, the controller will generate and send the flow tables and configuration files by executing routing and scheduling algorithms. The data plane includes the capture terminal, the front computing part, networking, the back computing part, and the display terminal. For the purpose of accelerating the computing process, we adopt INC, which can leverage the computing resource in edge switches.

The MTP latency is the most crucial parameter for evaluating holographic Quality of Service (QoS), as it represents the overall latency. We disregard equipment latency because it is typically a negligible constant. Therefore, the MTP latency equals the sum of the pre-computing latency, the network latency, and the post-computing latency, as shown in Eq. 8.

$$L_{MTP} = L_{pre\_computing} + L_{networking} + L_{post\_computing} \tag{8}$$

3.2 The Model with DRT

The relationships among these latencies are as follows. If we spend more computing time in point cloud registration, the front computing latency will be longer. And the network latency will be longer as well because the data size is bigger. However, the point cloud registration will bring down the difficulty of reconstruction and rendering algorithms, which represents that the back computing latency and the front computing latency will interact. Besides, if we spend more time in data compression, the data size will be smaller when forwarding in the network. Although the computing latency is longer, the network latency is shorter, which means the computing latency and network latency will affect each other.

These latencies have a complex relationship and interact with each other. For the purpose of analyzing these latencies better, we propose the deterministic computing and network resources tradeoff mechanism, DRT, to tradeoff computing resources and network resources and obtain the bounded MTP latency. Also, we build the optimization problem of DRT, as shown in formula (9).

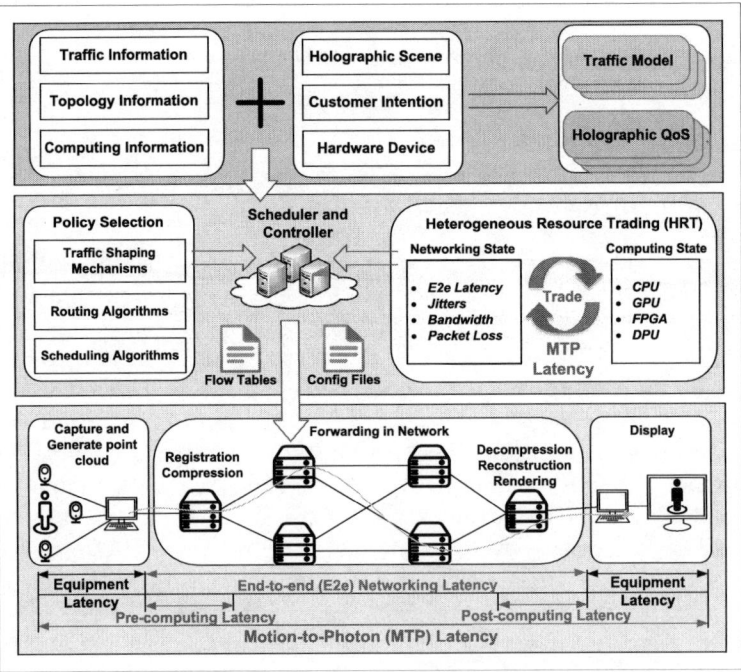

Fig. 3. The architecture of HTC system with DRT mechanism.

$$\min L_{\text{MTP}}$$
s.t.
$$L_{\text{MTP}} = L_{\text{computing}} + L_{\text{network}}$$
$$L_{\text{computing}} + L_{\text{network}} \leq \frac{1}{FPS_{\text{display}}} \quad (9)$$
$$L_{\text{network}} \leq \text{cycle} \times (\text{offset} + \text{hop\_count} + 1)$$
$$L_{\text{network}} \geq \text{cycle} \times (\text{offset} + \text{hop\_count} - 1)$$

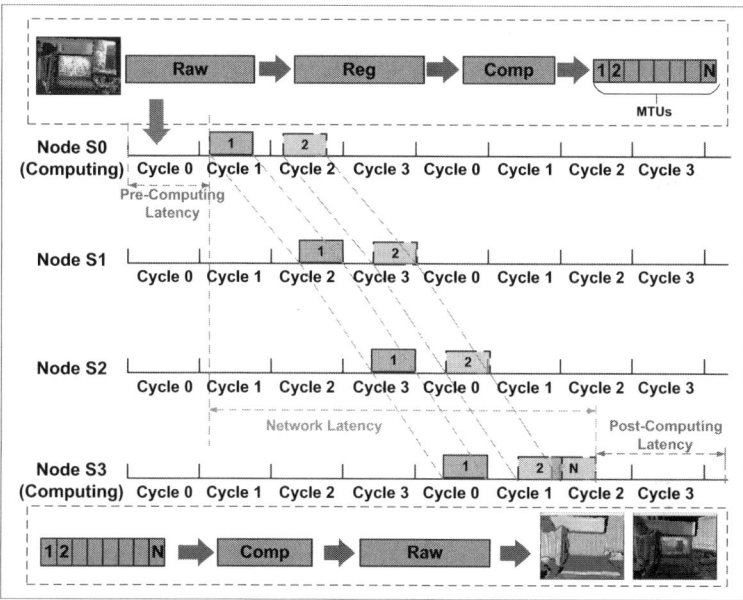

Fig. 4. The transmission of holographic data.

3.3 The Process of Transmission

The process of transmission is shown in Fig. 4. (1) The RGBD cameras capture the point cloud data. (2) The edge switch registers the point cloud data into a common coordinate system and compresses the data. (3) The switches adopt the CQF mechanism and provide the bounded latency for the holographic traffic. (4) When all packet groups are received at the destination node, the switch will converge the packets and decompress them. (5) After decompressing data, the node uses the computing resources to reconstruct and render the point cloud. (6) The display terminal shows the holographic stream.

4 Routing and Scheduling Algorithm

4.1 Scheduling Constraints

For accomplishing the routing and scheduling algorithm, we propose five constraints based on the DRT mechanism.

Cycle and Hypercycle Constraint: In CQF, the cycle serves as the minimum transmission unit. The cycle must not only exceed the sum of the sending delay, propagation delay, processing delay, and queuing delay but also be smaller than the frame interval. In a local area network, we simplify the propagation delay and processing delay, considering them negligible, and set the queuing delay as zero to determine the minimum cycle size. For the maximum cycle size, it can be the Greatest Common Divisor (GCD) of the periods of traffic sets. Therefore, the cycle size can be formulated as Eq. (10).

$$\frac{DS_{comp}}{bandwidth} \leq cycle = CD(F.period) \leq GCD(F.period) \quad (10)$$

The hypercycle is the set of cycles, which is equal to the Least Common Multiple (LCM) of periods of the traffic set, as depicted in Eq. (11).

$$hypercycle = LCM(F.period) \quad (11)$$

Offset Constraint: For the purpose of avoiding the buffer overflow, an offset constraint must be added to specify the initial sending cycle for packets. The offset of holographic frame f_i can be defined as (12).

$$\forall f_i \in F :$$
$$0 \leq \text{offset}_{f_i} \leq \frac{f_i.period}{cycle} - 1 \quad (12)$$

Network Resource Constraint: When the data streams forwarding in the network, we should ensure that the queue resource and bandwidth resource are enough. We use $O(f_i, cycle_k, SW_q, prot_p)$ to judge the packets of f_i whether exists in the $port_p$ of switch SW_q at $cycle_k$, as shown in (13).

$$O(f_i, cycle_k, SW_q, prot_p) = \begin{cases} 1 \longrightarrow packet\ exists \\ 0 \longrightarrow packet\ not\ exists \end{cases} \quad (13)$$

The networking resource constraint can be formulated as (14). R_{queue} represents the queue resources of the switches' queues.

$$\sum_{f_i \in F} DS_{comp} \times O(f_i, cycle_k, SW_q, prot_p) \leq R_{queue} \quad (14)$$

Computing Resource Constraint: The point cloud registration, compression, decompression, point cloud reconstruction, and rendering require computing resources, such as CPU, GPU, FPGA, and so on. In this paper, we assume that the equipment can provide enough computing and that the computing resource constraint can be satisfied.

Algorithm 1. Routing and Scheduling Algorithm for Holographic Traffic

---
Input: Holographic traffic set F, Topology G, Capture FPS $FPS_{capture}$, Display FPS $FPS_{display}$.
Output: Routing R_F, GCL.
1: Calculate cycle and hypercycle by formula (10) and (11);
2: **while** $f_i \in F$ **do**
3:     Generate routing R_F from the Dijkstra(G);
4:     Calculate the max offset by Offset Constraint;
5:     **while** offset $\in$ (offset$_{max}$, 0) **do**
6:        Calculate the MTP latency by MTP Latency Constraint;
7:        **if** Network resource constraint $\cup$ Computing resource constraint **then**
8:           Record the offset, routing and generate the GCL;
9:        **end if**
10:     **end while**
11: **end while**
12: **return** Routing and GCL;

4.2 Routing and Scheduling Algorithm

Based on the scheduling constraints, we have designed the routing and scheduling algorithm, as outlined in Algorithm 1. The input parameters include the holographic traffic set, network topology, capture FPS, and display FPS, while the output comprises routing results and GCL. Line 1 calculates the cycle and hypercycle based on constraints. Line 2 initiates the iteration over holographic traffic. Line 3 utilizes the Dijkstra algorithm to generate routing. Line 4 computes the maximum offset, and Line 6 iterates it. Lines 6 to 10 verify whether the scheduling result satisfies the MTP latency constraint, networking resource constraint, and computing resource constraint. Line 12 returns the routing and scheduling results.

5 Simulation Result

5.1 Experimental Setup

Experimental Environment: We utilize the Intel RealSense D455 as the capture camera and two Dell Precision 7960 workstations with RTX4090 as the data

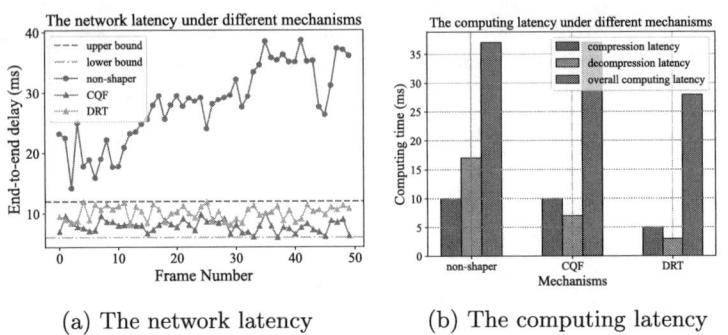

(a) The network latency (b) The computing latency

Fig. 5. The network latency and computing latency under different shaper mechanisms.

processing machines [16]. The capture FPS of the Intel RealSense D455 can be adjusted from 5 FPS to 60 FPS with a resolution of 848 × 480. The computing algorithms, such as registration, compression, decompression, reconstruction, and rendering, are deployed on the workstations. The topology structure mirrors the data plane in Fig. 3, comprising four high-speed forwarding switches, two workstations with computing resources, and six capture cameras.

Parameters Setting: By testing the holographic computing algorithms, the parameters W_{reg}, $Wcomp$, W_{decom} are set as 2.4 ms/MB, 1.2 ms/MB, 1.0 ms/MB in formula (5). For the purpose of simplifying the experiment, we assume that the computing latency of reconstruction and rendering is constant, nearly 20 ms.

5.2 Performance Evaluation

In this section, we evaluate the performance of the proposed approaches. Figure 5 compares the network latency and computing latency under the non-shaper mechanism, CQF, and DRT. The CQF and non-shaper mechanism aim to minimize network latency without considering the computing cost, resulting in the highest compression level. Conversely, DRT leverages the routing and scheduling algorithm and selects a lower compression level.

In Fig. 5(a), it is observed that the network latency is significantly high and the jitter fluctuates sharply with non-shaper mechanisms. This occurs because the bandwidth resources allocated to holographic traffic are occupied by other traffic, leading to a significant increase in queuing delay. When adopting the CQF mechanism, the network latency decreases, but the computing latency is high due to the use of the highest compression level. However, with the DRT mechanism, although the network latency slightly increases compared to CQF, the computing latency is well controlled, as depicted in Fig. 5(b). In a holistic view, DRT outperforms other mechanisms.

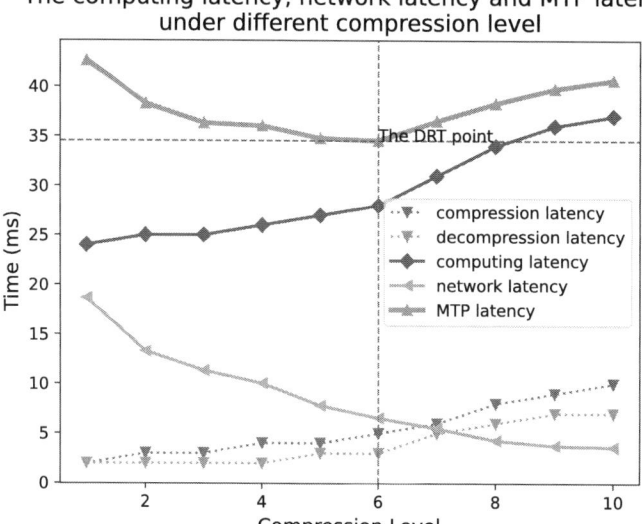

Fig. 6. The MTP latency, computing latency, and network latency under different compression level.

Figure 6 illustrates the computing latency, network latency, and the MTP latency under different compression levels. In this experiment, we use Draco to compress data and adopt DRT to investigate the effect of different compression levels on MTP latency [17]. The compression level with the minimum MTP latency is termed the DRT point, representing the best balance of network resources and computing resources. From Fig. 6, it is evident that a higher compression level results in better compression efficiency but consumes more computing resources and time. Comparing with the non-shaper mechanism and CQF mechanism, the DRT mechanism achieves the lowest MTP latency at 34.78 ms with the compression level equal to 6, providing superior performance and mitigating cybersickness.

Figure 7 illustrates the display FPS under different mechanisms in the prototype. Figure 7(a) displays the FPS of the capture camera at the source node, while Fig. 7(b)-(d) depict the FPS of the display at the sink node under the non-shaper mechanism, CQF, and DRT, respectively. The results indicate that the non-shaper mechanism can provide a maximum of only 12 fps. However, when leveraging CQF, the display FPS can reach 26 fps. On the other hand, using DRT, the display FPS can reach 32, which is suitable for normal visual experiences. At this time, the MTP latency of DRT (32 fps) is nearly three times lower than cases with non-shaper mechanism (12 fps).

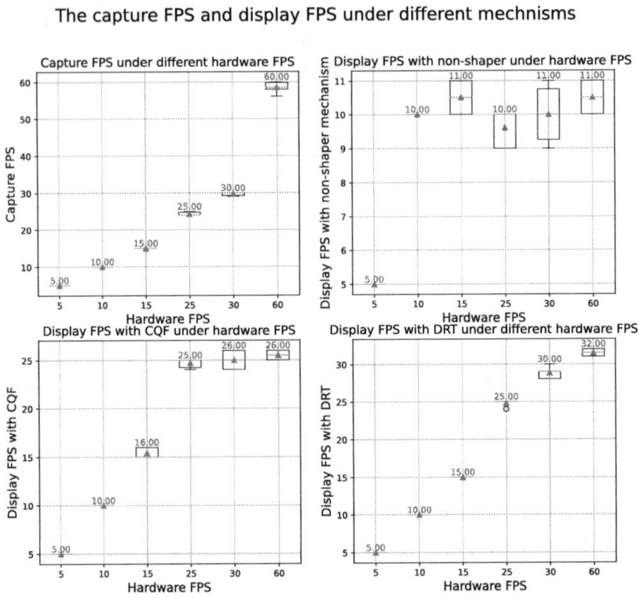

Fig. 7. The display FPS under different mechanisms.

6 Conclusion

This paper proposes the DRT mechanism, which achieves bounded network latency and computing latency by balancing computing resources and network resources. Experimental results demonstrate that DRT effectively ensures bounded MTP latency. The lowest MTP latency at approximately 34.78 ms, nearly three times lower than cases without DRT. The display in the prototype can reach around 32 fps, which can provide normal visual experience and avoid the cybersickness. In the future, we will explore and discuss other factors that will influence the MTP latency in the HTC system.

Acknowledgments. This work is supported by the National Key R&D Program of China under grant 2023YFB2904400, the Major Key Project of PCL under grant No. PCL2023A06, Fundamental Research Funds for the Central Universities under no. 2023JBGP003, Nature and Science Foundation of China under grant no. 62394321, 62072030, 92167204.

References

1. Petkova, R., et al.: Challenges in implementing low-latency holographic-type communication systems. Sensors **22**(24), 9617 (2022)
2. Tataria, H., Shafi, M., Molisch, A.F., Dohler, M., Sjöland, H., Tufvesson, F.: 6G wireless systems: vision, requirements, challenges, insights, and opportunities. Proc. IEEE **109**(7), 1166–1199 (2021). https://doi.org/10.1109/JPROC.2021.3061701

3. Mekuria, R., Blom, K., Cesar, P.: Design, implementation, and evaluation of a point cloud codec for tele-immersive video. IEEE Trans. Circuits Syst. Video Technol. **27**(4), 828–842 (2017). https://doi.org/10.1109/TCSVT.2016.2543039
4. Clemm, A., Vega, M.T., Ravuri, H.K., Wauters, T., Turck, F.D.: Toward truly immersive holographic-type communication: challenges and solutions. IEEE Commun. Mag. **58**(1), 93–99 (2020). https://doi.org/10.1109/MCOM.001.1900272
5. Aghaaliakbari, F., et al.: An architecture for provisioning in-network computing-enabled slices for holographic applications in next-generation networks. IEEE Commun. Mag. **61**(3), 52–58 (2023). https://doi.org/10.1109/MCOM.2200084
6. Huang, Y., Zhu, Y., Qiao, X., Tan, Z., Bai, B.: Aitransfer: progressive AI-powered transmission for real-time point cloud video streaming. In: Proceedings of the 29th ACM Int. Conf. Multimedia, Virtual Event, China, pp. 3989–3997 (Oct. 2021)
7. Akyildiz, Ian F., Hongzhi, G.: Holographic-type communication: a new challenge for the next decade. ITU J. Future Evolving Technol. **3**, 421–442 (2022)
8. Langa, S.F., Montagud, M., Cernigliaro, G., Rivera, D.R.: Multiparty holomeetings: toward a new era of low-cost volumetric holographic meetings in virtual reality. IEEE Access **10**, 81856–81876 (2022). https://doi.org/10.1109/ACCESS.2022.3196285
9. Hosseini, M.: View-aware tile-based adaptations in 360 virtual reality video streaming. In: IEEE Virtual Reality (VR). Los Angeles, CA, USA, pp. 423–424 (2017). https://doi.org/10.1109/VR.2017.7892357
10. Ravuri, H.K., Vega, M.T., Van Hooft, J.D., Wauters, T., De Turck, F.: Adaptive partially reliable delivery of immersive media over QUIC-HTTP/3. IEEE Access **11**, 38094–38111 (2023). https://doi.org/10.1109/ACCESS.2023.3268008
11. Marašević, J., Gavrovska, A.: Virtual Reality and WebRTC implementation for Web educational application development. In: 28th Telecommunications Forum (TELFOR). Belgrade, Serbia, vol. 2020, pp. 1–4 (2020). https://doi.org/10.1109/TELFOR51502.2020.9306513
12. Li, R., Dong, L., Westphal, C., Makhijani, K.: Qualitative communication for emerging network applications with new IP. In: 2021 17th International Conference on Mobility, Sensing and Networking (MSN), Exeter, United Kingdom, pp. 628–637 (2021). https://doi.org/10.1109/MSN53354.2021.00096.
13. Chong, H., Wu, Y., Chen, Z.: Network 2030 a blueprint of technology, applications and market drivers towards the year 2030 and beyond. Int. Telecommun. Union (2018)
14. Deng, L., et al.: A survey of real-time ethernet modeling and design methodologies: from AVB to TSN. ACM Comput. Surv. (CSUR) **55**(2), 1–36 (2022)
15. Nasrallah, A., et al.: Ultra-Low Latency (ULL) Networks: the IEEE TSN and IETF DetNet standards and related 5G ULL research. In: IEEE Commun. Surv. Tutorials **21**(1), 88–145 (2019). https://doi.org/10.1109/COMST.2018.2869350.
16. Zabatani, A. et al.: Intel®RealSense™ SR300 Coded Light Depth Camera. In: IEEE Transactions on Pattern Analysis and Machine Intelligence, vol. 42, no. 10, pp. 2333–2345 (1 Oct. 2020). https://doi.org/10.1109/TPAMI.2019.2915841.
17. Van Rensburg, B.J., Puech, W., Pedeboy, J.-P.: The first Draco 3D object crypto-compression scheme. IEEE Access **10**, 10566–10574 (2022). https://doi.org/10.1109/ACCESS.2022.3144533

Knowledge-Inspired Service

The State of Charge Predication of Lithium-Ion Battery Using Contrastive Learning

Yifeng Xiong[1(✉)], Ting He[1], Yingzhe Mao[2], Wenlong Zhu[1], and Yongxin Liao[1]

[1] School of Computer Science and Technology, Huaqiao University,
Xiamen 361021, China
shadow@stu.hqu.edu.cn

[2] College of Electronics and Information Engineering, University of Science and Technology Liaoning, Anshan 114000, China

Abstract. The State of Charge (SOC) plays a crucial role as an indicator of the current energy level in lithium-ion batteries. However, obtaining the precise value of SOC is challenging due to it being a hidden state quantity. Existing neural network models commonly employ an end-to-end prediction paradigm for SOC estimation, which fails to fully exploit the rich information present in the time-series battery data. To address this limitation, this paper developed a new SOC prediction method utilizing contrastive learning named CLDMM. The proposed approach utilizes data augmentation, multi-scale encoder, and multi-layer perceptrons to learn latent representations, which are subsequently employed for downstream predictive tasks. The Panasonic NCR18650PF dataset is used to evaluate the performance of the proposed method, and the results of experiments demonstrate that CLDMM outperforms the baseline methods and achieves an average mean absolute error (MAE) of 0.73%, and an average maximum error (MAX) of 2.54%.

Keywords: Lithium-ion battery · State of Charge · CLDMM

1 Introduction

As the global energy landscape increasingly pivots towards more sustainable solutions, lithium-ion batteries emerge as pivotal due to their high energy density, superior charging and discharging efficiencies, and rapid response kinetics. Consequently, lithium-ion battery technology has come to predominate the field of energy storage. In this context, the State of Charge (SOC) within an individual lithium-ion battery cell assumes critical importance as a key determinant in energy management systems. Accurately gauging the SOC is essential for optimizing power management strategies, enhancing energy utilization, preventing overcharging and overdischarging, ensuring operational safety, and extending the battery's service life.

However, SOC is inherently a latent state variable, whose precise quantification presents substantial challenges in state estimation. In response to these challenges, service computing emerges as a software-centric computing paradigm that offers a novel perspective and a robust technological framework for the efficient implementation of SOC estimation within Battery Management Systems (BMS).

The integration of contrastive learning models, deployed as services, significantly facilitates the maintenance and updating of these models. This approach is particularly advantageous in scenarios requiring frequent model updates to accommodate new data, such as in the estimation of SOC. By leveraging the service computing framework, these models can be dynamically updated and maintained, ensuring that they remain effective and accurate in real-time applications. This paradigm not only enhances the adaptability and scalability of the SOC estimation process but also improves the overall efficiency and reliability of battery management systems.

The main SOC estimation methods could be classified into the following four types: (i) Open circuit voltage method (OCV). This method establishes an OCV-SOC lookup table through discharge experiments. It estimates the battery SOC by measuring the battery OCV during operation and mapping it to the SOC based on the OCV-SOC relationship [1]. Accurate direct measurement of OCV requires the battery to remain at rest for a sufficient period of time. Therefore, this method is only applicable in laboratories or other specific environments and has certain limitations for online identification. (ii) Ampere-hour integral (AHI) method.AHI is the most widely used SOC estimation method. However, it is prone to being affected by noise, temperature drift, and other unknown random disturbances, resulting in accumulated errors and distorted results. (iii) Model-based method. Especially the equivalent circuit model method relies on parameter identification. The internal parameters of the battery (such as open circuit voltage and internal resistance) need to be re-identified before each use, resulting in poor generalization ability. (iv) Data-driven method, especially deep learning techniques, provides an effective solution to these problems.

As an important branch of machine learning, deep learning provides an effective solution to the above problems. We noticed that existing works have predominantly adopted an end-to-end deep learning prediction paradigm for SOC estimation, directly mapping battery operation-related parameters such as the observed voltage, current, and impedance to the output SOC value. However, such approaches do not fully leverage the rich information inherently contained within the time-series battery data.

Zhao et al [2]. utilized a gated recurrent unit (GRU) structure to better model the nonlinear behaviors exhibited over time by batteries. The GRU architecture, with its capability to recognize long-term dependency within time-series data, allowed for a more accurate representation of the temporal dynamics between battery inputs and outputs. Based on this, they developed current-input and power-input battery models for SOC estimation. Bian et al [3]. constructed an encoder-decoder model with bidirectional long short-term memory (LSTM) networks. The model is able to capture long-term dependencies within the measurement sequences from both past and future directions. This bidirectional approach aims to improve estimation accuracy by providing more contextual information across the whole input sequence compared to conventional unidirectional models. Wang et al [4]. developed a convolutional residual network model for SOC prediction of lithium-ion batteries. By stacking the values of several measurable variables obtained at various time instants as the model inputs. The suggested convolutional residual blocks can be used to efficiently extract the process information for the voltage or current production and their interrelations.

Our approach differs from the above methods in that it is inspired by well-developed contrastive learning algorithms [5–9]. We employ a contrastive learning approach to learn a higher level of representation. In contrast to directly applying prediction models, extracting salient features from the raw data in an unsupervised manner can better capture the underlying temporal dynamics and nonlinear relationships governing battery operation, improve the SOC estimation performance over existing end-to-end methods. The following is a summary of our main contributions:

1. A new SOC prediction method based on contrastive learning is proposed. This approach leverages data augmentation, multi-scale encoder and multi-layer perceptrons to learn latent representations within the embedded space, with the learned representations subsequently utilized for downstream predictive tasks.
2. In order to more effectively extract latent features from the raw battery data, we thoroughly considered the characteristics of battery charging and discharging data and designed a targeted data augmentation method accordingly.
3. The prediction performance of our model was verified using the Panasonic NCR18650PF datasets. The experimental results show that the proposed method accurately estimates the SOC sequence at different ambient temperatures, with an average mean absolute error (MAE) of 0.73% and an average maximum error (MAX) of 2.54% at varying temperatures. We evaluated the effectiveness of our proposed data augmentation techniques and contrastive learning framework by comparing them with other advanced neural network models.

The rest of this work is organized as follows: The detailed presentation of the proposed approach for predicting SOC using contrastive learning is outlined in Sect. 2; The experimental results are reported in Sect. 3; Finally, this work are summarized and directions for future research are discussed in Sect. 4.

2   Model Design

The overall architecture of CLDMM is shown in Fig. 1. To achieve more accurate SOC prediction, our model performs two parts of work separately: perform battery data feature learning and representation extraction based on contrastive learning, and use the representation learning output as the input to perform

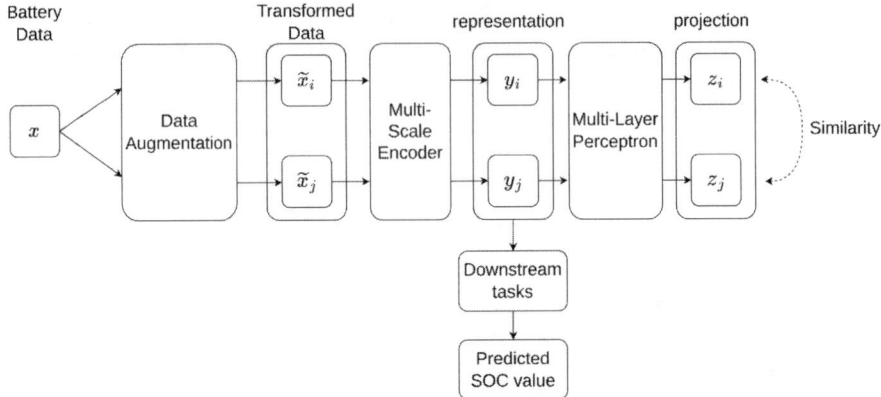

Fig. 1. Overall structure of the proposed model

SOC prediction. We focus on learning feature representations from observed data, with the goal of improving predictive performance.

- Given a battery data series $x = [x_1, x_2, ..., x_T] \in \mathbb{R}^{C \times T}$), where C is the number of features (current, voltage, temperature, etc.) and T denotes the sequence length.
- Two augmented data $\tilde{x}_i$ and $\tilde{x}_j$ of x are created by applying randomly selected augmentation techniques.
- The augmented data is subsequently encoded in the representations y_i and y_j using a multi-scale encoder, yielding a two headed approach.
- As in BYOL [6], the representations y_i and y_j are projected to smaller spaces z_i and z_j by a multi-layer perceptron (MLP) network.
- For each pair of projection representation vectors z_i and z_j, we treat them as positive pairs and calculate their similarity:

$$loss_{i,j} = -log \frac{exp(sim(z_i, z_j)/\tau)}{\sum_{k=1}^{2N} \mathbb{1}_{k \neq i} exp(sim(z_i, z_k)/\tau)} \quad (1)$$

where $\mathbb{1}_{k \neq i} \in [0,1]$ is the indicator function, which corresponds to 1 if $k \neq i$, otherwise 0. And sim($\cdot$) represents the cosine similarity. The loss is further tunable with an additional temperature parameter τ.
- At the end of training, the learned representations y_i and y_j are used as inputs in downstream tasks. In this paper, the Autoformer model uses them to perform the task of predicting the SOC of batteries.

2.1 Data Augmentation for Battery Data

Traditional data augmentation techniques like cropping, scaling, and rotation, commonly used in image tasks, cannot be directly applicable to battery charging or discharging data. Inspired by approaches like SimCLR [5] and CoST [7], we adopted the following data augmentation techniques.

Left-to-Right Flipping. The most right data values become the most left in a left-to-right flip, which is conceptualized as a rotation of the data around the y-axis (channel-axis). This can be expressed as in matrix representation:

$$\widetilde{x} = xJ \qquad (2)$$

where x is the original data, $\widetilde{x}$ denotes the augmented data and $J \in \mathbb{R}^{T \times T}$ is an exchange matrix, then the elements of J are:

$$J_{i,j} = \begin{cases} 1, & \text{\&if } i+j = n+1 \\ 0, & \text{\&if } i+j \neq n+1 \end{cases} \qquad (3)$$

A battery's charging and discharging curves resemble a mirrored pair with very minor variations. By highlighting the differences between mirrored data and real charge/discharge data, allowing the model to more accurately identify the current operating state.

Blockout. We choose at random a region of $m \in T$ adjacent items inside the time-series signal and set all values to 1 for the blockout augmentation. Beginning with data position k, then:

$$\widetilde{x}_{i,j} = \begin{cases} 1, & \text{if } k \leq i \leq k+m \text{ and } k \leq j \leq k+m \\ x_{i,j}, & \text{otherwise} \end{cases} \qquad (4)$$

The SOC of a battery can only reach 1 when it is fully charged. The purpose of blockout augmentation is to enhance the model's awareness of abnormal data.

Jittering. Every time step is augmented with I.I.D. Gaussian noise, derived from a distribution $e \sim \mathcal{N}(0, 0.1)$, where each time step is now:

$$\widetilde{x} = x + e \qquad (5)$$

We selected a 10% range for Gaussian jittering injection due to the inherent inaccuracies in battery SOC monitoring. By perturbing the sequences within this range, the model's ability to generalize was improved while preserving the underlying trends of the original sequences.

2.2 Multi-scale Encoder

The structure of the encoder network is vital for learning a meaningful representation. As illustrated in Fig. 2, we used a convolutional network with multiple filters capable of extracting both global and local information. This network consisted of several filters with different kernel sizes. First, a convolutional projection layer is applied to each input time series. By utilizing the projection layer, we are able to project time series data into a latent space [7,8]. This projection enables us to capture abstract information and identify consistent intra-time relationships between features that may not be readily evident from the raw data itself. Second, we added a set of parallel convolutional layers on top of the projection layer. For augmented data $\tilde{x}$ with length T, we designed $m = [log_2 T]+1$ convolution layers in parallel. The kth convolution has kernel size 2^k, where $k \in \{0, 1, ..., m\}$. This design allowed us to capture information at different scales. After extracting the latent features from the projection layer, each convolution k produces a representation $\hat{y}_{(k)}$. By averaging over $\hat{y}_{(0)}, \hat{y}_{(1)}, ..., \hat{y}_{(m)}$, the final multi-scale representation y is produced.

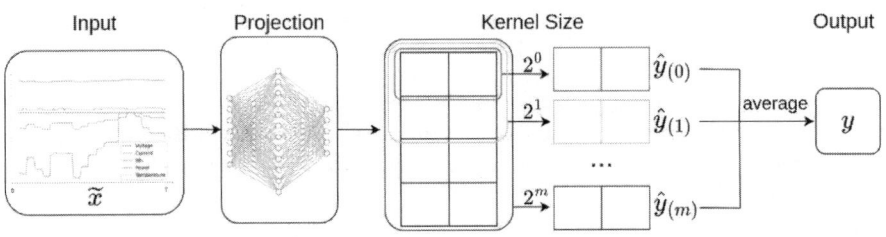

Fig. 2. Structure of Multi-scale Encoder

2.3 MLP Layer

Multi-Layer Perceptrons (MLP) is the most basic neural network architecture. Compared to directly computing the contrastive loss on the representation vectors y, mapping y to a lower-dimensional space z via an MLP and defining the contrastive loss in z can achieve better results. This MLP consists in a linear layer with output size 4096 followed by batch normalization, rectified linear units (ReLU) , and a final linear layer with output dimension 256:

$$z = W^{(2)} ReLU(BN(W^{(1)} y)) \tag{6}$$

where y is multi-scale representation vector, BN is a batch normalization layer, $ReLU$ is a ReLU nonlinearity, $W^{(1)}$ is the first fully connected layer, and $W^{(2)}$ is the second fully connected layer.

Specifically, BatchNorm calculates the batch mean and standard deviation, mapping each sample's feature values to a space where the mean is 0 and standard deviation is 1. It compares each sample to the batch average, realizing positive and negative contrast, performing implicit contrastive learning and enhancing the contrast effect.

3 Experiments and Results

3.1 Dataset and Experimental Setup

The Li-ion battery data used in this paper are from University of Wisconsin-Madison [10]. The dataset contains data from a 2.9 Ah nickel cobalt aluminum chemistry Li-ion battery (Panasonic NCR18650PF). The measured data were collected during experimental tests conducted under varied ambient temperature conditions. For each test, the battery cell was initially brought to a full SOC. The battery was charged after each test at a 1C rate to 4.2V, 50mA cut off, with battery temperature 12°C or greater. The cell was cycled according to nine different driving schedules: US06, HWFET, UDDS, LA92, neural network (NN), and Cycles 1 to 4, under ambient temperatures of 25°C, 10°C, 0°C, −10°C, and −20°C.

As previously indicated, Cycles 1 to 4 were used as the training dataset. NN driving schedule was specially designed to help train neural networks, its related data were used as the validation set. Finally, the data of the US06 and HWFET were retained for model testing.

The experiments were conducted on Ubuntu 22.04 system, Python 3.8.18, and Pytorch framework 2.1.1. Training was performed on a single NVIDIA RTX A4000 GPU, with a batch size of 32, and lasted for 10 epochs. A dynamic learning rate was utilized in this study, starting with an initial value of 0.0001. Following the first epoch, the learning rate was halved at the beginning of each subsequent epoch.

3.2 Evaluation Metrics

To accurately evaluate the performance of the proposed method, the MAE and MAX were used as evaluation criteria. Their mathematical representations are as follows:

$$MAE = \frac{1}{N} \sum_{i=1}^{N} \left| \widehat{SOC} - SOC \right| \qquad (7)$$

$$MAX = max_{i=1,\dots,N}(\left| \widehat{SOC} - SOC \right|) \qquad (8)$$

where SOC and $\widehat{SOC}$ represent the measured and the estimated values of the SOC, respectively, and N is the total number of samples.

3.3 Comparison of Experiment Results

As shown in Fig. 3, temperature greatly affects battery performance. During low-temperature discharge, the battery discharge voltage drops sharply and reaches the discharge cutoff voltage more quickly. The available capacity at 0°C is 80%, only 70% at −10°C. At lower temperatures, this leads to greater prediction errors for the state of charge.

In order to verify the validity of the proposed model, the following four sophisticated neural network models are selected for comparison. Including BLSTM-ED [3], CRN [4], SBLSTM [11] and SPA-ED [12], the experimental results are shwn in Table 1. Given the disparities in the data used by the aforementioned models, we opted to conduct comparative analyses solely based on the shared 25°C, 10°C, and 0°C samples.

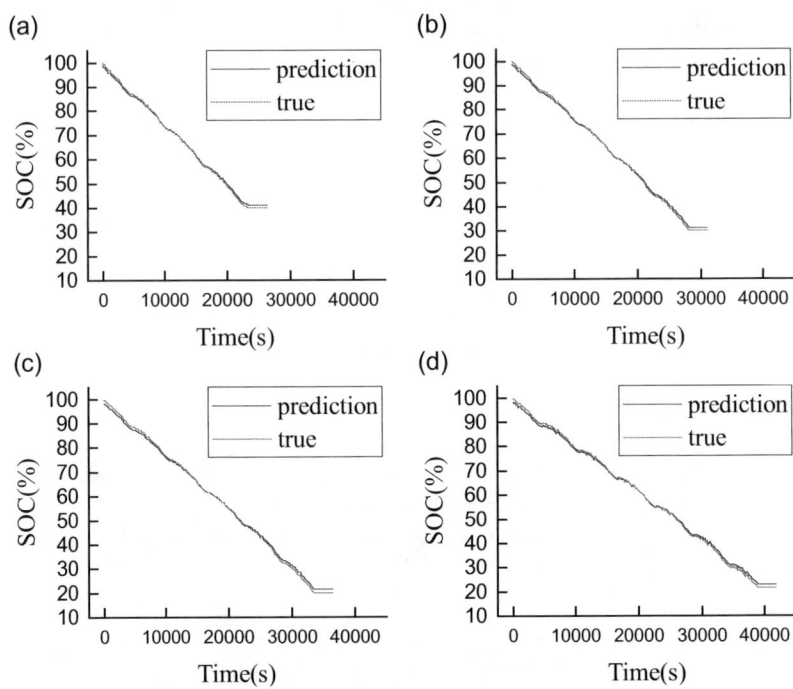

Fig. 3. SOC prediction results of different temperatures: (a)−20°C, (b)−10°C, (c)0°C and (d)10°C on the US06 conditions.

Table 1. Comparison results with different temperatures tested on the US06 and HWFET driving cycles(SPA-ED didn't give results of other temperature in the paper).

Models	Temperature					
	25°C		10°C		0°C	
Metric	MAE	MAX	MAE	MAX	MAE	MAX
SBLSTM [11]	0.73	3.04	1.00	4.75	1.13	5.71
BLSTM-ED [3]	0.77	3.85	1.04	4.02	1.11	4.17
SPA-ED [12]	0.77	1.98	–	–	–	–
CRN [4]	0.51	1.92	0.75	2.68	0.936	2.672
CLDMM	**0.56**	**2.01**	**0.76**	**2.28**	**0.89**	**3.33**

As shown in Table 1, at 25°C, CLDMM achieves MAE of 0.56% and MAX of 2.01%, outperforming LSTM-based methods including SBLSTM [11], BLSTM-ED [3] and SPA-ED [12]. As the temperature decreases to 10°C, the MAE of CLDMM remains essentially the same as the CRN [4] model. However, CLDMM achieves a lower MAX error of 2.28% compared to 2.68% for the CRN model. This indicates that CLDMM enhances the ability to identify the detrimental effects of lowered temperature on battery dynamics and characteristics. Similarly, at the lowest temperature of 0°C, CLDMM achieves the lowest MAE of 0.89% amongst all compared methods. This suggests that the contrastive learning-based framework adopted by CLDMM facilitates a more comprehensive extraction and utilization of intrinsic temporal dependencies and contextual information encapsulated within battery data. By learning a higher level representation and extracting salient features from the raw data in an unsupervised manner, it can better capture the underlying temporal dynamics and nonlinear relationships governing battery operation, thereby improving the accuracy of SOC.

4 Conclusion

Accurate estimation of SOC is paramount for ensuring the safety and reliability of lithium-ion batteries. however, the SOC is inherently unmeasurable and exhibits nonlinear variations influenced by multiple factors. Traditional neural network models, which have predominantly employed an end-to-end prediction paradigm for SOC estimation, often fail to fully exploit the rich temporal information embedded within battery data sequences. In this paper, we introduce a novel SOC prediction method utilizing contrastive learning, termed CLDMM. This method enhances learning by employing data augmentation and a multi-scale encoder designed to capture latent representations within an embedded space. These representations subsequently utilized for downstream predictive tasks. By integrating contrastive learning models as services within BMS, we propose a dynamic, robust, and scalable framework capable of adapting promptly to new data inputs and changing operational conditions. This service-oriented deployment facilitates continuous model improvement and real-time data processing, which are crucial for maintaining system reliability and performance. Experimental results demonstrate that the CLDMM method can precisely estimate the SOC sequence under varying ambient temperatures. Future research will focus on further refining the model structure to enhance its performance across diverse temperature conditions.

References

1. Yu, Q., et al.: An open circuit voltage model fusion method for state of charge estimation of lithium-ion batteries. Energies **14**(7), 1797 (2021)
2. Zhao, R., Kollmeyer, P.J., Lorenz, R.D., Jahns, T.M.: A compact methodology via a recurrent neural network for accurate equivalent circuit type modeling of lithium-ion batteries. IEEE Trans. Ind. Appl. **55**(2), 1922–1931 (2018)
3. Bian, C., He, H., Yang, S., Huang, T.: State-of-charge sequence estimation of lithium-ion battery based on bidirectional long short-term memory encoder-decoder architecture. J. Power Sources **449**, 227558 (2020)
4. Wang, Y.C., Shao, N.C., Chen, G.W., Hsu, W.S., Wu, S.C.: State-of-charge estimation for lithium-ion batteries using residual convolutional neural networks. Sensors **22**(16), 6303 (2022)

5. Chen, T., Kornblith, S., Norouzi, M., Hinton, G.: A simple framework for contrastive learning of visual representations. In: International Conference on Machine Learning, pp. 1597–1607. PMLR (2020)
6. Grill, J.B., et al.: Bootstrap your own latent-a new approach to self-supervised learning. Adv. Neural. Inf. Process. Syst. **33**, 21271–21284 (2020)
7. Woo, G., Liu, C., Sahoo, D., Kumar, A., Hoi, S.: CoST: contrastive learning of disentangled seasonal-trend representations for time series forecasting. arXiv preprint arXiv:2202.01575 (2022)
8. Zheng, X., Chen, X., Schürch, M., Mollaysa, A., Allam, A., Krauthammer, M.: SimTS: rethinking contrastive representation learning for time series forecasting. arXiv preprint arXiv:2303.18205 (2023)
9. Yue, Z., et al.: TS2Vec: towards universal representation of time series. In: Proceedings of the AAAI Conference on Artificial Intelligence, vol. 36, pp. 8980–8987 (2022)
10. Kollmeyer, P.: "Panasonic 18650PF Li-ion Battery Data" (Jun 2018). https://doi.org/10.17632/wykht8y7tg.10jk
11. Bian, C., He, H., Yang, S.: Stacked bidirectional long short-term memory networks for state-of-charge estimation of lithium-ion batteries. Energy **191**, 116538 (2020)
12. Wu, L., Zhang, Y.: Attention-based encoder-decoder networks for state of charge estimation of lithium-ion battery. Energy **268**, 126665 (2023)

A Feature Dataset of Microservices-Based Systems

Weipan Yang[1], Bingyu Song[2], Yongchao Xing[1], Yiming Lyu[1], Huihui Cui[2], Zhihao Liang[1], and Zhiying Tu[1](✉)

[1] School of Computer Science and Technology, Harbin Institute of Technology, Weihai 264209, China
{23S030135,22B903085,2201110523,2201110520}@stu.hit.edu.cn,
tzy_hit@hit.edu.cn
[2] Weichai Power Co., Ltd., Weifang, China
{songby,cuihuihui}@weichai.com

Abstract. Microservice architecture has become a dominant architectural style in the service-oriented software industry. Poor practices in the design and development of microservices are called microservice bad smells. In microservice bad smells research, the detection of these bad smells relies on feature data from microservices. However, there is a lack of an appropriate open-source microservice feature dataset. The availability of such datasets may contribute to the detection of microservice bad smells unexpectedly. To address this research gap, this paper collects a number of open-source microservice systems utilizing Spring Cloud. Additionally, feature metrics are established based on the architecture and interactions of Spring Boot style microservices. And an extraction program is developed. The program is then applied to the collected open-source microservice systems, extracting the necessary information, and undergoing manual verification to create an open-source feature dataset specific to microservice systems using Spring Cloud. The dataset is made available through a CSV file. We believe that both the extraction program and the dataset have the potential to contribute to the study of microservice bad smells.

Keywords: Microservice · Spring Cloud · Bad Smell · Dataset

1 Introduction

Microservice architecture has become a dominant architectural style in the service-oriented software industry [1]. Microservice architecture achieves the decoupling of a complex business into multiple small-grained microservices. Each microservice operates in its own process, allowing independent deployment, scalability, and testing, while fulfilling a specific functional responsibility. The communication between microservices relies on lightweight mechanisms [2, 3].

Since the rise of microservice architectures, research on poor practices in designing and developing microservices has followed, and such research is known as microservice bad smells [4] or microservice-based antipattern research [5]. The research methodology can be broadly classified into two categories: static analysis based on source code [6, 7] and analysis during system runtime [8]. The former is the primary focus of relevant research. Regrettably, most studies in this field have primarily focused on establishing a set of metrics for detecting bad smells based on bad smells definitions. Subsequently, they evaluate the presence of bad smells by analyzing the metrics data. However, there is a relative scarcity of studies that comprehensively analyze the structure of microservice systems, extract more comprehensive feature metrics, evaluate the granularity of microservices, their design, and the interactions between different microservices based on the architecture and interaction of microservices, and subsequently explore the occurrence of poor practices within and between microservices. Additionally, it is necessary to explore the quality attributes defined in ISO25010:2023 [9], such as system modularity and maintainability, in the context of microservices. This exploration should be based on metrics extracted from the diverse fundamental elements of microservices. To address the current gap, this paper analyzes the architecture and interactions of microservices based on Spring in various Spring Cloud style microservice systems, establishes the relevant metrics of various fundamental elements of microservices in Spring Boot style, which are based on the three-tier architecture, collects open-source microservice systems, implements the extraction program[1], and constructs a dataset containing microservice feature data, which in turn paves the way for exploring poor practices within and between different microservices through machine learning, heuristic algorithms, and other means. To achieve this objective, the paper presents and resolves the following three problems.

RQ1: How can an amount of Spring Cloud style microservice systems be collected as data sources and organized into a catalog for constructing feature dataset?

RQ2: How to identify the various basic elements that need to be extracted for Spring Cloud style microservice systems and extract them accordingly?

RQ3: How can the accuracy of the extracted data be validated to create a reliable dataset?

This paper presents the following studies and solutions in response to the three questions.

1. For RQ1, Spring Cloud style microservice systems are initially screened on GitHub by applying specific search conditions. Third-party libraries, frameworks, and development tools like Low-Code development platforms are excluded. Subsequently, from the remaining open-source projects, the more mature projects are selected to compile an open-source catalog[2] of Spring Cloud style microservice systems.
2. For RQ2, we analyze Spring Boot style microservices in Spring Cloud style microservice system[3]. Focusing on the three-tier architecture of individual microservices and adhering to their respective naming conventions, we identify crucial classes and interface files within microservices. On this basis, we define fourteen metrics to capture the fundamental aspects of individual microservices and derive nine supplementary metrics from the initial fourteen. By utilizing these twenty-three metrics, an initial

---
[1] https://github.com/yang66-hash/BSStaticAnalysis.git.
[2] https://github.com/yang66-hash/microservice-catalog.git.
[3] https://spring.io/microservices

evaluation can be conducted on the granularity, design, and interactions between different microservices. Finally, the extraction program for the metrics is implemented with the aid of toolkits like JavaParser, JGit, and Maven-Model.
3. For RQ3, this paper verifies the extracted data manually to ensure its accuracy. A part of the verification results is presented in Table 2. Ultimately, the manually verified data is curated as the feature dataset of open-source microservice systems. The dataset is made available through a .csv file[4].

The rest of the paper is structured as follows: Sect. 2 introduces the related work of this paper, Sect. 3 introduces how to construct the catalog of microservice systems, Sect. 4 introduces how to establish the twenty-three metrics as well as the extraction logic of the program and the important algorithms. Section 5 elaborates on the feature data and validates its accuracy, Sect. 6 discusses the limitations of this research, and Sect. 6 concludes the paper by summarizing the findings and suggesting future work based on the feature dataset and extraction program.

2 Related Work

In the research of code bad smells, researchers have extracted relevant metrics data from various open-source projects to build different datasets [10–12]. A dataset focusing on technical debts and code bad smells is created by establishing 30 distinct software metrics [10]. This was done by analyzing 33 open-source Apache Software Foundation Java projects with the aid of third-party tools like SonarQube. Tighilt et.al.[13] attempts to detect code bad smells by machine learning.

In recent years, the research on microservice bad smells has expanded extensively, resulting in continuous extensions of the bad smells catalog [14, 15]. Moreover, the related detection methods for these bad smells have been continuously updated, which roughly include static analysis [7, 16] and detection based on runtime data [8]. There also have attempts to apply machine learning algorithms in detection [17, 18]. An open-source dataset was formed through an analysis of the effective lines of code and dependencies in 20 open-source microservice systems [17]. Abid et.al. [18] confirm the feasibility of establishing metrics, generating association rules using machine learning, and detecting the quality of web service. This confirmation indirectly supports the feasibility of integrating metrics and machine learning for the detection of microservice bad smells. However, there is a lack of work on extracting comprehensive metrics data tailored to microservice systems, and the absence of an open-source dataset that captures microservice characteristics. This constraint impedes the application of machine learning to microservice bad smell detection and limits the scope of investigating the correlation between the design, implementation of microservice systems and their associated quality attributes. To bridge this gap, this paper concentrates on establishing the extraction of metrics for various fundamental elements of microservices based on Spring Boot three-tier architecture in Spring Cloud style microservice systems. We implement an extraction program, collect data from open-source systems, conduct extraction and manual verification, and create an open-source dataset comprising microservice system feature data.

---

[4] https://github.com/yang66-hash/Spring-Cloud-Microservice-Dataset.git.

This dataset will serve as a fundamental resource for the application of machine learning algorithms and further research in the domain of microservice bad smell detection.

Table 1. A subset of selected microservice systems.

Name	Service number	Multiple tags	Introduction	Stars
apollo	5	Yes	Apollo is a reliable configuration management system suitable for microservice configuration management scenarios	28.7K
gpmall	10	No	E-commerce platform based on microservices	4.8k
mogu_blog_v2	7	Yes	Microservices-based open-source blog system	1.5k
mall4cloud	11	Yes	Microservices-based mall system	5.5k
microservice-recruit	7	No	Microservices-based open-source intelligent recruitment system	209
siam-cloud	9	No	Microservices-based open-source takeaway delivery system	27
Scblogs	5	Yes	Microservices-based open-source campus blog system	318
Seckillcloud	4	Yes	Microservices-based mall system	36
spring-petclinic-microservices	7	Yes	Distributed version of the Spring Pet-Clinic Sample Application	1.5k
train-tickets	41	Yes	The project is a train ticket booking system based on microservice architecture which contains 41 microservices [20]	627

3 Microservice System Selection

Ewan Tempero et al. [19] curate and make available a collection of Java projects. However, to date, there has been no research undertaken to select and organize open-source Spring Cloud style microservice systems. We select open-source projects based on microservice architecture from GitHub, the open-source code hosting platform, as the primary source for feature data extraction. These projects are microservice systems developed based on the Java Spring Cloud framework. In this paper, we curate and share a catalog comprising 55 microservice systems. Among these projects, 13 systems have multiple versions, and 14 systems have more than 1000 Stars on GitHub, which are diverse, encompassing backend management systems, e-commerce platforms, blog systems, and other types.

In the specific search and retrieval process, the following strings were used to initially screen relevant projects: "topic:microservices language:Java" and "topic:spring-cloud language:Java".

We filter 2800 microservice system projects based on the former search condition and an additional 2700 microservice projects based on the latter. Subsequently, we exclude projects that are duplicated and other projects, including third-party libraries, frameworks and Low-Code development tools. From the remaining microservice systems, we further filter and select 55 systems for data extraction purposes. The specific screening rules are as follows.

1. The microservice system should consist of four or more microservices, and the business division among microservices should be logically sound.
2. The system should have service registration and service discovery mechanisms.
3. The preferred selection is open-source systems with multiple stable versions, meaning that the associated GitHub repository should have multiple release tags.
4. The most microservices in the system should be developed on Spring Boot.

The prioritization of selecting open-source microservice systems with at least 4 microservices and multiple versions aims to ensure that the chosen systems possess a certain level of maturity in terms of project scale and development standards. As for the fourth rule, we found the most open-source microservice systems based on Spring Cloud satisfy this. Table 1 presents the top 10 most representative open-source projects that were collected and utilized for this research, along with their corresponding introductions.

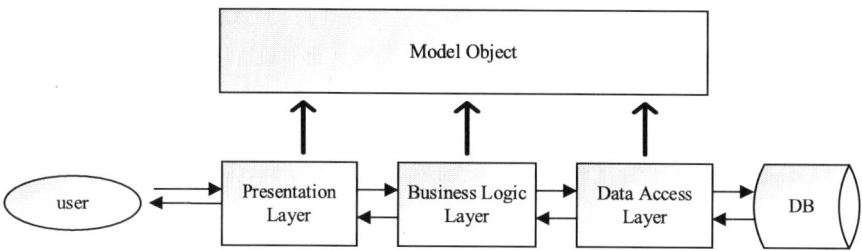

Fig. 1. Three-tier architecture of microservice based on Spring Boot

4 Extraction Strategy

4.1 Establishing Extraction Metrics

Spring Cloud is built upon the foundations of the Spring and Spring Boot frameworks. Although the microservices architecture of Spring Cloud is inherently distributed, individual microservices, which are vertically partitioned based on business logic, are commonly developed using Spring Boot and adhere to the widely adopted three-tier architecture (shown in Fig. 1). The microservice systems collected in Sect. 3 also confirm this. The architecture primarily involves the following four aspects:

- **The presentation layer** is responsible for receiving and handling user requests, as well as presenting results to the users. In Spring Boot style microservices, this mainly refers to the controller layer, which is typically annotated with @RestController or @Controller. We establish a series of metrics including controllerNum, serviceImplCall, and others about APIs.
- **The business logic layer** is responsible for handling the business logic and rules of the application. In Spring Boot style microservices, this mainly refers to the service layer, which coordinates and processes the business workflows. It is annotated with @Service. We establish the metric of serviceClassNum and interfaceNum.
- **The data access layer** is responsible for interacting with the database and performing data persistence and retrieval operations. In Spring Boot style microservices, this mainly refers to repositories, which encapsulate database operations such as data manipulation (CRUD). Spring Data JPA or other ORM frameworks are commonly used for data access implementation. We also add up the data access operation interfaces to interfaceNum.
- **Model** objects are Java objects used for encapsulating and transferring data. They represent business data in the microservice and are responsible for operations such as data retrieval, storage, and modification. We establish a series of entity-related metrics and Data Transfer Object metrics.

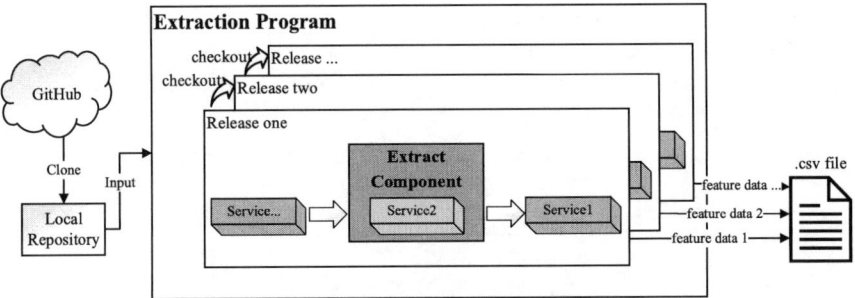

Fig. 2. Extraction program working framework.

Besides the metrics mentioned above, we also establish other metrics, such as codeSize, serviceCall, serviceCalled, to show the effective lines of source code of microservices, and the invocation relationships among microservices. All these metrics enable an evaluation of the microservices' granularity, design, and interaction relationships. Detailed information regarding these metrics is presented in Table 2. Among them, fourteen metrics are directly extracted, while the remaining nine metrics are calculated and derived based on these fourteen metrics.

Table 2. Introduction of metrics.

Name	Introduction	Classification
codeSize	The effective lines of source code in all .java files of the microservice	Code lines
entityNum	The number of object classes used for persistent storage in the microservice	Classes
entityAttributeNum	The number of attributes contained in the microservice entity classes	
controllerNum	The number of controllers in the microservice	
interfaceNum	The number of interfaces in the microservice	
abstractClassNum	The number of abstract classes in the microservice	
serviceClassNum	The number of service implementation classes in the microservice	
dtoClassNum	The number of Data Transfer Object classes in the microservice	
APINum	The number of APIs exposed by the microservice	APIs
maxParaNum	The maximum value of the parameter list size of all APIs exposed	
APIVersionSet	The collection of versions for APIs exposed by the current microservice. It's a set of Strings representing versions	
serviceImplCall	The data structure is a map, where the keys correspond to the methods of service implementation classes invoked in the controller classes within the microservice. The values in the collection represent the count of internal invocations for each method	Interaction
serviceCall	The data structure is $Map < serviceA, < ServiceB, times > >$, where ServiceA acts as the primary key, ServiceB serves as the nested key, and the associated value, times, denotes the frequency of ServiceA invoking ServiceB	

(*continued*)

Table 2. (*continued*)

Name	Introduction	Classification
serviceCalled	The data structure is $Map < serviceA, < ServiceB, times >>$, where ServiceA acts as the primary key, ServiceB serves as the nested key, and the associated value, times, denotes the frequency of ServiceA being invoked by ServiceB	
aveEntityAttribute	The ratio obtained by dividing the total number of attributes in entity classes by the total number of entity classes	Classes
APIVersionNum	The size of APIVersionSet	APIs
serviceImplCallNum	The total number of times the controller layer invokes methods within the service implementation layer	Interaction
maxServiceCall	The maximum number of times the current microservice invokes other microservices	
serviceCallCate	The number of distinct microservices invoked by the current microservice	
serviceCallPer	The percentage of distinct microservices invoked by the current microservice out of the total number of microservices in the system	
maxServiceCalled	The maximum number of times the current microservice is called by other microservices	
serviceCalledCate	The number of distinct microservices that invoke the current microservice	
serviceCalledPer	The percentage of distinct microservices that invoke the current microservice out of the total number of microservices in the system	

4.2 Extraction Program for Metrics

The microservice systems gathered in Sect. 3 consist of Maven projects based on Spring Cloud style. We parse and extract feature data from each microservice system. The working framework for the extraction program is illustrated in Fig. 2. Firstly, the microservice system is cloned from GitHub to the local repository, and then the extraction program is executed to obtain feature data for each release of the repository. Lastly, the extracted data from each release is aggregated into a .csv file and stored in a predetermined file path.

The most important part of the extraction program is the **extract component**, which consists of the following four small parts of the extraction functionality.

Extract Code Count. Drawing inspiration from existing open-source tool cloc[5] for counting effective lines of source code.

---
[5] https://github.com/AlDanial/cloc.git.

Extract Feature Data About Various Classes Related to Spring Boot Style Microservices. The extraction of different classes primarily involves analyzing the programming conventions of the traditional three-tier architecture in Spring Boot. This analysis combines package naming conventions with regular expressions for filtering and matching, and also includes the direct identification of classes with specific annotations. The main classes comprise controller, serviceImpl, interface, Entity, DTO, and abstract. The Controller corresponds to the Presentation Layer, serviceImpl corresponds to the Business Logic Layer, interface corresponds to the Data Access Layer's data operation interfaces, Entity corresponds to the database mapping and persistence objects in the Model, and DTO corresponds to the data transfer objects between the Presentation Layer and Business Logic Layer in the Model. Among them, accurately identifying the quantity of Entity and DTO classes poses a relative challenge, whereas the remaining parts can be accurately identified based on their corresponding annotations.

- Entity classes: Entity refers to the object classes, which are utilized for mapping and persistence with the database. In this study, we perform initial filtering of Java files by applying regular expressions (1) to the package path. Subsequently, the presence of relevant annotations is determined based on the utilized data access dependencies. If these annotations are detected, the class is classified as an entity. For instance, when employing the Spring Data JPA, the presence of the @Entity annotation in the file is verified to classify it as an entity class.

$$[/\backslash\backslash\backslash\backslash](?i)(entity|pojo|model|domain|bean)[/\backslash\backslash\backslash\backslash] \qquad (1)$$

- Data Transfer Object classes: Serve as data transfer objects between the Presentation Layer and Business Logic Layer. By matching class names that start or end with the string "dto" or by using regular expression (2) to match all class files within the package named "dto" in the package path.

$$[/\backslash\backslash\backslash\backslash](?i)dto[/\backslash\backslash\backslash\backslash] \qquad (2)$$

Feature Data About APIs Exposed. Each method within the Controller classes is parsed, to identify annotations such as @RequestMapping (or its variants for Get, Post, Put, Delete, Patch) that associate HTTP requests with the "public" declaration. If these criteria are met, the method is considered a valid API and documented accordingly. Additionally, the maximum value of the parameter list size for each API is recorded, and the API version is detected by capturing the HTTP path and matching regular expression (3).

$$/(?i)v\backslash d + (\backslash.\backslash d+)? \qquad (3)$$

Interaction Between Microservices The extraction of this part is challenging. We aim to extract the invocation relationships among microservices in a microservice system. These invocation relationships provide insight into the system's internal interactions and assist in identifying some potential microservice bad smells. Currently, most microservices communicate with each other using either RestTemplate or Feign.

```
private String getServiceUrl(String serviceName) { return "http://" + serviceName; }

@Override
public Response createFoodDeliveryOrder(FoodDeliveryOrder fd, HttpHeaders headers) {
    String stationFoodStoreId = fd.getStationFoodStoreId();

    String station_food_service_url = getServiceUrl( serviceName: "ts-station-food-service");  // 1.detect method call
    ResponseEntity<Response<StationFoodStoreInfo>> getStationFoodStore = restTemplate.exchange(
            url: station_food_service_url + "/api/v1/stationfoodservice/stationfoodstores/bystoreid/" + stationFoodStoreId,
            HttpMethod.GET,   2. replace field/variable and method call recursivly
            new HttpEntity(headers),
            new ParameterizedTypeReference<Response<StationFoodStoreInfo>>() {
    });
```

Fig. 3. Explanation of the image depicting the detection method.

For the method of the RestTemplate class, we utilizes the JavaParser to parse methods in Java classes, aiming to determine whether the methods of the RestTemplate class are invoked for HTTP requests and to extract the first parameter representing the URL. However, when extracting the first parameter directly, the result may be a combination of a variable name or method call with part of a URL, rather than the actual URL. This may result in inaccuracy in the analysis of microservice invocations. Hence, we employ a method that recursively extracts and replaces the value of the variable or method call, effectively transforming the URL expression into a concatenated string format. And then matching the microservice name with the regular expression (4) for counting. An example is shown in Fig. 3. Firstly, the exchange method call should be detected. After that, variable station_food_service_url should be replaced by the method call of getServiceUrl, and then this method call will be replaced by "http://" + "ts-station-food-service" in recursively. Finally, the microservice name will be matched by the regular expression.

$$\backslash\backslash S * (service|Service|SERVICE) \qquad (4)$$

Algorithm 1 describes the process of extracting the method call of the RestTemplate class and matching regular expression (4) for the microservice name being invoked. In our implementation, we parse on each Java class, get a list of fields (with each field corresponding to a FieldDeclaration object) and methods (with each method corresponding to a MethodDeclaration object), which are the input of Algorithm 1. And then we conduct a search within the fieldDeclarations list to identify the declaration of RestTemplate objects. If such declaration is found, we iterate through each MethodDeclaration associated with that class, applying Algorithm 1 to extract the collection of expressions representing method calls of the RestTemplate class within each method. We further analyze the URL parameters of each method call statement within the expressions. Then employ a recursive approach to substitute any remaining NameExpr (variable expression in JavaParser) and MethodCallExpr (method call expression) until the URL parameter is transformed into a concatenated string format. Subsequently, put the microservice name and call times into callMap. Finally, this approach enhances the precision of static analysis when establishing microservice invocation relationships. However, it is crucial to recognize that the scope of this URL parameter parsing method is limited to variables and method calls within the confines of the Java class in question. It is essential to note that if there are references to static constants or functions external to the class, the possibility of misjudgment arises.

Algorithm 1: Extract service call in method.

Input: The set of field declarations for parsed class currently: filedDeclarations. The set of method declarations for parsed class: methodDeclarations. The position of the method being analyzed in methodDeclarations currently: i.
Output: The map of microservice calls, the key is the microservice name while the call times is value: callMap.
1: expressions ← ∅;
2: callMap ← ∅;
3: method ← methodDeclarations.get(i);
4: **if** get restTemplateName methodCallExpr in method **do**
5:   add methodCallExpr to expressions;
6: **end if**
7: **for** expr in expressions **do**
8:   urlExpr ← parse first argument in expr;
9:   url ← replace variables and method Calls in urlExpr in recursive;
10: serviceName ← matching url with regular expression (6);
11: callMap.put(serviceName,callMap.getOrDefault(serviceName, 0) + 1);
12:**end for**
13:**return** callMap;

When detecting microservice communication using Feign, our approach involves searching for classes or interface files that are annotated with @FeignClient. From these files, we extract the respective microservice name by retrieving the value stored in the "value" or "name" field. Subsequently, we analyze the outcome of invoking these feign clients within other Java classes.

4.3 Validate of Extracted Data

The feature extraction program was executed on 55 microservice systems, yielding a total of 1446 data points. Subsequently, after removing data from the registry center, gateway, and instances of misjudgment, a remaining set of 1180 data points was obtained. We conducted a correctness verification of each data point by cross-referencing it with the source code manually. Figure 4 illustrates the distribution and presence of outliers for each numerical metric within this refined dataset. The median is represented by a red solid line, while the mean is denoted by a blue dashed line. Notably, the data exhibits a power-law distribution. The data distribution of each metric exhibits a notable concentration within a narrow range. For example, upon conducting statistical analysis of metric data from various classes, it becomes evident that most data points reside within the lower range. However, a considerable number of data points also exhibit outlier characteristics. This phenomenon can be attributed to the coexistence of both small-scale open-source microservice systems and larger, more intricate ones, such as the Apollo-Portal within Apollo and select microservices within the Train-Ticket system. The former is much more numerous than the latter. Although these larger microservices are relatively scarce in number, their presence beyond the scale of most microservices businesses contributes to the existence of outliers in the final microservice dataset.

Table 3. Display of System Data Compared with Manual Verification.

System	Data size	EN	EAN	CN	IN	AN	SN	DTON	APIN	MPN	SIC	SC	SCD
gpmall	10	30%	30%	100%	100%	100%	100%	100%	100%	100%	100%	100%	100%
mogu_blog_v2	42	100%	100%	100%	100%	100%	100%	100%	100%	100%	100%	100%	100%
mall4cloud	55	100%	100%	100%	100%	100%	100%	100%	100%	100%	100%	90.90%	90.90%
Scblogs	18	100%	83.33%	100%	100%	100%	100%	100%	100%	100%	100%	100%	100%
Seckillcloud	20	66.67%	66.67%	100%	100%	100%	100%	100%	100%	100%	100%	100%	100%
spring-petclinic-microservices	66	100%	100%	100%	100%	100%	100%	100%	100%	100%	100%	85.71%	71.43%
train-tickets	338	100%	100%	100%	100%	100%	100%	100%	100%	100%	100%	100%	100%

EN: entityNum. EAN: entityAttributeNum. CN: controllerNum. IN: interfaceNum. AN: abstractClassNum. SN: serviceClassNum. DTON: dtoClassNum. APIN: APINum. MPN: maxParamNum. SIC: serviceImplCall. SCS: serviceCall. SCD: serviceCalled.
Data Size: the number of data points extracted from the microservice system.

In the previous text, it was mentioned that a manual verification of the source code was conducted for each data point. To demonstrate the effectiveness and accuracy of the extraction program, we compare the metric data obtained from representative systems with the manually inspected results (details shown in Table 3), which may have errors, but very few and close to the true answers. Therefore, we consider the results of manually inspected as the correct answers. The codeSize metric, extracted based on the inspiration of cloc, yielded similar results with cloc. Therefore, it is not presented in the comparison. Additionally, only the directly extracted metrics are presented, excluding nine metrics deriving from them.

The data in Table 3 reveals that extraction errors primarily occur in entity classes associated with the data access layer and the invocation relationships among microservices. Some errors in detecting microservice invocation relationships arose due to the communication ways of a few open-source microservice systems being updated to WebClient, which is recommended by Spring (for instance, spring-petclinic-microservices). Another set of errors was identified due to the presence of references to static variables from other files when using RestTemplate or Feign. Currently, our extraction program cannot detect this part of the invocation relationships accurately. Consequently, this results in some omissions or errors during the detection process, which were corrected manually during the later stage of human inspection.

The detection errors of entityNum and entityAttributeNum in the gpmall microservice system occurred due to non-standardized package naming. The package was named "entitys", resulting in a significant number of entity classes missed. As for the error in entityAttributeNum of Scblogs, certain entity classes in some microservices extend basic classes from the common sharing project, but the attributes in base classes are missed, resulting in the loss of some attributes from the base classes. Additionally, another issue was encountered when detecting entity classes. Some entity classes are defined in the common sharing project and are imported through dependencies while corresponding

XML files are in the respective system projects of the microservices. Seckillcloud, for instance, experienced the problem. Because our program analyzes each microservice individually, the aforementioned project structure will result in analysis errors. The data extracted for the above-mentioned issues was rectified during the manual inspection phase.

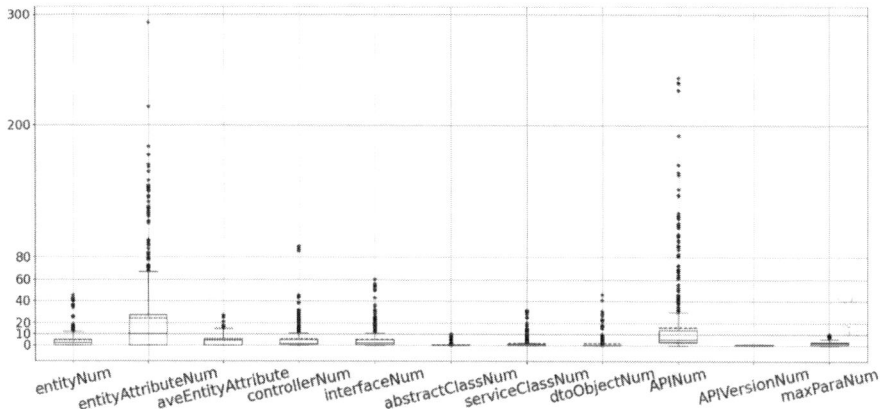

Fig. 4. Distribution of data points in each metric.

Lastly, we can give a simple example of using this dataset. Nano Service mentioned by Tighilt et.al. [14], which means overly fine-grained service granularity, can be evaluated comprehensively by considering metrics such as the number of entity classes, the number of controller classes, and the number of APIs exposed in the microservices. We can label the dataset with the bad smell in design and apply machine learning, heuristic algorithms, or other means to validate the effectiveness of the dataset being labeled and compare the efficiency of these different detection means and get the better one.

5 Threats to Validity

The data in this paper is derived from open-source microservice systems. The limitation of our search criteria may have led to the exclusion of exceptional open-source microservice systems. Moreover, during the collection process, we observed that some open-source microservice systems are primarily developed for demonstration purposes. It means that they cannot represent the whole open-source ecosystem and the scale, and the scale and maturity of these collected microservice systems differ significantly compared to the large-scale micro-service systems used by Internet companies in the real world. This implies that the extracted data would require validation for its effectiveness if used for machine learning purposes.

Furthermore, the challenges encountered in Sect. 4 also highlight the variations in technology and development standards among microservice systems developed by different teams. Accomplishing 100% accurate automatic extraction poses a difficult challenge, given the diverse external technologies and development standards employed in microservice systems. The effectiveness of the extraction program should be validated for various external technologies and development standards, along with its external validity in the Spring Cloud style microservice systems applied in the real world. Meanwhile, the detection of entity classes for NoSQL was not considered, indicating a limitation in the research.

Nevertheless, this paper believes that the collected microservice systems can, to some extent, embody the structure and development standards of Spring Boot style microservice. The extraction program has also shown good effectiveness in application, and this work holds practical significance.

6 Conclusions and Future Work

In this paper, we have collected 55 Spring Cloud style microservice systems based on Maven from GitHub, forming a catalog. To intuitively evaluate the granularity of microservices, their design, and the interactions between different microservices, we devised extraction metrics based on microservices with the Spring Boot three-tier architecture and developed an extraction program. Based on the collected microservice systems, the established metrics were extracted, and manual verification was performed, resulting in a feature dataset derived from open-source microservice systems. This dataset can contribute to the application of machine learning and heuristic algorithms in microservice bad smell research, as well as provide a foundational sample dataset for comparing the efficiency of different microservice bad smell detection methods. We believe that this dataset will facilitate further research in the domain of microservice bad smells.

Our future work will focus on expanding the catalog of microservice systems, continuously modifying, and improving the feature extraction program, and expanding the dataset. Additionally, attempts will be made to label the dataset for specific sets of microservice bad smells and apply machine learning algorithms to research in the domain of microservice bad smells. The curation of a catalog of microservice bad smells that can be detected using the feature dataset presented in this paper is underway.

References

1. Thönes, J.: Microservices. IEEE Softw. **32**(1), 116 (2015)
2. Dragoni, N., et al.: Microservices: yesterday, today, and tomorrow. In: Mazzara, M., Meyer, B. (eds.) Present and ulterior software engineering, pp. 195–216. Springer International Publishing, Cham (2017). https://doi.org/10.1007/978-3-319-67425-4_12
3. Wolff, E.: Microservices: Flexible Software Architecture. Addison-Wesley Professional (2016)
4. Taibi, D., Lenarduzzi, V.: On the definition of microservice bad smells. IEEE Softw. **35**(3), 56–62 (2018)
5. Bogner, J., Boceck, T., Popp, M., et al.: Towards a collaborative repository for the documentation of service-based antipatterns and bad smells. In: 2019 IEEE International Conference on Software Architecture Companion (ICSA-C), pp. 95–101. IEEE (2019)
6. Fontana, F.A., Pigazzini, I., Roveda, R., et al.: Arcan: A tool for architectural smells detection. In: 2017 IEEE International Conference on Software Architecture Workshops (ICSAW), pp. 282–285. IEEE (2017)

7. Walker, A., Das, D., Cerny, T.: Automated code-smell detection in microservices through static analysis: a case study. Appl. Sci. **10**(21), 7800 (2020)
8. Liu, L., Tu, Z., He, X., et al.: An empirical study on underlying correlations between runtime performance deficiencies and "bad smells" of microservice systems. In: 2021 IEEE International Conference on Web Services (ICWS), pp. 751–757. IEEE (2021)
9. ISO/IEC 25010:2023: Systems and software engineering Systems and software Quality Requirements and Evaluation (SQuaRE) Product quality model
10. Lenarduzzi, V., Saarimäki, N., Taibi, D.: The technical debt dataset. In: Proceedings of the Fifteenth International Conference on Predictive Models and Data Analytics in Software Engineering, pp. 2–11 (2019)
11. Palomba, F., Di Nucci, D., Tufano, M., et al.: Landfill: An open dataset of code smells with public evaluation. In: 2015 IEEE/ACM 12th Working Conference on Mining Software Repositories, pp. 482–485. IEEE (2015)
12. Madeyski, L., Lewowski, T.: MLCQ: industry-relevant code smell data set. In: Proceedings of the 24th International Conference on Evaluation and Assessment in Software Engineering, pp. 342–347 (2020)
13. Pecorelli, F., Palomba, F., Di Nucci, D., et al.: Comparing heuristic and machine learning approaches for metric-based code smell detection. In: 2019 IEEE/ACM 27th International Conference on Program Comprehension (ICPC), pp. 93–104. IEEE (2019)
14. Tighilt, R., Abdellatif, M., Moha, N., et al.: On the study of microservices antipatterns: a catalog proposal. In: Proceedings of the European Conference on Pattern Languages of Programs 2020, pp. 1–13 (2020)
15. Taibi, D., Lenarduzzi, V., Pahl, C.: Microservices anti-patterns: a taxonomy. Microserv. Sci. Eng., 111–128 (2020).https://doi.org/10.1007/978-3-030-31646-4_5
16. Tighilt, R., Abdellatif, M., Trabelsi, I., et al.: On the maintenance support for microservice-based systems through the specification and the detection of microservice antipatterns. J. Syst. Softw. **204**, 111755 (2023)
17. Imranur, M., Panichella, S., Taibi, D.: A curated dataset of microservices-based systems. In: Joint Proceedings of the Summer School on Software Maintenance and Evolution. Tampere (2019)
18. Abid, C., Kessentini, M., Wang, H.: Early prediction of quality of service using interface-level metrics, code-level metrics, and antipatterns. Inf. Softw. Technol. **126**, 106313 (2020)
19. Tempero, E., Anslow, C., Dietrich, J., et al.: The qualitas corpus: a curated collection of java code for empirical studies. In: 2010 Asia Pacific Software Engineering Conference, pp. 336–345. IEEE (2010)
20. Zhou, X., Peng, X., Xie, T., et al.: Benchmarking microservice systems for software engineering research. In: Proceedings of the 40th International Conference on Software Engineering: Companion Proceedings, pp. 323–324 (2018)

Crawling and Exploring RESTful Web APIs from RapidAPI

Wen Li[1,2], Hongshuai Ren[1,2], Yamei Nie[1,2], Zihao Liu[1,2], Guosheng Kang[1,2(✉)], Jianxun Liu[1,2], and Zhenlian Peng[1,2]

[1] School of Computer Science and Engineering, Hunan University of Science and Technology, Xiangtan, China
guoshengkang@gmail.com
[2] Hunan Provincial Key Lab. for Services Computing and Novel Software Technology, HNUST, Xiangtan, China

Abstract. RapidAPI serves as a marketplace and management platform that integrates a wide range of Web APIs, offering developers access to a rich pool of API resources. More and more researchers are delving into ways to maximize the value created by leveraging these resources. Thus, acquiring the Web API data and knowing the details is of significance for researchers and ordinary users. In this paper, we propose the methodology of crawling Web APIs from RapidAPI (https://rapidapi.com/hub) and provide rich visualizations and statistical analysis for the crawled dataset. The crawling code and the crawled dataset are open for public access (https://github.com/IntelligentServiceLab/RESTful-API-Crawler) so that researchers and users can acquire them with no effort. Moreover, the use cases of RESTful Web APIs are provided as a usage reference for users and developers.

Keywords: RESTful Web API · Web API Crawling · Web API Exploration · RapidAPI

1 Introduction

With the rapid development and widespread adoption of service-oriented computing technology, the number of Web services is continuously growing. Furthermore, the REST architecture style emerges, and Web services gradually turn to be designed as RESTful APIs. A RESTful API is an architectural style for an application program interface (API) that uses HTTP requests to access and use data. The data can be used by sending GET, PUT, POST, and DELETE requests to certain service providers, which refers to the reading, updating, creating, and deleting of operations concerning resources [1]. RESTful APIs play a crucial role in fields such as commerce, social interaction, and entertainment, since APIs are easy to be composed into Mashups by users or developers. The emergence of RESTful APIs has not only transformed people's lifestyles but also driven innovation in software development methodologies [2].

Web APIs facilitate communication and data exchange between various applications. They offer a flexible means for developers to leverage the functionalities and data of other services, thereby accelerating the development process of applications. With the popularity of cloud computing and mobile internet, an increasing number of Web APIs are being developed, providing developers with a wealth of functionalities and resources. It allows developers to focus more on the core logic of their applications without needing to build all functionalities and services from scratch. However, with the continuously increasing number and variety of Web APIs, it would be a challenge for developers to effectively manage and use these APIs from various API markets [3]. As for researchers, it is significant to obtain available data for research purposes. RapidAPI serves as a marketplace and management platform integrating various Web APIs, providing developers with a convenient and resource-rich environment [4]. Through RapidAPI, developers can easily discover and use a variety of APIs, thereby speeding up the development process and enhancing the functionality and innovation of their applications. However, the Web API data from RapidAPI is not provided in the collection, and the characteristics of the dataset are still unclear to people so far.

Based on the above discussion, this paper aims to introduce the process of crawling Web APIs from RapidAPI and conduct a detailed analysis of the obtained Web API dataset, providing an open Web API dataset from RapidAPI and the basis for the visualization and understanding. The rest of the paper is organized as follows. Section 2 reviews the related work. We present our crawling method in Sect. 3, including the process of data acquisition and processing. Section 4 demonstrates the characteristics and visualizations of the crawled dataset, and also provides some use cases of Web APIs. Finally, the discussion and analysis of the potential applications and value of Web APIs in software development is outlined in Sect. 5.

2 Related Work

Our work focuses on crawling Web APIs and analysis of Web API data. Thus, we will explore the related work from the above two aspects. Next, we will review them one by one.

Web API Crawling. The web crawler is a component of a search engine that gathers information from the internet, allowing the indexer to construct data indexes [5]. Crawlers can be roughly divided into two types: focused crawlers [6] and thematic crawlers [7]. Focused crawlers have been developed to prioritize crawling based on specific conditions or topics of interest provided by user, rather than simply collecting all links crawled [8]. To optimize performance and address the disparity between available information in digital libraries and on the web, Pant et al. [9] introduced a lexical and link analysis approach. Shchekotykhin et al. [10] suggested utilizing composite technology to identify and utilize Website navigation structures, enabling focused crawling based on hub and authority information. To prevent mistakenly leaving relevant web pages during crawling, Aggarwal et al. [11] proposed an intelligent crawler that learns the characteristics of the WWW link structure. Additionally, Liu et al. [12] developed a method for crawling based on user behavior using soft computing technology. While focused crawler technologies prioritize the acquisition of relevant information, they may not necessarily prioritize structuring the data they acquire. This can lead to the acquisition of unstructured data, which can present significant challenges for any subsequent data analysis.

Analysis of Web API Data. In contrast, thematic crawling concentrates solely on particular areas of interest. Focused crawling operates under the assumption that some marked examples of relevant and irrelevant web pages are already present [6]. Chung et al. [13] put forward a hash-based approach to classify web pages into themes and assign them to designated crawlers. They recommended collaborative crawling to expedite the process. Noh et al. [14] utilized TF-IDF entropy and compilation rules to determine the relevance of web pages and implemented thematic crawlers. Qin et al. [15] tackled the problem of focused crawlers getting stuck in limited subgraphs by using search-enhanced focused crawling. While topic-based crawler technology is useful for retrieving specific information, there is a dearth of research on retrieving information for individual URLs.

To summarize, the existing work mainly focuses on the Web API data from ProgrammableWeb[1], while ProgrammableWeb has shut down operations. As a result, more and more work should transfer their focus to RapidAPI [16]. However, there is still little work on Web API crawling and public exploration from RapidAPI until now. Thus, we propose the Web API crawling methodology with respect to RapidAPI and offer the crawled dataset to the public.

3 RESTful Web API Crawling

We initially choose RapidAPI as our data source, which serves as a marketplace and management platform integrating a variety of Web APIs, providing developers with access to a diverse range of API resources. Before starting the scraping process, we conduct a comprehensive investigation of RapidAPI, gaining insights into its site structure, data presentation methods, and potential anti-scraping mechanisms.

This study employs Python along with a suite of related libraries and technologies, including Selenium, Pandas, and CSV file handling, to crawl Web API data from RapidAPI and conduct subsequent analysis. Given the dynamic content loading on RapidAPI, traditional static Web scraping methods may prove ineffective. Selenium is chosen to mimic browser actions and fetch dynamically loaded data as it automates interactions with web pages, enabling users to control web browsers programmatically. Selenium provides powerful tools and APIs enabling the emulation of user actions such as clicking and text input, thereby facilitating the scraping of dynamic Web pages [17]. Web scraping is a sophisticated technique employed for the systematic extraction of data from Websites, playing a pivotal role as the primary method in retrieving content from RapidAPI for this study [18]. The Web scraping process is divided into 3 stages as shown in Fig. 1.

The web crawler's workflow, illustrated in Fig. 1, outlines the process of extracting data from the target website, RapidAPI. Initially, the crawler targets the specific URL of RapidAPI to retrieve all HTML documents associated with the website. These documents

---

[1] https://www.programmableweb.com/.

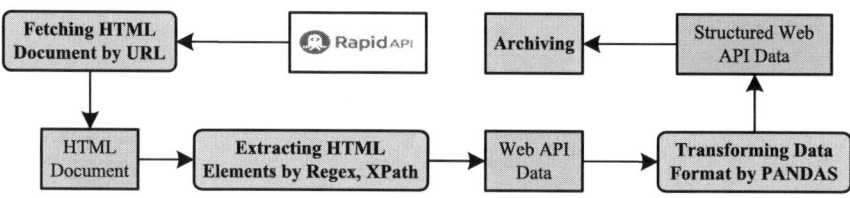

Fig. 1. Web scraping process

are then parsed to locate the desired elements using XPath, enabling the extraction of relevant data points. Following the extraction phase, tools such as pandas are used to clean and transform the obtained data into a structured format, ensuring consistency and usability. This transformation step is crucial for organizing the data into a format suitable for analysis and further processing. Ultimately, the structured data is saved as a CSV file, consolidating the extracted information into a coherent dataset. This final dataset serves as a valuable resource for subsequent analysis and exploration of the offerings provided by RapidAPI.

3.1 Locating Specific Elements Based on XPath

XPath, is a language for locating nodes in XML and HTML documents, offering potent and flexible selectors for element localization [19]. In Selenium, XPath selectors are a commonly employed method for effortlessly locating and manipulating page elements [20]. XPath selectors consist of nodes, operators, and functions. We used slashes '/' to specify an absolute path from the root node or double slashes '//' to denote a relative path, adding conditions in square brackets '[]' to filter nodes, for instance, '[@class = 'classname']'.

However, certain Web pages have unique structures, and as we conduct our research, the Websites also underwent frequent updates to their page layouts. These factors pose challenges during the data scraping process. To address these issues, it is necessary to use XPath judiciously. We prioritize using relative paths rather than absolute paths to locate elements. Relative paths offer greater flexibility, making them more likely to remain stable when there are changes in the Webpage structure.

Additionally, we make efforts to use unique identifiers of elements, such as IDs, class names, or data attributes, to construct the XPath expressions when possible. This ensures the accuracy of XPath-based element targeting, and in cases where the Webpage structure changes, unique identifiers are often among the last elements to be modified [21]. By employing these methods, we can retrieve the desired data content with reasonable accuracy during our research process.

3.2 Configuring the Waiting Time for Loading of Webpage

Waiting time refers to the duration from the initiation of Webpage loading to the point where the content becomes accessible for scraping. This period is critical as Web pages often employ technologies like JavaScript and Ajax for asynchronous loading, rendering traditional synchronous scraping methods ineffective.

The *WebDriverWait* feature in Selenium is a valuable tool designed to address waiting time by pausing execution until specific conditions are met. For instance, using practical scenarios such as *visibility_of_element_located*, Selenium can wait for specific elements to become visible on the page before executing corresponding actions. This approach ensures that asynchronous content fully loads before considering the page as loaded.

However, the absence of meticulous waiting strategies undermines the reliability and effectiveness of Selenium-based Web scraping activities. Inadequate waiting times may prompt Selenium to attempt locating elements before they are fully loaded, resulting in a *NoSuchElementException* error. Moreover, insufficient waiting periods make Selenium scripts vulnerable to instability, as they depend on Webpage loading speed and network responsiveness. Slow page loading or unstable connections can lead to script failures, system crashes, or abnormal terminations. To mitigate these issues, setting an implicit wait time in Selenium allows for automatic waiting throughout the session. If an element is found within the specified wait time, the operation proceeds immediately; otherwise, a *NoSuchElementException* error is triggered. This approach ensures seamless waiting for asynchronous content to load, enhancing the reliability and robustness of Web scraping activities. By setting an implicit wait time, Selenium will wait for a fixed period when searching for elements. If the element is found within that time, the operation will be executed immediately; otherwise, a *NoSuchElementException* error will be thrown. This enables automatic waiting for asynchronous content to load throughout the entire session, without the need for explicit waits in each operation.

3.3 Anti-Crawling for IP Blocked in Web Scraping

The issue of IP blocking during Web scraping is a common challenge, especially when dealing with large-scale data extraction tasks [22]. Websites often detect abnormal traffic patterns and subsequently block the corresponding IP addresses, which disrupts or prevents access to the desired content. With the continuous advancement of technology, there are various methods employed to block IP addresses in customer service. Here are some of the methods we utilize during our research.

Virtual Private Networks (VPNs) play a crucial role in addressing IP blocking issues. When a website blocks a specific IP, VPNs enable users to bypass the IP blocking measures by changing their network nodes. This allows them to continue data scraping and maintain the continuity of data extraction. VPNs encrypt internet traffic, ensuring the security and privacy of data transmitted between the user's device and the VPN server [23]. This encryption is crucial when handling sensitive information during Web scraping activities. Another method to address this issue is to reduce the frequency of crawling requests sent to the target Website's server. By adhering to predefined request limits within each time unit, limiting the rate helps prevent server overload and reduces the likelihood of triggering anti-crawling mechanisms. Choosing an appropriate frequency contributes to the stable operation of the Web crawler script and ensures continuous data acquisition.

Lastly, we introduce pauses between consecutive crawling requests to address the issue of IP blocking. By introducing pauses, the delayed crawling reduces the strain on the target server and mimics human browsing behavior. This approach helps distribute scraping traffic more evenly over time and minimizes the risk of detection or retaliation by Website administrators. After retrieving the data from RapidAPI, it becomes imperative to process and analyze the dataset effectively. To efficiently handle and organize large-scale datasets, the study employs the Pandas library, with its DataFrame structure extensively utilized. After multiple program crashes and a thorough investigation of the issues, we opt for an appropriate waiting time that allows the program to run efficiently and stably. The study initially utilizes Pandas' *read_excel* function to read data from Excel files containing API information. This step significantly simplifies the data import process, allowing us to easily import external data into the analysis environment. The DataFrame plays a pivotal role throughout the data wrangling and scraping process. With the DataFrame, users can iterate over API links, and scrape and extract relevant data for each API.

In this process, the DataFrame not only provides an efficient data storage structure but also simplifies the organization and management of data. After scraping and processing, the study obtains structured data, including API names, links, hosts, endpoint names, descriptions, categories, required parameters, and optional parameters. The DataFrame is used to organize this information into tabular form and ultimately save it as a CSV file. This structured data storage approach provides robust support for subsequent analysis and visualization. The Pandas library's DataFrame demonstrates outstanding performance in data processing and wrangling. Owing to its powerful functionality, we can efficiently import, wrangle, and store data, providing a clear and reliable data foundation for subsequent analysis.

4 RESTful Web API Exploration

In this section, we first present the description of the crawled Web API dataset. Then, a comprehensive analysis is introduced from the statistical perspective. Finally, several use cases are provided for the usage of RESTful Web APIs, including the use for single Web API and the use for Web API composition.

4.1 Description of Dataset

The crawled dataset comprises 50,000 API information obtained from RapidAPI. The dataset encompasses a wide range of attributes, including *API Name, Update Time, API Author, API URL, API Popularity, API Latency, API Service Level, API Host, Endpoint Name, Endpoint Category, Endpoint Description, Required Endpoint Parameters, Optional Endpoint Parameters*. The attribute list and examples for each field are demonstrated in Table 1. Next, we explain each attribute in detail as follows.

a. API Name

The API Name serves as a unique identifier for each API, facilitating reference and identification.

b. Update Time

The Update Time indicates the most recent update time of the API, providing insights into the update frequency and timeliness of the API's documentation and functionality.

Table 1. List of data set fields and examples

Field Name	Example
API Name	SEO Automations
Update Time	2023-02
API Author	Eduard Kleine
API URL	https://rapidapi.com/BigFoxMedia/api/seo-automations/
API Popularity	9.5
API Latency	13,540 ms
API Service Level	90%
API Host	seo-automations.p.rapidapi.com
Endpoint Name	GET: Extract Sitemap XML as JSON
Endpoint Category	Tier 2 APIs (Fast)
Endpoint Description	Are you looking for an API that can quickly and easily download and parse sitemap.xml files into JSON format?
Required Endpoint Parameters	{'Parameters': ['your-API-key', 'shortcode'], 'Parameters Type': ['STRING', 'STRING'], 'Parameter precautions ': ['Your API Key provided by Workable', 'Retrieve detailed job information, including the job description. The shortcode is a unique identifier for each job and can be seen by invoking "/jobs"]}
Optional Endpoint Parameters	{"Parameters": ['address', 'lng', 'lat', 'note'], 'Parameters Type ': ['STRING', 'STRING', 'STRING', 'STRING'], 'Parameter precautions ': ['An optional human-readable address string where the QR Code will be attached', 'An optional longitude of where the QR Code will be attached, 'An optional latitude of where the QR Code will be attached, 'An optional note']}

c. API Author

The API Author field specifies the individual or organization responsible for creating or maintaining the API.

d. API URL

The API URL is a URL that directs users to the API resource, enabling access to detailed information and relevant documentation.

e. API Popularity

API Popularity reflects the usage frequency or level of an API. It may be quantified using numerical metrics or expressed by descriptive ratings.

f. API Latency

The API Latency attribute quantifies the delay or response time experienced when utilizing the API, typically measured in milliseconds.

g. API Service Level

API Service Level denotes the reliability and stability of the API. It may include metrics such as availability percentage or other indicators of service quality.

h. API Host

The API Host specifies the server or domain where the API is hosted or deployed, providing insights into the technical infrastructure supporting the API.

i. Endpoint Name.

APIs often consist of multiple endpoints, each serving a distinct functionality or operation. The Endpoint Name field identifies these individual endpoints within the API.

j. Endpoint Category

The Endpoint Category describes the operations or functionalities provided by each endpoint, such as data retrieval, modification, deletion, or other specific actions.

k. Endpoint Description

The Endpoint Description offers detailed information about each endpoint, including its purpose, input/output specifications, and any additional relevant details.

l. Required Endpoint Parameters

The Required Endpoint Parameters that must be provided when invoking each endpoint. These parameters are essential for the proper functioning of the endpoint.

m. Optional Endpoint Parameters

The Optional Endpoint Parameters field lists additional parameters that can be provided to the endpoint, offering extended functionality or customization options.

This dataset serves as a valuable resource for researchers, developers, and stakeholders seeking insights into the characteristics, functionalities, and performance of various APIs. Through analysis of this dataset, trends, popularity, and domain-specific applications of diverse APIs can be identified. Moreover, the dataset can facilitate the development of API directories and aggregation platforms, as well as support API-related research and analysis.

4.2 Statistical Analysis

This subsection presents a comprehensive visual analysis of the Web API dataset obtained from RapidAPI. The dataset is subjected to exploratory data analysis to uncover patterns, trends, and insights into the world of Web APIs. Through various visualization techniques, a general understanding of the dataset and several insights for software development are provided. Before proceeding with the visual analysis, data cleaning is conducted to address the missing values, duplicates, and inconsistencies, ensuring the integrity and accuracy of the dataset.

Figure 2 illustrates the cumulative number of APIs published on RapidAPI over time, with "Time" represented on the x-axis in years and the vertical axis depicting the quantity of APIs. Overall, there is a discernible upward trend indicating a steady increase in the availability of APIs over the years. Notably, the year 2020 exhibits the lowest point on the graph, suggesting a comparatively slower rate of API releases during that period. However, from 2022 to 2023, there is a significant spike in the number of APIs, indicating a surge in growth during this period. This trend reflects the growing popularity and demand for web services in recent years.

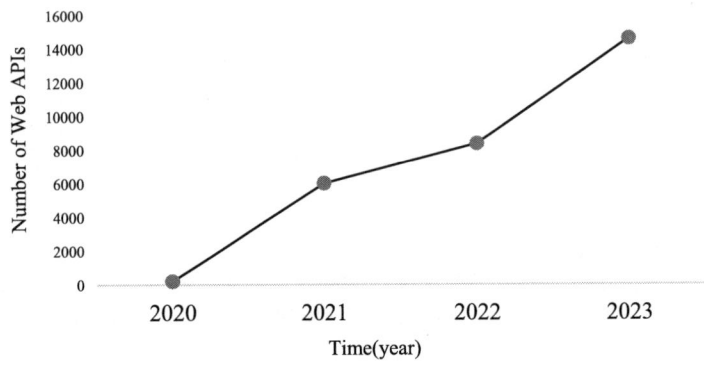

Fig. 2. Number of Web APIs from 2020 to 2023

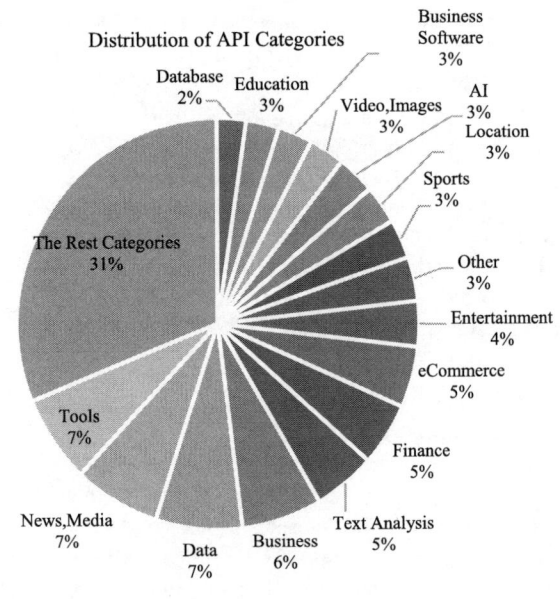

Fig. 3. The proportion of Web API categories

Figure 3 presents a breakdown of API categories based on their proportion in the dataset. Categories accounting for more than 2.2% of the total are individually displayed, while those representing less than 2.2% collectively fall under "Minor Categories". This categorization allows for a clearer visualization of dominant API categories alongside a comprehensive view of less prevalent ones. The categories of News, Media, Tools, and Data APIs collectively account for a significant proportion of 7% of the dataset. Additionally, the categories of Business, E-commerce, and Finance APIs individually represent proportions of 6%, 5%, and 5% respectively. This indicates the high relevance and significance of these categories within the overall dataset.

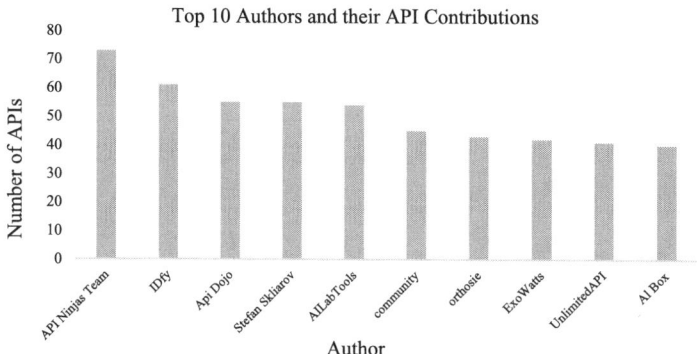

Fig. 4. Top 10 developers and their API contributions

Figure 4 depicts the correlation between the quantity of APIs provided by authors on RapidAPI. The horizontal axis corresponds to the authors' names, while the vertical axis reflects the number of APIs contributed by each author. This visual representation exclusively showcases the top ten authors, ordered by their respective API contribution counts, thereby offering valuable insights into how API contributions are distributed among the most prolific authors on the platform. By analyzing Fig. 4, we can know that the *API Ninjas Team* has emerged as the most prolific API developer on RapidAPI, contributing 73 Web APIs until the year of 2023. Following closely behind are developers *IDfy* and *Api Dojo*, among others, who have also made significant contributions to the platform in terms of API development. This ranking provides valuable insights into the top contributors and highlights the notable achievements of these developers in expanding the API ecosystem on RapidAPI.

Figure 5 visually presents the relationship between the number of endpoints associated with individual APIs on RapidAPI. The x-axis displays the names of the APIs, while the y-axis shows the corresponding count of endpoints linked to each API. This graphical representation specifically focuses on the top ten APIs, ordered by their endpoint counts, thereby offering valuable insights into how endpoints are distributed among the most extensively featured APIs on the platform. *Aspose.PDF Cloud* stands out as the API with the highest number of endpoints, boasting an impressive total of 363 endpoints. Following closely behind are APIs such as *Flickr* and *MailSlurp Email Testing*. Studying this distribution provides significant insights for developers and platform administrators, helping them identify APIs that offer a wide range of functionalities and integrations, and facilitating informed decisions regarding API selection and utilization (Fig. 6).

The word cloud visually represents the frequency of words found in the descriptions of APIs available on RapidAPI [24]. In this visualization, the size of each word corresponds to its frequency, with the most commonly occurring words displayed in larger

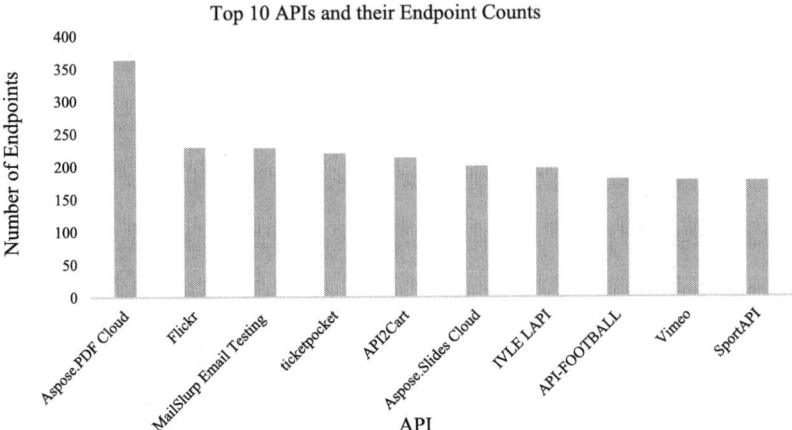

Fig. 5. Top 10 APIs and their Endpoint counts

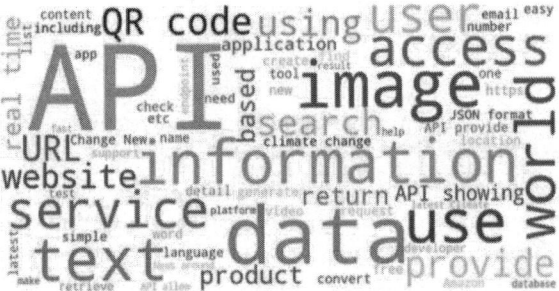

Fig. 6. The word cloud of API descriptions

font sizes. The word cloud offers a snapshot of 70 words, presenting valuable insights into prevalent themes and keywords within API descriptions. This analysis not only provides a glimpse into the common trends and focal points across various APIs but also serves as a useful tool for understanding the prominent features and functionalities that developers are seeking within the RapidAPI ecosystem.

4.3 Use Case of RESTful Web API

In today's Web development environment, creating dynamic and interactive applications using Web APIs has become ubiquitous [25]. A single API can do many things. However, as applications grow in complexity and functionality, a single API may not be enough to meet all requirements. Therefore, you need to leverage multiple Web APIs and orchestrate their integration to form a comprehensive service. This part discusses the strategies and technologies involved in this process. The following three use cases are given. The first use case specifically describes the calling process of a single API, and the second and third use cases specifically describe the calling process of multiple API combinations.

Use Case 1. In RapidAPI, there are code snippets for each API with various programming languages, such as Python and Java, to illustrate the example of invocation. Subscribers are required to click on the "Subscribe" button to obtain the corresponding API Key for accessing the desired Web API. This key is essential for enabling the usage of the API functionalities. The utilization process of a single API is depicted in Fig. 7 and the invocation code is shown in Fig. 8.

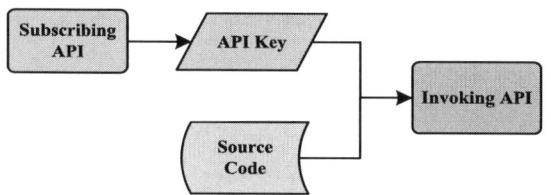

Fig. 7. Use Case 1: Invoking a Web API

```
url = "https://yummly2.p.rapidapi.com/feeds/auto-complete"
querystring = {"q":"chicken"}
headers = {'x-rapidapi-key': "9f3e0e429cmsh63526b5a2cc832cp13d3f0jsnfbfcd3cc961d",
           'x-rapidapi-host': "yummly2.p.rapidapi.com"}
response = requests.request("GET", url, headers=headers, params=querystring)
```

Fig. 8. Use Case 1: Invocation code of a Web API

Use Case 2. This use case is to illustrate the invocation of a composited API, i.e., Mashup. The selected Mashup includes two APIs: *Text Translator* and *OpenAI*. The data flow for this use case is shown in Fig. 8, and the invocation code is shown in Fig. 9. The main functionality of the Invocation is to use *Text Translator* to translate our questions into English and then pass them to *OpenAI*. Then answer our questions and output the corresponding results. The following is the main Invocation of the service composition use case. The use case imports the request module for sending HTTP requests and defines two functions: *translate_text()* for translating Text using *Text Translator*, and *ask_question()* for calling *OpenAI* to answer the question. The *translate_text()* function is then called to translate the Chinese question into English, and the translated text is passed as input to the *ask_question()* function. In addition, the context information "the current date is November 17, 2023" provides *OpenAI* for inference. The *ask_question()* function sends the translated question, along with context information, to *OpenAI* and retrieves the API's response. Finally, print out the answer to *OpenAI*. This approach implements service composition by sequentially calling *Text Translator* to translate a question and then passing it to *OpenAI* to get an answer. The combination of these steps demonstrates the seamless integration and functionality offered by the different APIs.

Use Case 3. This use case is to illustrate the invocation of a composited API, i.e., Mashup. The selected Mashup includes two APIs: *OTT Details/Search, IMBD API-Internet Movie Database/Film, DouBan,* and *Text Sentiment Analysis Method.* In the

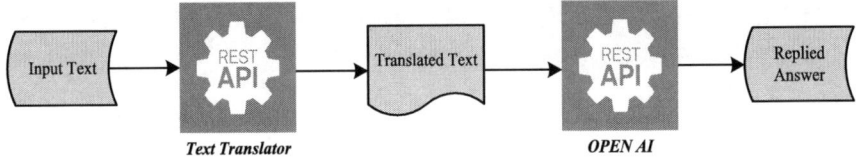

Fig. 9. Use Case 2: Invoking a Web API composition

```
// Invocation code of Text Translator
    url_1 = "https://text-translator2.p.rapidapi.com/translate"
    headers_1 = { "content-type": "application/x-www-form-urlencoded",
                  "X-RapidAPI-Key": api_key,
                  "X-RapidAPI-Host": "text-translator2.p.rapidapi.com" }
    payload_1 = { "source_language": source_language,
                  "target_language": target_language,
                  "text": text}
    response_1 = requests.post(url_1, data=payload_1, headers=headers_1)
// Invocation code of Open AI
    url_2= "https://open-ai21.p.rapidapi.com/qa"
    headers_2 = {"content-type": "application/json",
                 "X-RapidAPI-Key": api_key,
                 "X-RapidAPI-Host": "open-ai21.p.rapidapi.com" }
    payload_2 = {"question": question,"context": context }
    response_2 = requests.post(url_2, json=payload_2, headers=headers_2)
```

Fig. 10. Use Case 2: Invocation code of a Web API composition

digital era, there's a growing demand for movies, with people seeking easy access to various movie-related information including basic details, reviews, and sentiment analysis. Concurrently, the internet's evolution has led to the emergence of numerous movie databases and review platforms, offering abundant data resources. However, these data are typically scattered across different platforms, necessitating users to navigate between multiple websites to obtain desired information. Thus, we present a use case demonstrating the process of this service composition, as depicted in Fig. 10 and the invocation code is shown in Fig. 11.

The user inputs the movie title, triggering the first step of the service composition. Then, *OTT Details/Search* is called, which is used to retrieve the basic information and IMBD ID of the movie. After obtaining the basic movie information, users have the option to input the IMBD ID into the *IMBD API-Internet Movie Database/Film* API to obtain more detailed movie information. Users may also choose to input the IMBD ID to retrieve reviews from the Douban platform, which can provide additional perspectives and evaluations about the movie. Finally, the *Text Sentiment Analysis Method* API is called, allowing users to input reviews and conduct sentiment analysis to understand the sentiment orientation of reviewers towards the movie. This can assist users in better understanding the movie's popularity and reception (Fig. 12).

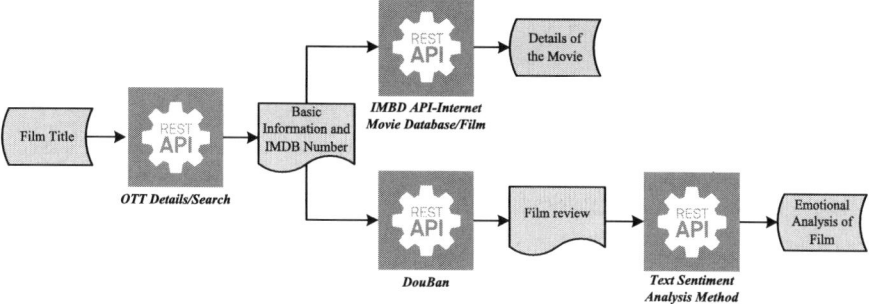

Fig. 11. Use Case 3: Invoking a Web API composition

```
// Invocation code of OTT details/Search
url_1 = "https://text-sentiment.p.rapidapi.com/analyze"
payload_1 = "text=I%20am%20not%20really%20happy"
headers_1 = {
'content-type': "application/x-www-form-urlencoded",
'x-rapidapi-key': "9f3e0e429cmsh63526b5a2cc832cp13d3f0jsnfbfcd3cc961d",
'x-rapidapi-host': "text-sentiment.p.rapidapi.com"}
response_1 = requests.request("POST", url_1, data=payload_1, headers= headers_1)
// Invocation code of IMDB - Internet Movie Database (Unofficial)/Film
url_2 = "https://imdb-internet-movie-database-unofficial.p.rapidapi.com/film/tt>12292428"
headers_2 = {
'x-rapidapi-key': "9f3e0e429cmsh63526b5a2cc832cp13d3f0jsnfbfcd3cc961d",
'x-rapidapi-host':"imdb-internet-movie-database-unofficial.p.rapidapi.com"}
response_2 = requests.request("GET", url_2, headers=headers_2)
// Invocation code of Text Sentiment Analysis Method
url_3 = "https://ott-details.p.rapidapi.com/search"
querystring_3 = {"title":"Endgame","page":"1"}
headers_3 = {
'x-rapidapi-key': "9f3e0e429cmsh63526b5a2cc832cp13d3f0jsnfbfcd3cc961d",
'x-rapidapi-host': "ott-details.p.rapidapi.com"}
response_3 = requests.request("GET", url_3, headers=headers_3, params=querystring_3)
```

Fig. 12. Use Case 3: Invocation code of a Web API composition

5 Conclusion and Discussion

This study presents the specific methodology for scraping the required data from RapidAPI and conducts a visualization analysis of the obtained dataset. The insights gained from this analysis are invaluable for developers, businesses, and researchers, offering guidance for the utilization, development, and innovation of Web APIs. The visualization analysis results serve as indispensable references and foundational knowledge for the future advancement of the Web API domain.

While this study offers an initial introduction and analysis of the Web API dataset, there are several promising avenues for future research. One potential direction involves expanding the dataset size to encompass a broader range of API entries. This expansion would contribute to a more comprehensive and diverse dataset, facilitating a deeper understanding of the overall API ecosystem and enabling the exploration of additional trends and patterns. Furthermore, while this study provides a preliminary analysis of API functionality and performance, future research could focus on specific domains or types of APIs to delve deeper into their functional and performance characteristics. This could involve conducting more detailed comparisons and evaluations to identify strengths, weaknesses, and opportunities for improvement. Future work may entail the evaluation of API quality, encompassing assessments of the completeness and accuracy of API documentation, experimental tests on the reliability and stability of APIs, and quantitative evaluations of API performance and response time. By systematically evaluating API quality, developers and businesses can make informed decisions regarding API selection and integration, ultimately enhancing the overall reliability and effectiveness of their applications.

The findings and suggestions outlined in this study lay the foundation for continued exploration and advancement in the field of Web APIs. As the demand for interconnected services continuing to grow, ongoing research efforts will play a crucial role in shaping the future of API development and utilization.

Acknowledgments. This work is supported by Educational Commission of Hunan Province of China under Grant No: 23A0359, Natural Science Foundation of Hunan Province under Grant No: 2022JJ30262, and Project of Hunan Province Ordinary Higher Education Reform under Grant No. HNJG-2021-0650. The corresponding author is *Guosheng Kang*.

References

1. Pautasso, C., Wilde, E.: RESTful web services: principles, patterns, emerging technologies. In: Proceedings of the 19th International Conference on World Wide Web, pp 1359–1360 (2010)
2. Kang, G., Liu, J., Xiao, Y., Cao, B., Xu, Y., Cao, M.: Neural and attentional factorization machine-based web API recommendation for mashup development. IEEE Trans. Netw. Serv. Manag. **18**(4), 4183–4196 (2021)
3. Wang, Y., Xiang, J., Cheng, H., Chen, W., Xiao, Y., Kang, G.: Towards dynamic evolutionary analysis of programmable web for API-mashup ecosystem. In: 2023 26th International Conference on Computer Supported Cooperative Work in Design, pp 1716–1721. IEEE (2023)
4. Bülthoff, F., Maleshkova, M.: RESTful or RESTless – current state of today's top web APIs. In: Presutti, V., Blomqvist, E., Troncy, R., Sack, H., Papadakis, I., Tordai, A. (eds.) ESWC 2014. LNCS, vol. 8798, pp. 64–74. Springer, Cham (2014). https://doi.org/10.1007/978-3-319-11955-7_6
5. Kumar, M., Bhatia, R., Rattan, D.J.W.I.R.D.M., Discovery, K.: A Survey of Web Crawlers For Information Retrieval. Surv. Web Crawlers Inf. Retrieval **7**(6), e1218 (2017)
6. Chakrabarti, S., Van den Berg, M., Dom, B.: Focused crawling: a new approach to topic-specific web resource discovery. Comput. Netw. **31**(11–16), 1623–1640 (1999)
7. Yu, H.L., Bingwu, L., Fang, Y.: Similarity computation of web pages of focused crawler. In: 2010 International Forum on Information Technology and Applications, pp. 70–72. IEEE (2010)
8. Cho, J., Garcia-Molina, H., Page, L., Systems, I.: Efficient crawling through URL ordering. Comput. Netw. **30**(1–7), 161–172 (1998)

9. Pant, G., Tsioutsiouliklis, K., Johnson, J., Giles, C.L.: Panorama: extending digital libraries with topical crawlers. In: Proceedings of the 4th ACM/IEEE-CS Joint Conference on Digital Libraries, pp. 142–150 (2004)
10. Shchekotykhin, K., Jannach, D., Friedrich, G.: XCrawl: a high-recall crawling method for web mining. Knowl. Inf. Syst. **25**, 303–326 (2010)
11. Aggarwal, C.C., Al-Garawi, F., Yu, P.S.: On the design of a learning crawler for topical resource discovery. ACM Trans. Inf. Syst. **19**(3), 286–309 (2001)
12. Liu, H., Milios, E., Janssen, J.: Focused crawling by learning hmm from user's topic-specific browsing. In: IEEE/WIC/ACM International Conference on Web Intelligence (WI'04), p. 732. IEEE (2004)
13. Chung, C., Clarke, C.L.: Topic-oriented collaborative crawling. In: Proceedings of the Eleventh International Conference on Information and Knowledge Management, pp. 34–42 (2002)
14. Noh, S., Choi, Y., Seo, H., Choi, K., Jung, G.: An intelligent topic-specific crawler using degree of relevance. In: Yang, Z.R., Yin, H., Everson, R.M. (eds.) IDEAL 2004. LNCS, vol. 3177, pp. 491–498. Springer, Heidelberg (2004). https://doi.org/10.1007/978-3-540-28651-6_72
15. Qin, J., Zhou, Y., Chau, M.: Building domain-specific web collections for scientific digital libraries: a meta-search enhanced focused crawling method. In: Proceedings of the 4th ACM/IEEE-CS Joint Conference on Digital Libraries, pp. 135–141 (2004)
16. Wang, S., Zhou, Y., Ding, Z.: Automated restful API service discovery with various interface features. In: Troya, J., Medjahed, B., Piattini, M., Yao, L., Fernández, P., Ruiz-Cortés, A. (eds.) ICSOC 2022. LNCS, vol. 13740, pp. 54–70. Springer, Cham (2022). https://doi.org/10.1007/978-3-031-20984-0_4
17. De Smedt, T., Daelemans, W.: Pattern for Python. J. Mach. Learn. Res. **13**(1), 2063–2067 (2012)
18. Sapre, A., Vartak, S.: Scientific computing and data analysis using NumPy and Pandas. Int. Res. J. Eng. **7**, 1334–1346 (2020)
19. Gottlob, G., Koch, C., Pichler, R.: Efficient algorithms for processing XPath queries. ACM Trans. Database Syst. **30**(2), 444–491 (2005)
20. Yuan, S.: Design and visualization of Python web scraping based on third-party libraries and selenium tools. Acad. J. Comput. Inf. Sci. **6**(9), 25–31 (2023)
21. Singjai, A., Zdun,: Conformance assessment of architectural design decisions on API endpoint designs derived from domain models. J. Syst. Softw. **193**, 111433 (2022)
22. Haque, A., Singh, S.: Anti-scraping application development. In: 2015 International Conference on Advances in Computing, Communications and Informatics, pp. 869–874. IEEE (2015)
23. Ezra, P.J., Misra, S., Agrawal, A., Oluranti, J., Maskeliunas, R., Damasevicius, R.: Secured communication using virtual private network. In: Cyber Security and Digital Forensics, pp. 309–319 (2022)
24. Dong, M., Lu, J., Wang, G., Zheng, X., Kiritsis, D.: Model-based systems engineering papers analysis based on word cloud visualization. In: 2022 IEEE International Systems Conference, pp. 1–7. IEEE (2022)
25. Adeleye, O., Yu, J., Yongchareon, S., Han, Y.: Constructing and evaluating an evolving web-API network for service discovery. In: Pahl, C., Vukovic, M., Yin, J., Yu, Q. (eds.) ICSOC 2018. LNCS, vol. 11236, pp. 603–617. Springer, Cham (2018). https://doi.org/10.1007/978-3-030-03596-9_44

Trustworthy Services

A Trustworthy Service Transaction Framework for Privacy Protection

Ziyu Li[1], Tong Mo[1(✉)], Weiping Li[1], and Zhiying Tu[2]

[1] Peking University, Beijing, China
motong@ss.pku.edu.cn
[2] Harbin Institute of Technology, Harbin, China

Abstract. Servitization is one of the important trends in reshaping the information world in recent years. With the development of division of labor in today's service-oriented society, all parties involved need to gather data and collaborate on training. However, it is difficult to gather data from all parties involved, and each party in the transaction is fighting on its own, forming a complex digital service network. In this network, trading parties need to collaborate with multiple parties while engaging in multi-party games. The key issue faced by this complex service network is how to achieve coordination of overall interests, that is, to achieve multi-party cooperation among all parties involved in the entire transaction process, and to accurately trace problems. Therefore, this paper proposes a trustworthy service transaction framework for privacy protection. To address the differences in service content openness, degree, and standards among different service providers in digital service networks, a service sharing model training system based on federated learning is constructed. By combining deep neural network algorithms and large language models, service recommendation and risk assessment can be implemented to safeguard and regulate service transaction behavior while ensuring data and model privacy. Distributed verification of data and service chains in the service transaction process is carried out through blockchain technology for various transaction records stored in multiple service entities and service terminals. A case study on credit services in a large state-owned bank is given to demonstrate the application of the framework.

Keywords: Trustworthy service transaction framework · Complex service network · Federated learning · Blockchain · Service recommendation

1 Introduction

In recent years, servitization has become one of the key trends in reshaping the information world. However, with the continuous evolution of the division of

Supported by the National Key R&D Program of China [2022YFF0902703].

labor in service oriented society, serviceization has also encountered some challenges, such as the integration and collaborative training of data from all parties, as well as the balance of overall interests among all parties, which have gradually become prominent. Fortunately, the rise and development of technologies such as federated learning and large language model have injected new vitality into service oriented development, opening up more possibilities for development.

The Large Language Model (LLM) has become a powerful tool in the field of Natural Language Processing (NLP) and has recently received great attention in the field of recommendation systems. These models have been trained using self supervised learning on a large amount of data and have achieved significant success in learning general representations, potentially enhancing various aspects of recommendation systems through effective transfer techniques such as fine-tuning and hint tuning. The key to utilizing the power of language models to improve recommendation quality is to utilize their high-quality representation of text features and extensive coverage of external knowledge to establish correlations between projects and users.

When applying LLM in practical applications such as finance, law, and medicine, it is essential to use domain specific data to fine tune LLM. Fine tuning can enrich LLM's domain knowledge, enhance its specific capabilities, and improve the fairness and reliability of output. However, fine-tuning LLM has a high demand for computing resources and a large amount of domain data, which may not be shared due to privacy issues. Federated learning (FL) is a promising paradigm that can use decentralized data for collaborative model training. When multiple entities have similar interest tasks but cannot directly share their local data due to privacy regulations, federated learning is the mainstream solution to utilize data from different entities.

However, federated learning using a central server has some drawbacks, such as the unreliability of uploading model parameters to the server and the lack of incentive measures. And blockchain technology can solve the problems existing in federated learning. Blockchain technology is a decentralized distributed ledger technology, which can be understood as a collectively maintained shared ledger and database, not controlled by central institutions or individuals, but jointly maintained and verified by many participating parties. Blockchain technology has the characteristics of openness, transparency, immutability, full traceability, and traceability.

Therefore, our research has the following contributions:

(1) We use blockchain technology to conduct distributed verification of data and service chains during service transactions, achieving transparent and accurate traceability.
(2) We implement a service sharing model system from different sources through federated learning.
(3) And we combine blockchain based federated learning with large language models to achieve efficient and accurate recommendation of shared services, combine with graph neural networks to achieve risk identification, and build a trustworthy service transaction framework for privacy protection.

This paper is organized as follows: Sect. 1 introduces the background; Sect. 2 discusses related work; Sect. 3 introduces the overall architecture of a trusted service transaction framework for privacy protection; Sect. 4 presents case studies; Sect. 5 is the summary section.

2 Related Work

2.1 Federated Learning

Mcmahan [23] first proposed the concept of federated learning, which aims to achieve collaborative model learning by collecting participant data without compromising privacy. Unlike traditional centralized machine learning techniques, data is fixed locally rather than collected on central servers, which poses many systemic privacy risks and costs [15]. Therefore, federated learning is a promising approach to address this data isolation challenge. The commonly used training algorithm for federated learning is FedAvg, where each client downloads the current model from a central server, calculates updates by performing local calculations on its dataset, and returns the updates to the server. The server aggregates updates between clients to update the global model, and returns the updated model to the local client to achieve the goal of collaborative learning without directly accessing training data on each user's mobile device. However, there are certain issues with federated learning using a central server. The most important reason is the unreliability of uploading model parameters to the server and the lack of incentive measures. Blockchain technology can solve the problems in federated learning.

2.2 Blockchain Technology

Blockchain technology allows any data and digital assets to be placed into the blockchain, which uses a series of immutable records with timestamps to store information and is managed by computer clusters. It is precisely due to the decentralization and immutability of blockchain that it has become an important technology for secure data storage systems [3,30,31]. For a three tiered supply chain, upstream sellers provide trade credit to cash strapped downstream buyers. Wang [27] focused on the implementation of blockchain technology. Li [18] introduced Fabric-SCF, a blockchain based secure storage system designed and implemented through distributed consensus. Lin [21] proposed a new concept of Decentralized Conditional Anonymous Payment (DCAP) and its corresponding security standards.

Overall, blockchain technology is a fundamental technology with broad application prospects in ensuring service transactions. By using blockchain technology for distributed verification of data and service chains during service transactions, transparent and accurate traceability is achieved.

2.3 LLM-Based Recommendation

Large Language Model (LLM) has become a powerful tool in the field of Natural Language Processing (NLP) and is a large-scale language model developed based on pre trained language models (PLMs). Researchers studying the scaling laws of PLM have noticed that increasing the parameters and training data of PLM can have a positive impact on its performance, especially when dealing with complex tasks. Therefore, they developed LLM and observed that LLM exhibited emerging capabilities that PLM did not have [28]. The training of LLM includes three stages [32]: pre training, adaptive fine-tuning, and usage.

In the pre training stage, the basic model is trained on unlabeled text from a large corpus to learn language patterns and acquire language knowledge. The main purpose of pre training is to generate useful sequence representations through unsupervised or self supervised methods, which is equivalent to the first stage of the self supervised learning (SSL) paradigm [2]. After pre training, the model can be fine tuned in downstream tasks or specific fields to professionalize its knowledge and adapt to specific use cases. However, due to the large scale of the model and the need to annotate data, the computational cost of direct fine-tuning may be high. In order to reduce computational costs, current mainstream research has adopted efficient parameter methods [5], such as adapter tuning [14], prefix tuning [20], lora [13], and prompt tuning [17]. These methods involve freezing the backbone network parameters and only adjusting some of them. In the utilization stage, LLM uses zero-shot or few-shot [6] to further improve its generalization ability for downstream tasks and enhance inference ability. The main technique used in this stage is prompt learning [22], which optimizes the interaction between users and models through carefully designed prompts. These prompts can stimulate the model's reasoning ability, thereby improving the performance of downstream tasks.

LLM is used as a recommendation system to understand project text features and improve recommendation performance [16]. Most existing LLM based recommenders are tuning-free and utilize pretraining knowledge to generate the next item recommendation [10]. For example, ChatREC [7] utilizes ChatGPT to understand user preferences and improve interactive and interpretable recommendations. Another suggestion flow based on LLM focuses on designing tuning strategies for subtasks (such as rating prediction) to further improve performance [12]. For example, TallRec [1] executes instruction adjustments to determine whether a certain project should be recommended.

3 Overall Framework

The trustworthy service transaction framework for privacy protection is shown in Fig. 1, which uses blockchain technology to perform distributed authentication on the data chain and service chain during the service transaction process. Miners exchange and verify all local model updates, and then run Proof of Work (PoW); Once the miner completes PoW, it will generate a block that records validated local model updates. Finally, the generated blocks for storing and aggregating local model updates are added to the blockchain (also known as a distributed ledger) and downloaded by the device. Each device calculates global model updates from the new module. Next, using federated learning to achieve service sharing and data privacy protection from different sources, and implementing precise and effective recommendations through large language model based on prompt tuning. Local users use a lightweight prompt generator tailored to their local dataset. Initially, local users use the prompt generator to generate appropriate prompts and send the prompts and local data to LLM. After receiving the input, LLM will respond with the corresponding output. For each service recommendation task, after one cycle of local training, the local model will be transmitted to the central server for aggregation. Then, the local user obtains the updated model parameters as the initial state for the next round of training. Finally, by combining federated learning with graph neural networks, risk identification and service pricing and billing can be achieved.

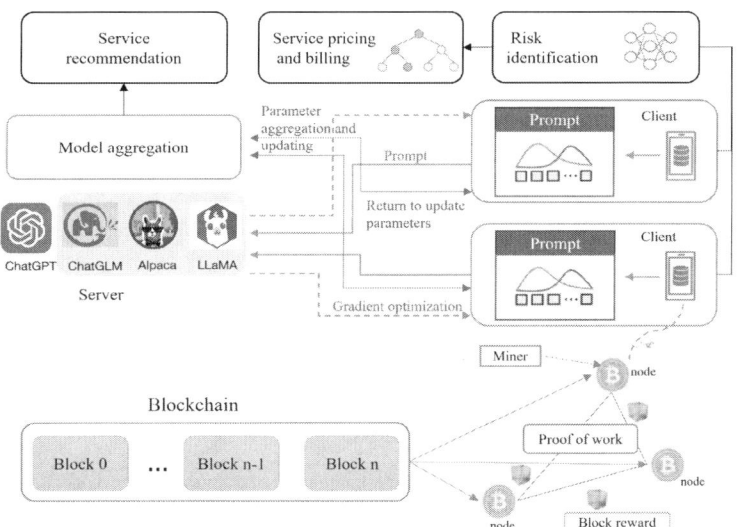

Fig. 1. Overall framework.

3.1 Federated Learning and Blockchain

Federated learning is a promising distributed machine learning framework that can train models without sharing local data while protecting privacy. In the federated learning paradigm, the central server and local terminal devices maintain the same model by exchanging model updates instead of raw data, so as not to directly leak the privacy of data stored on terminal devices. Through this approach, privacy violations caused by collecting more and more sensitive data can be alleviated. However, federated learning using a central server has some drawbacks, such as the unreliability of uploading model parameters to the server and the lack of incentive measures. And blockchain technology is a great solution.

In blockchain based federated learning, servers are replaced by blockchain networks. In blockchain based federated learning, miners M are used to generate and validate blocks, and their function is to exchange updates of local models between a distributed ledger and a local model. The architecture is shown in Fig. 2.

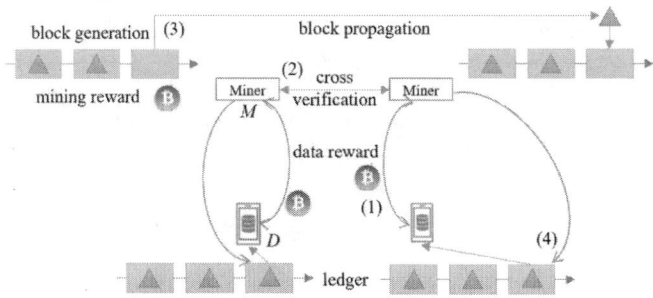

Fig. 2. Blockchain based federated learning architecture.

The client of federated learning consists of a set of devices $D = \{1, 2, ..., N_D\}$, where $|D| = N_D$. The data of the device D_i is represented as S_i, where $|S_i| = N_i$. Each device's data is not shared with other devices, and only local models are trained. The update of the local model of device D_i will be uploaded to its associated miner M_j, which is randomly selected from a group of miners $M = \{1, 2, ..., N_M\}$. In federated learning, device D_i uploads its local model updates to the central server, and global model updates are calculated by the server.

Therefore, the implementation of blockchain based federated learning can be divided into the following steps. a. Update of local models; b. Upload local model update data, randomly associate a miner M_i with the device D_i, and upload the updated local model data and corresponding local calculation time to the associated miner; c. Verification, miners broadcast local model updates obtained, while miners verify local model updates received from their related devices or other miners. The validated local model updates are recorded in the candidate blocks of miners until it reaches the size of the block or the maximum waiting time T_{wait}; d. Block generation, where each mining machine starts running consensus algorithms until it finds the value of a random term or receives a generated block; e. Block broadcasting, first find the candidate blocks of miners with random item values as new blocks and broadcast them to all miners; f. Global device download, where the device downloads the latest generated blocks from its associated miners; g. Global model update data is calculated locally by the device, and the local model is updated by aggregating global weight values in the generated blocks. The above process is iterated continuously until convergence.

3.2 LLM-Based Service Recommendation

For large-scale recommendation datasets, the size of project scope can often reach millions. Therefore, a common solution is to use a two-stage framework, where a fast retriever effectively generates potential candidates and a more powerful model ranks the retrieved candidates to obtain recommendation sequences. So, we adopt a two-stage framework to implement a recommendation model based on LLM. The process is shown in Fig. 3.

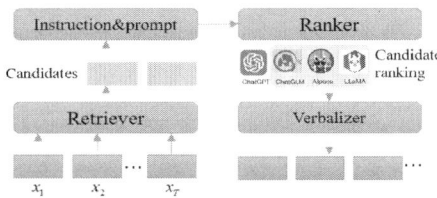

Fig. 3. LLM-based service recommendation flowchart.

Retrieval. In the retrieval stage, we use a retrieval model to obtain top-n recommendations from users based on their historical interactions. Based on these recommendation items, we construct prompts to input LLM for precise recommendations in the next stage. Specifically, in the retrieval stage, the input is the user interaction history x in the dataset X, where x represents a series of historical interaction projects $[x_1, x_2, ..., x_T]$ in chronological order. Each term is defined in the term space I. During the retrieval stage, due to the large amount of item data, the item is represented by a unique ID. As for the ranking stage, we use item titles to understand user behavior and transition patterns.

LLM Ranker. We use LLM as the basic model for recommendation. Specifically, we use LLM to rank among the candidate items in the previous retrieval stage. Although instructions are used to prompt LLM, the generated output does not directly provide ranking scores for candidates. We use a simple language expression to effectively convert the output of the LLM header into the score ranking of candidate items. The output is the ranking scores $\hat{y} \in R^{|I|}$, with the ground truth denoted by $y \in I$. The model with f is parameterized by θ (i.e., $\hat{y} = f(\theta; x)$). Ideally, the highest ranked item in $\hat{y}$ should be the basic real project y. Therefore, the goal of the model is to maximize the ground truth project score. And we seek to minimize the expectation of negative log likelihood loss L parameters θ over X:

$$\min_{\theta} E_{(x,y) \sim X} [L(f(\theta; x), y)] \qquad (1)$$

3.3 Risk Identification and Service Pricing and Billing Based on Graph Neural Network

Our default risk identification model constructs a heterogeneous graph network with users as nodes and different association relationships as edges. The input of the model is the user's own characteristics, neighbor node characteristics, and the user's default label to predict the probability of user default. The overall structure of the model includes the following three parts. The process is shown in Fig. 4.

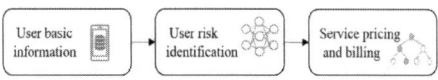

Fig. 4. Risk identification and service pricing and billing flowchart.

Firstly, all nodes in the association network are projected onto a unified feature space. In each semantically homogeneous network, a node level attention mechanism is applied to learn the importance weights of different neighboring nodes, and the node hidden layer representation is obtained by weighted sum of neighboring nodes. Before aggregating neighbor node information from a semantically homogeneous network for each node, it should be noted that neighbors in different semantic networks of each node play different roles and exhibit different importance in learning specific tasks. Based on this, we introduce a node level attention mechanism to learn the importance of neighbors under the same semantics to each node in the associated network, and aggregate these meaningful neighbor representations to form a hidden layer representation of the node. Specifically, the original node features are marked as h_i, and the transformed node features are marked as h'_i:

$$h'_i = MLP(h_i) \qquad (2)$$

Then, we use self attention mechanism to calculate the weights of each node:

$$e_{ij}^{\Phi} = att_{node}(h'_i, h'_j, \Phi) \qquad (3)$$

Then, normalize and calculate the weight coefficients:

$$\alpha_{ij}^{\Phi} = softmax_j(e_{ij}^{\Phi}) \qquad (4)$$

Finally, the embedding of node i can be obtained by multiplying the transformed features of neighboring nodes with their corresponding weight coefficients:

$$z_i^{\Phi} = \sigma(\sum_{j \in N_i^{\Phi}} \alpha_{ij}^{\Phi} \cdot h'_j) \qquad (5)$$

Then, the weight of each semantic homogeneous network is jointly learned through the semantic level attention mechanism, and the hidden layer representation of nodes under different semantics is fused to obtain the final node representation vector. The nodes in the heterogeneous map may contain multiple semantic information, but the semantic specific node level attention mechanism can only reflect the node information from one aspect. In order to learn more comprehensive node representation, it is necessary to integrate multiple semantics contained in the heterogeneous map, so semantic level attention is used to automatically learn the importance of different semantics. Specifically, each semantic weight learned by the model can be represented as:

$$(\beta_{\Phi_0}, \beta_{\Phi_1}, ..., \beta_{\Phi_P}) = att_{sem}(Z_{\Phi_0}, Z_{\Phi_1}, ..., Z_{\Phi_P}) \quad (6)$$

For semantics Φ_r, the semantic importance calculation method is as follows:

$$w_{\Phi_0} = \frac{1}{|V|} \sum_{i \in V} q^T \cdot tanh(W \cdot z_i^{\Phi_r} + b) \quad (7)$$

Then, by normalizing with the softmax function, the weights corresponding to each meta path are obtained.

Finally, the prediction category of nodes is obtained through multi-layer perceptron calculation, and the classification loss is calculated and end-to-end optimization is carried out.

Based on the graph convolution neural network framework, we explore the correlation network between users, establish a risk early warning model, predict the risk probability of the product users' duration overdue, and timely warn potential overdue customers, so as to improve the customer's post loan risk early warning rate and optimize the duration management.

We achieve reasonable service pricing and billing by effectively identifying risks and integrating multiple machine learning models.

4 A Case Study

4.1 Overview

With the development of today's information age, the way banks predict loan outcomes has undergone tremendous changes. The diversity and intricate nature of the data, as well as the vast repository of information, allow banks to delve deeper into the complexities of the lending space. In the financial industry, smart finance has become the mainstream of loan product recommendation, default risk identification, and personalized pricing of bank loans in the financial industry, providing customized financial services for consumer groups with good credit.

Based on this, we demonstrated the application of a trustworthy service transaction framework through research on credit services in a large state-owned bank. First, based on the user's interaction history, we recommend personalized loan products to the user. After the user chooses to purchase a suitable credit product, the user's default risk is identified, and a loan pricing and billing model is constructed for the user based on the default risk identification and loan-related information. Among them, the loan pricing model refers to the prediction model used by banks to determine loan interest rates. The billing model here refers to the way users choose to repay principal and interest when they are ready to purchase a loan product. Moreover, the above-mentioned transaction process uses federated learning to protect data privacy, and uses blockchain for distributed certificate verification to further protect users' transaction behavior.

Loan product recommendation in banks predicts the user's next item of interest by modeling the user's past behavior in chronological order, that is, sequential recommendation. Sequential recommendation systems play a crucial role in personalized platforms such as Netflix [25] and Amazon [19], and these recommendation systems have made significant progress over time, ranging from Markov chains [8,24] and other traditional methods to deep neural networks such as convolutional neural network (CNN) [26,29] and recurrent neural network (RNN) [11]. Afterwards, self-attention recommendation system (SAR) inspired by transformers and their variants [4] further improved training efficiency and recommendation accuracy [9].

Recently, Large language models have received great attention in the field of recommendation systems. These models, trained on large amounts of data using self-supervised learning, have achieved significant success in learning universal representations and have the potential to enhance various aspects of recommendation systems through some effective transfer techniques.

With the development of machine learning and artificial intelligence technology, research on the identification and pricing of bank loan default risks has gradually attracted attention. Many scholars and researchers in the financial field use machine learning and data mining technologies to predict users' loan default risks. Banks can use loan pricing prediction models to price more accurately, thereby better meeting customer needs, improving customer satisfaction, enhancing the bank's competitiveness, while also reducing the bank's risks and saving manpower and time costs.

However, there is currently no unified financial service transaction system for bank loans research, nor has it taken into account the privacy protection of bank data. Therefore, we comprehensively consider the loan product recommendations, default risk identification, loan pricing and billing of bank users to construct a trustworthy financial service transaction framework to protect privacy. Due to the relative confidentiality of bank data information, which involves sensitive data such as personal information and finance, in order to protect the security of user information, banks cannot share data with other participants. Federated learning is a promising distributed machine learning framework that can train models without sharing local data while protecting privacy. Therefore, we introduce federated learning into the service transaction framework. And use blockchain technology to conduct distributed verification of user purchase loan product records, further protecting user transaction behavior.

4.2 System Design and Implementation

Our system includes two roles: user and administrator. It includes the following modules: loan product display module, loan product purchase module, user purchase details module, user repayment record module, user basic information module, and user management module. Table 1 gives the system functional module.

Table 1. System function module.

Module	Description
Loan product display module	The loan product display module includes a display of loan products on the homepage. Users who have not registered and logged in can browse some loan products on the homepage. After the user registers and logs in, the loan product display on the homepage will be a personalized recommended product sequence for that user. Users can choose the loan product they want to purchase and enter the loan product purchase module
Loan product purchase module	The loan product purchase module includes some basic introductions to loan products. Users can choose the loan product they want to purchase, set the limit, interest rate, and repayment method, and finally decide to purchase the product
User purchase details module	In the user purchase details module, users can see the history of purchased loan products and also query the purchased loan products
User payment record module	In the user repayment record module, users can see the repayment status of their previously purchased loan products, including the repayment amount, principal, interest, and other information for each installment
User basic details module	In the user basic details module, users can see some basic information they have filled out and can also make modifications to certain information
User management module	In the user management module, administrators can perform user information maintenance and administrator information maintenance

The loan product display module includes a display of loan products on the homepage. Users can browse some loan products on the homepage before logging in. After logging in, the loan product display on the homepage will be a recommended product sequence for the user. Users can choose the loan product they want to purchase and enter the loan product purchase module.

The loan product purchase module includes the user's selection of loan product limits. The system calculates and displays the interest rate of the product to the user through a pricing model, as well as the repayment and billing methods that the user can choose, and finally determines the purchase of the product.

In the user purchase details module, users can see the history of the loan products they have purchased.

In the user repayment record, users can see the repayment status of each previous loan product, including the repayment amount, principal, interest for each installment, as well as the remaining amount, principal, interest, and other information.

In the user basic information module, users can see some basic information they have filled out and can also make modifications to certain information.

In the user management module, administrators can add, modify, search, and delete users, as well as set up accounts and maintain administrator information.

The overall process of the system mainly revolves around the purchase of loan products by users, and various modules work together to achieve efficient financial service transaction management. After entering the system, if the user

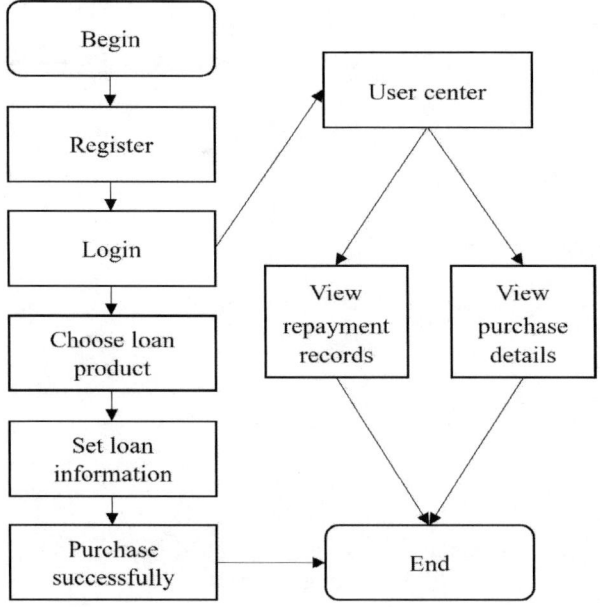

Fig. 5. Flow chart.

has not registered, they can only browse some loan products displayed on the homepage. After registering and logging in, the user can choose the loan products they want to purchase, and then select and set the corresponding product limit, interest rate, and repayment method. After successfully purchasing the loan product, users can view the purchase details and repayment records in their own user center. The system flowchart is shown in Fig. 5.

5 Conclusion

In order to ensure the security and credibility of the service trading market in digital service networks, we propose a trustworthy service transaction framework for privacy protection. To address the differences in service content openness, degree, and standards among different service providers in digital service networks, a service sharing model training system based on federated learning is constructed. By combining deep neural network algorithms and large language models, service recommendation and risk identification can be implemented to safeguard and regulate service transaction behavior while ensuring data and model privacy. Distributed verification of data and service chains in the service transaction process is carried out through blockchain technology for various transaction records stored in multiple service entities and service terminals. Through the study of credit services in a large state-owned bank, the application of a trustworthy service transaction framework is demonstrated.

Specifically, we comprehensively consider the loan product recommendation, default risk identification, loan pricing and billing of bank users, and constructs a trustworthy financial service transaction framework for privacy protection. This framework takes banks as the background and targets individual industrial and commercial households of banks. Firstly, based on the user's transaction history, provide personalized loan product recommendations for the user. After users choose to purchase suitable credit products, they are subjected to default risk identification, and a loan pricing and billing model is constructed based on default risk identification and loan related information for users. Among them, the loan product recommendation model is based on the large language model for recommendation, and the recommendation system is enhanced by fine-tuning the big language model. The default risk identification model adopts a recognition model based on graph neural networks, while loan pricing combines default risk and loan related information to predict interest rates. Due to the relatively private nature of bank data, which involves sensitive data such as personal and financial information, in order to protect user information security, banks are unable to share data with other participants. Federated learning is a promising distributed machine learning framework that can train models without sharing local data while protecting privacy. Therefore, we will introduce federated learning into the service transaction framework. Moreover, adopting blockchain technology for distributed certificate verification further ensures the transaction behavior of users.

References

1. Ba, J.L., Kiros, J.R., Hinton, G.E.: Layer normalization. arXiv preprint arXiv:1607.06450 (2016)
2. Balestriero, R., et al.: A cookbook of self-supervised learning. arXiv preprint arXiv:2304.12210 (2023)
3. Berdik, D., Otoum, S., Schmidt, N., Porter, D., Jararweh, Y.: A survey on blockchain for information systems management and security. Inf. Process. Manag. **58**(1), 102397 (2021)
4. Devlin, J., Chang, M.W., Lee, K., Toutanova, K.: BERT: pre-training of deep bidirectional transformers for language understanding. arXiv preprint arXiv:1810.04805 (2018)
5. Ding, N., et al.: Parameter-efficient fine-tuning of large-scale pre-trained language models. Nat. Mach. Intell. **5**(3), 220–235 (2023)
6. Gu, Y., Han, X., Liu, Z., Huang, M.: PPT: pre-trained prompt tuning for few-shot learning. arXiv preprint arXiv:2109.04332 (2021)
7. Harper, F.M., Konstan, J.A.: The movielens datasets: history and context. ACM Trans. Interact. Intell. Syst. (TIIS) **5**(4), 1–19 (2015)
8. He, R., McAuley, J.: Fusing similarity models with Markov chains for sparse sequential recommendation. In: 2016 IEEE 16th International Conference on Data Mining (ICDM), pp. 191–200. IEEE (2016)
9. He, Z., Zhao, H., Lin, Z., Wang, Z., Kale, A., McAuley, J.: Locker: locally constrained self-attentive sequential recommendation. In: Proceedings of the 30th ACM International Conference on Information and Knowledge Management, pp. 3088–3092 (2021)
10. He, Z., Zhao, H., Wang, Z., Lin, Z., Kale, A., Mcauley, J.: Query-aware sequential recommendation. In: Proceedings of the 31st ACM International Conference on Information and Knowledge Management, pp. 4019–4023 (2022)
11. Hidasi, B., Karatzoglou, A.: Recurrent neural networks with top-k gains for session-based recommendations. In: Proceedings of the 27th ACM International Conference on Information and Knowledge Management, pp. 843–852 (2018)
12. Hidasi, B., Karatzoglou, A., Baltrunas, L., Tikk, D.: Session-based recommendations with recurrent neural networks. arXiv preprint arXiv:1511.06939 (2015)
13. Hu, E.J., et al.: Lora: low-rank adaptation of large language models. arXiv preprint arXiv:2106.09685 (2021)
14. Hu, Z., et al.: LLM-adapters: an adapter family for parameter-efficient fine-tuning of large language models. arXiv preprint arXiv:2304.01933 (2023)
15. Kairouz, P., et al.: Advances and open problems in federated learning. Found. Trends® Mach. Learn. **14**(1–2), 1–210 (2021)
16. Kang, W.C., McAuley, J.: Self-attentive sequential recommendation. In: 2018 IEEE International Conference on Data Mining (ICDM), pp. 197–206. IEEE (2018)
17. Lester, B., Al-Rfou, R., Constant, N.: The power of scale for parameter-efficient prompt tuning. arXiv preprint arXiv:2104.08691 (2021)
18. Li, D., Han, D., Crespi, N., Minerva, R., Li, K.C.: A blockchain-based secure storage and access control scheme for supply chain finance. J. Supercomput. **79**(1), 109–138 (2023)
19. Li, J., et al.: Coarse-to-fine sparse sequential recommendation. In: Proceedings of the 45th International ACM SIGIR Conference on Research and Development in Information Retrieval, pp. 2082–2086 (2022)

20. Li, X.L., Liang, P.: Prefix-tuning: optimizing continuous prompts for generation. arXiv preprint arXiv:2101.00190 (2021)
21. Lin, C., He, D., Huang, X., Khan, M.K., Choo, K.K.R.: DCAP: a secure and efficient decentralized conditional anonymous payment system based on blockchain. IEEE Trans. Inf. Forensics Secur. **15**, 2440–2452 (2020)
22. Liu, X., et al.: P-tuning v2: prompt tuning can be comparable to fine-tuning universally across scales and tasks. arXiv preprint arXiv:2110.07602 (2021)
23. McMahan, B., Moore, E., Ramage, D., Hampson, S., Arcas, B.A.: Communication-efficient learning of deep networks from decentralized data. In: Artificial Intelligence and Statistics, pp. 1273–1282. PMLR (2017)
24. Rendle, S., Freudenthaler, C., Schmidt-Thieme, L.: Factorizing personalized Markov chains for next-basket recommendation. In: Proceedings of the 19th International Conference on World Wide Web, pp. 811–820 (2010)
25. Steck, H., Baltrunas, L., Elahi, E., Liang, D., Raimond, Y., Basilico, J.: Deep learning for recommender systems: a Netflix case study. AI Mag. **42**(3), 7–18 (2021)
26. Tang, J., Wang, K.: Personalized top-n sequential recommendation via convolutional sequence embedding. In: Proceedings of the Eleventh ACM International Conference on Web Search and Data Mining, pp. 565–573 (2018)
27. Wang, C., Chen, X., Xu, X., Jin, W.: Financing and operating strategies for blockchain technology-driven accounts receivable chains. Eur. J. Oper. Res. **304**(3), 1279–1295 (2023)
28. Wei, J., et al.: Emergent abilities of large language models. arXiv preprint arXiv:2206.07682 (2022)
29. Yan, A., Cheng, S., Kang, W.C., Wan, M., McAuley, J.: Cosrec: 2D convolutional neural networks for sequential recommendation. In: Proceedings of the 28th ACM International Conference on Information and Knowledge Management, pp. 2173–2176 (2019)
30. Yang, F., Qiao, Y., Qi, Y., Bo, J., Wang, X.: BMP: a blockchain assisted meme prediction method through exploring contextual factors from social networks. Inf. Sci. **603**, 262–288 (2022)
31. Yang, F., Qiao, Y., Wang, S., Huang, C., Wang, X.: Blockchain and multi-agent system for meme discovery and prediction in social network. Knowl.-Based Syst. **229**, 107368 (2021)
32. Zhao, W.X., et al.: A survey of large language models. arXiv preprint arXiv:2303.18223 (2023)

Towards Efficient Backdoor Attacks Against Federated Self-supervised Learning as a Service Through Intra-Union Aggregation

Shuchi Wu[1], Chuan Ma[2(✉)], Kang Wei[3], Ming Ding[4], Jiyun Yang[2], and Yuwen Qian[1]

[1] Nanjing University of Science and Technology, Nanjing, China
[2] Chongqing University, Chongqing, China
chuan.ma@cqu.edu.cn
[3] The Hong Kong Polytechnic University, Hong Kong, China
[4] CSIRO, Data61, Eveleigh, Australia

Abstract. Compared with classical federated learning (FL) with label supervision, federated self-supervised learning (FSSL) has shown soaring performance in representation learning, making it promising to be deployed as a service. Despite the FSSL-as-a-service can collaboratively train a model using unlabeled data across numerous clients, it introduces vulnerabilities to backdoor attacks due to its distributed nature. To complete a backdoor attack in FSSL, several malicious clients upload crafted local models for aggregation so that a target prediction can be activated by a pre-defined trigger pattern. However, the training process of FSSL is beyond the control of malicious clients, which may terminate at any point. Therefore, a backdoor attack with higher efficiency is preferred. In this paper, we propose an efficient backdoor attack on FSSL-as-a-service named *United Backdoor Attacks (UBA)*. Specifically, UBA aggregates models within the union of participating malicious clients to initialize their models in each epoch, which can significantly enhance the attack efficiency. For example, UBA can achieve 20 to 70 times higher attack success rate on CIFAR100 compared to baselines after the same 20 attacking rounds. Furthermore, we demonstrate that UBA can evade the current state-of-the-art defense mechanisms in FL. To mitigate embedded backdoors inside the global model, we also investigate the effectiveness of a general-purpose defense strategy, i.e., fine-tuning, and explore the impacting factors. Our code is available at https://github.com/wsc2000/UBA.

Keywords: Backdoor attacks · Federated Learning · Self-Supervised Learning

1 Introduction

With the exponential proliferation of edge devices (e.g., smartphones) owned by individuals and groups, there has been a remarkable surge in the volume of

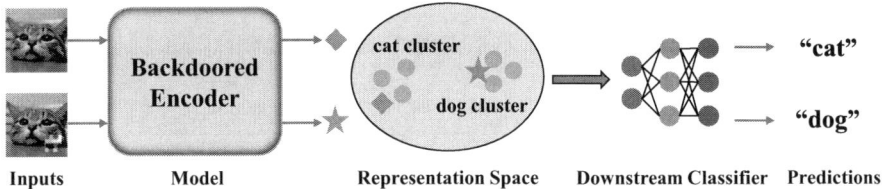

Fig. 1. Illustration of backdoor attacks on the global model of FSSL system. When the backdoor is embedded into the global self-supervised learning (SSL) model, it will be misled to produce an embedding that does not belong to its intrinsic class but the attacker's desired target class (see the representation space above). Consequently, any downstream classifiers that are built based on the poisoned global model will classify inputs with the attacker-specified trigger to the target class (taking "dog" as the target class for example).

data they generate, which bears immense value for machine learning. Nevertheless, these data cannot be centrally collected due to privacy constraints, nor can they be directly utilized to train a model owing to the absence of annotations. In this context, federated self-supervised learning (FSSL) employing a decentralized learning approach exhibits tremendous potential. It possesses the ability to leverage distributed datasets for the training of a high-achieving global model that accommodates all data contributors, all without necessitating labels or direct access to their unprocessed data. [13,18,35]. In this regard, it becomes promising for FSSL to be deployed as a service, which can benefit lots of organizations and individual data owners.

Despite the remarkable achievements of FSSL (e.g., video understanding [21] and disease diagnosis [30,33]), there may exist malicious participants in the FSSL-as-a-service system aiming to implant a backdoor into the global model. This backdoor can lead to misclassification of inputs that contain a specific trigger (e.g., a white square at the bottom right of an image) as a predefined target while functioning normally for clean inputs, as depicted in Fig. 1. Existing works have revealed the susceptibility of traditional federated supervised learning (FSL) to backdoor attacks [1,26,32]. However, such attacks against FSSL remain largely unexplored. Moreover, as [32] recommended, backdoor attacks should be executed when the global model is close to convergence to minimize the negative impact on the model's performance on its primary task. Therefore, it is desirable to devise an efficient backdoor approach as the training process may terminate at any point if the global model is close to convergence.

In this paper, we propose a backdoor attack method that can achieve high efficiency against FSSL, named *United Backdoor Attacks (UBA)*. Specifically, at the beginning of each training round, UBA updates the local models of malicious clients by aggregating models from all participating malicious clients, rather than initializing them to the current global model. This practice can alleviate the dilution effect on models uploaded by malicious clients caused by the global aggregation. Our experimental results show that UBA can significantly acceler-

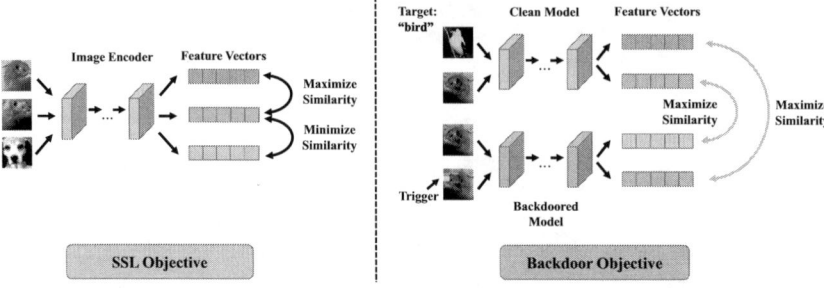

Fig. 2. Illustration of the SSL (left) and Backdoor (right) training objectives, respectively. SSL objective pulls/pushes embeddings for two augmentation views of the same/different image(s) close/away. The blue arrow in backdoor objectives indicates the stealthiness (Eq. (3)) goal, while the pink arrow indicates the effectiveness (Eq. (2)) goal. (Color figure online)

ate the convergence speed of attack success rates (ASR) while simultaneously preserving the model's accuracy on clean inputs. Furthermore, we show that UBA also is resilient to several state-of-the-art defense mechanisms designed for federated learning (FL). To mitigate backdoors that have been embedded in the global model, we evaluate a general-purpose post-training defense, i.e., fine-tuning the global model with a set of clean data, which exhibits notable efficacy if the fine-tuning data's distribution is close to the pre-training data and fine-tuning time is long enough.

In conclusion, our main contributions are three-fold:

- To the best of our knowledge, we are the first to investigate efficient backdoor attacks against FSSL.
- We reveal that existing defense algorithms are inadequate in combating our proposed backdoor method.
- We show that fine-tuning is an effective approach to mitigate backdoors embedded in poisoned SSL models and further explore several impacting factors.

2 Preliminary

2.1 Federated Self-supervised Learning

The fusion of FL capabilities, enabling multiple clients to collaborate in training a sophisticated joint model while preserving the confidentiality of individual private data, along with the label-free nature of SSL, has witnessed a surge in the prominence of FSSL within academic research. For instance, [35] integrated classical SSL techniques such as SimCLR [4] and BYOL [9] into the federated framework, introducing a novel aggregation principle attuned to the FL context, centered on the discrepancies among locally uploaded models. To address the challenges posed by heterogeneous data in FSSL, SSFL [10] personalized the training approach for distinct local clients. Nowadays, FSSL has found applications across diverse domains including computer vision [21], acoustics [6], and medical diagnostics [33], underscoring the bright prospects of FSSL-as-a-service.

2.2 Backdoor Attacks

Adversaries seeking to perpetrate a backdoor attack typically commence by selecting a secret trigger and subsequently leveraging it to contaminate a subset of the victim's training data. The contamination process generally consists of two stages: first, embedding the trigger into the designated data, followed by altering their labels to correspond to the attacker-desired class, known as the target class. Nevertheless, with the absence of labeled data in SSL, the conventional attack strategy outlined above becomes impracticable, prompting the emergence of novel methodologies for backdooring SSL. Thanks to the spontaneous usage of data augmentations by SSL (e.g., contrastive learning [11]), [23] pasted a trigger on images belonging to the target class, thereby SSL will naturally foster associations between the trigger and the target class since cropping may make only one view of two augmentations of a trigger image contains the trigger. Conversely, BadEncoder [14] assumed access to a pre-trained encoder and employed a shadow dataset with a trigger to fine-tune it to manipulate its behaviors on triggered data, which exhibits more effectiveness. Within the FL scenarios, plenty of research has demonstrated its fragility to backdoor attacks [1,26,28,32]. For instance, DBA [32] disperses multiple distinct triggers among malicious local clients, yielding expedited convergence speed and heightened resilience against defense mechanisms.

Despite extensive efforts in scrutinizing the vulnerabilities of traditional FL and centralized SSL frameworks, FSSL remains inadequately explored. This paper endeavors to address this research gap, and proposes an efficient attacking method.

2.3 Defense Algorithms

Backdoor attacks are notorious for their stealthiness and substantial latent harm, rendering the protection of the model training process against such attacks a challenging endeavor. On one front, inverse-engineering-based approaches [7,27] strive to decipher the embedded trigger within backdoored models and discern the designated target class. Nonetheless, this defense strategy necessitates extensive computational resources. Conversely, defense mechanisms in FL predominantly rely on the statistical attributes of uploaded local models (e.g., gradients [7], activation values [22,29]) to identify and eliminate potentially tainted models, ensuring computational efficiency. However, this type of defense relies on appropriate prior knowledge of the backdoor attacks.

In this work, we have examined the effectiveness of six defense algorithms for mitigating backdoor attacks in FSSL, including three designed for combating untargeted attacks [3,34], two designed for countering backdoor attacks [8,20], and one general-purpose defense [2].

3 System Framework

Typically, the FL training process consists of a local training phase conducted by numerous local clients and a global aggregation phase conducted by a central server. We consider an FSSL setting in which there are N local clients, with each having a private local training dataset $\mathcal{D}_i$ of size $|D_i|, i \in \mathcal{N} = \{1, 2, \cdots, N\}$. For attacking, we assume there are M malicious clients among the total N clients colluding together to backdoor the global model. The union of malicious clients is denoted as $\mathcal{M}$. Their attack objectives and capabilities are summarized as follows:

- Malicious clients' objectives: Malicious clients need to make the injected backdoor effective while ensuring its stealthiness. Effectiveness indicates that the backdoored model should classify triggered inputs to the target class with a high probability, i.e., a high attack success rate. Stealthiness implies that the backdoor should not make the model's performance on primary tasks have a perceptible degradation so that the injection of backdoors can not be perceived easily. The ultimate goal of malicious clients in FSSL is to mislead the global SSL model to exhibit backdoor behaviors.
- Malicious clients' capabilities: Malicious clients have complete control of their models, training processes, and datasets while being agnostic to the aggregation rule the server uses and model updates from benign clients. If selected in the current training round, they can also download the broadcasted global model from the central server for the subsequent local training.

Next, we explicate the local training phase and global aggregation phase as follows:

Local Training Process. In each communication round, benign clients follow the standard practice of training their local models using an SSL method, for which we use SimCLR [4] by default. Specifically, SimCLR is designed based on contrastive learning, which pulls together two augmentations of the same image (denoted as a positive pair) while pushing apart that of two different images (denoted as a negative pair) in the embedding space, as shown in the left part of Fig. 2.

For malicious clients, they strive to train a model that fulfills the aforementioned two objectives, i.e., effectiveness and stealthiness. We will elaborate on them in Sect. 4.

Global Aggregation Phase. After the local training phase, clients upload their individual models to the central server, and the server aggregates these models using the FederatedAveraging (FedAVG) [19] aggregation algorithm by default. Formally, FedAVG performs the aggregation in the following manner:

$$\boldsymbol{\theta}^{t+1} = \sum_{i \in \mathcal{N}/\mathcal{M}} \frac{|\mathcal{D}_i|}{|\mathcal{D}|} \cdot \boldsymbol{\theta}_i^t + \sum_{i' \in \mathcal{M}} \frac{|\mathcal{D}_{i'}|}{|\mathcal{D}|} \cdot \boldsymbol{\theta}_{i'}^t, \tag{1}$$

where $\boldsymbol{\theta}^{t+1}$ represents the aggregated global model for the next round, $\boldsymbol{\theta}_{i/i'}^t$ denotes the trained model of client i/i' at the current round, and $|\mathcal{D}|$ represents the total size of datasets across all clients.

4 Backdoor Method

Given that SSL models exclusively generate feature vectors (embeddings) rather than providing labels, malicious clients are compelled to modify the model representations for inputs with triggers to align them with the intended target class, thus fulfilling their effectiveness goal [14,17]. Additionally, as a crucial step to enhance the attack's efficiency, adversaries must ensure that their local models can accurately recognize the target. Based on [14], the effectiveness objective of malicious client $i' \in \mathcal{M}$ can be formally expressed as follows:

$$\mathcal{L}_{i',\mathrm{E}} = -\frac{1}{|\mathcal{D}_{i'}|} \sum_{x \in \mathcal{D}_{i'}} s\left(f\left(x \oplus e_{i'}, \tilde{\boldsymbol{\theta}}_{i'}\right), f\left(x_\mathrm{t}, \tilde{\boldsymbol{\theta}}_{i'}\right)\right) \\ - s\left(f\left(x_\mathrm{t}, \tilde{\boldsymbol{\theta}}_{i'}\right), f\left(x_\mathrm{t}, \boldsymbol{\theta}\right)\right), \tag{2}$$

where $s(\cdot, \cdot)$ is a cosine similarity measuring function, $f(\cdot, \cdot)$ represents the output feature vector of the model, $x \oplus e_{i'}$ indicates a clean image stamped with a trigger $e_{i'}$, $\tilde{\boldsymbol{\theta}}_i$ refers to the backdoored model i' aims to train, x_t is an image of the target class used as a reference for manipulating the model representation and $\boldsymbol{\theta}$ is a clean model used as a reference to ensure that the backdoored model $\tilde{\boldsymbol{\theta}}_i$ maintains its ability to correctly identify the target.

To achieve the stealthiness objective, malicious clients should ensure the backdoored global model produces similar feature vectors for clean inputs as the clean model. This can be formally expressed as:

$$\mathcal{L}_{i',\mathrm{S}} = -\frac{1}{|\mathcal{D}_{i'}|} \sum_{x \in \mathcal{D}_{i'}} s\left(f\left(x, \tilde{\boldsymbol{\theta}}_{i'}\right), f\left(x, \boldsymbol{\theta}\right)\right). \tag{3}$$

Finally, the optimization objective for malicious clients to mount a backdoor attack can be summarized as follows:

$$\arg\min_{\tilde{\boldsymbol{\theta}}_{i'}} \mathcal{L}_{i'} = \lambda_1 \cdot \mathcal{L}_{i',E}\left(\tilde{\boldsymbol{\theta}}_{i'}\right) + \lambda_2 \cdot \mathcal{L}_{i',S}\left(\tilde{\boldsymbol{\theta}}_{i'}\right), \tag{4}$$

where λ_1 and λ_2 are preset weights to balance the two goals. The backdoor objective of malicious clients is illustrated in the right part of Fig. 2.

To mount a more efficient backdoor attack, [26,32] demonstrate that increasing the trigger size, prolonging the backdoor epochs, and poisoning more data are applicable. In this paper, we think from a different perspective: the model

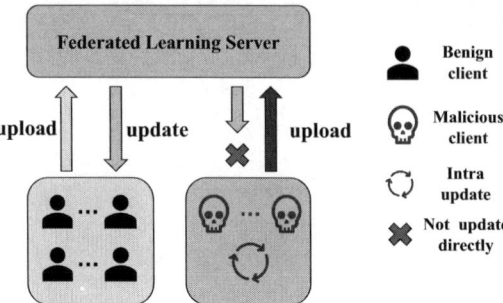

Fig. 3. Illustration of UBA. When selected to participate in the current training round, UBA does not initialize local models of malicious clients to the current global model broadcasted by the server as benign clients do. In contrast, UBA updates each malicious client's local model by only doing aggregation intra the malicious clients union, with the weight of each malicious model decided by its divergence with the current global model.

initialization strategy that malicious clients adopt. In previous works [1,32], malicious clients typically initialize their local models as the current global model at the beginning of each training round. However, we argue that this practice will diminish the efficiency of the attack since the backdoors tend to get diluted after the server aggregates both the models from benign and malicious clients. Therefore, to alleviate such a dilution effect, we propose a novel approach called United Backdoor Attacks (UBA), where malicious clients initialize their models by only aggregating backdoored models from all participating malicious clients in each round, as illustrated in Fig. 3. However, aggregating models from malicious clients with the AVG algorithm naively may make the aggregated model deviate from the global model and thus pose a higher risk that uploaded backdoored models are detected as outliers by anomaly detection algorithms [3,8,20,34]. To address this divergence, we calculate the weight p'_i for each backdoored model within the aggregated model based on its dissimilarity with the global model transmitted by the server. Formally, p'_i is calculated as follows:

$$p'_i = \frac{d\left(\boldsymbol{\theta}^{t+1}, \tilde{\boldsymbol{\theta}}^t_{i'}\right)}{\sum_{i' \in \mathcal{M}} d\left(\boldsymbol{\theta}^{t+1}, \tilde{\boldsymbol{\theta}}^t_{i'}\right)}, \qquad (5)$$

where $d(\cdot, \cdot)$ is a function used for measuring the model divergence. We set both $d(\cdot, \cdot)$ and $s(\cdot, \cdot)$ to cosine similarity in our paper. Finally, each malicious client $i' \in \mathcal{M}$ initializes its model for the next round as follows:

$$\tilde{\boldsymbol{\theta}}^{t+1}_{i'} = \sum_{i' \in \mathcal{M}} p'_i \cdot \tilde{\boldsymbol{\theta}}^t_{i'}. \qquad (6)$$

After finishing the local training epochs, malicious clients upload their respective backdoored models to the server for aggregation.

5 Experiments

5.1 Settings

Datasets and Models. We conduct experiments on three classical benchmark datasets, including CIFAR10 [15], STL10 [5], and CIFAR100 [16], with mainly using ResNet18 [12] as the backbone. Besides ResNet18, Fig. 6 also demonstrates the high efficacy of UBA on another two backbones, i.e., ResNet34 [12] and VGG19_bn [25]. We consider a non-i.i.d setting, in which each client has 2,000 images sampled from the training set. The 2,000 images only consist of two classes of CIFAR10 or four classes of CIFAR100. For STL10, since most images in the training set are unlabeled, we randomly sample 2,000 for each client.

Training and Attacking Setup. We consider an FSSL system consisting of 25 clients, of which 20 are benign and 5 are malicious. In each round, the server randomly selects 10 clients for local training and global aggregation. This implies that selected malicious clients' numbers and identities vary across rounds. Following [32], we begin to attack when the global model is close to convergence, i.e., after 200 rounds of pretraining in our setup. We consider two attack scenarios: in the first scenario, all malicious clients use the same trigger to mount a backdoor (SBA), while in the second scenario, a global trigger is decomposed and distributed among malicious clients, i.e., DBA [32]. We set both λ_1 and λ_2 in Eq. (4) to 1 across all experiments. The training process lasts for 20 communication rounds, in each of which we set the local training epochs of clients to 2. Accordingly, when exploring UBA in the SBA and DBA scenarios, we denote the attack as S-UBA and D-UBA, respectively.

Defense Setup. We consider five state-of-the-art defense algorithms designed for safeguarding FL in our experiments to evaluate the proposed UBA, i.e., Krum [3], Trimmed-Mean [34], Median [34], Foolsgold [8], and FLAME [20]. In addition, we also examine the effectiveness of a general-purpose defense mechanism, i.e., fine-tuning, in mitigating backdoors embedded in the global SSL model.

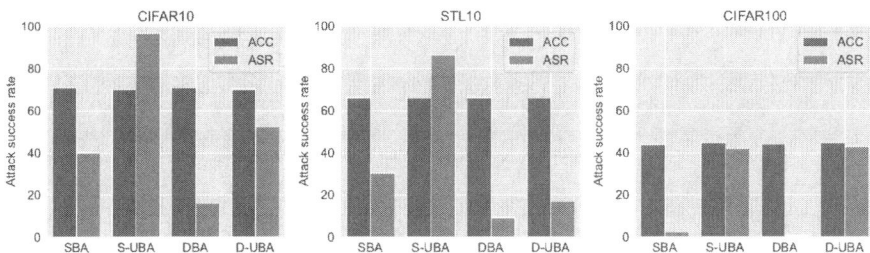

Fig. 4. Performances of backdoor attacks on FSSL after 20 rounds of injecting backdoors. S-UBA and D-UBA indicate the integration of UBA with SBA and DBA, respectively. The results show that our proposed UBA can significantly improve the attacking efficiency of both SAB and DBA.

Table 1. S-UBA under existing state-of-the-art defense methods (the left is ACC and the right is ASR).

Dataset	Clean	AVG	Krum [3]	Trimmed-Mean [34]	Median [34]	Foolsgold [8]	FLAME [20]
CIFAR10	70.5/13.0	70.0/96.7	67.5/44.5	70.1/95.9	70.0/84.3	68.5/100.0	69.9/97.4
STL10	66.0/8.8	66.0/86.1	64.8/100.0	65.9/95.1	65.8/88.9	65.3/100.0	65.9/13.5
CIFAR100	45.2/0.8	44.8/41.9	40.9/9.1	44.7/41.9	44.7/25.7	43.9/3.3	44.5/54.5

Evaluation Metrics. Following the classical settings used in existing backdoor studies [1,32], we consider the attack success rate (ASR) and the primary task accuracy (ACC) to verify the effectiveness of the proposed methods. Since we need to monitor the results in each round, we use the KNN accuracy [31] to measure the two metrics.

5.2 Attack Results

As depicted in Fig. 4, DBA exhibits a consistently low ASR across the three datasets. This is because triggers used in DBA are smaller than in SBA, thus the dilution effect caused by global aggregation is more prominent. Moreover, since each malicious client in DBA uses a different trigger, it suffers from catastrophic forgetting [24] as one malicious client can not always be chosen to participate. Though SBA can mount a more effective attack, the final ASR remains below 40% on CIFAR10 and STL10, and below 5% on CIFAR100. In contrast, both S-UBA and D-UBA demonstrate higher efficiency compared to their respective counterparts after the same attacking rounds. Specifically, the final ASRs achieved by S-UBA and D-UBA on CIFAR10 and STL10 are more than 2 times higher than their counterparts. On CIFAR100, S-UBA achieves about **20** times higher ASR than SBA (41.89% vs 2.26%), while D-UBA achieves about **70** times higher ASR than DBA (42.86% vs 0.61%). These results illustrate that UBA can significantly enhance the backdoor efficiency in both scenarios. Additionally, we note that ACCs remain uncompromised (Clean vs AVG in Table 1). We attribute this preservation of ACCs to $L_{i',S}$ (Eq. (3)), which maintains the model's ability to classify clean inputs correctly.

5.3 Defense Results

To assess the robustness of UBA against existing defense algorithms, we evaluated S-UBA against five state-of-the-art defenses. The results (we report the final results at the 20th round since the attack) are presented in Table 1 in the format of ACC/ASR. It can be observed that none of these defense algorithms exhibit consistent robustness across the three datasets. In addition, some defenses may inadvertently facilitate the attack (e.g., FLAME [20] in CIFAR100), while some may severely degrade the primary task accuracy (e.g., Krum [3] in CIFAR100). Most of these algorithms identify malicious clients by analyzing the statistical attributes of the parameters found within the uploaded local models and

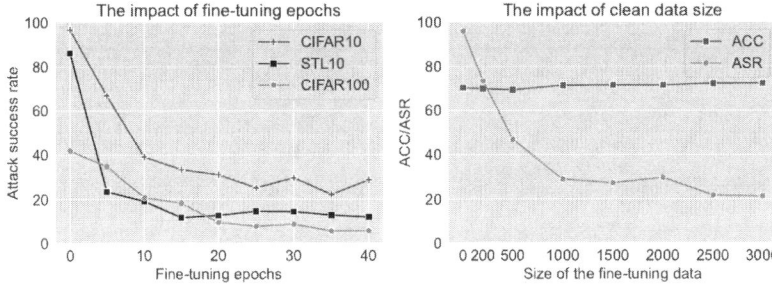

Fig. 5. The performance of fine-tuning with the varying fine-tuning epochs (left) and clean data size (right).

devised for the FSL. In this regard, our UBA considers the divergence between each malicious model and the global model as the benchmark for deciding its weight in the aggregation phase, thereby making malicious models more similar to benign models. Moreover, $L_{i',S}$ tries to minimize the change to the malicious model, which also contributes to the failure of these defenses. Our experimental results indicate that future explorations on effective defense algorithms against backdoor attacks in FSSL should be considered from other perspectives.

5.4 Fine-Tuning Results

Recently, the work in [2] demonstrated that fine-tuning is an effective approach for mitigating backdoors in pre-trained multimodal models. Therefore, we investigate the effect of fine-tuning as a defense for mitigating backdoors. Specifically, we consider a user will fine-tune the pre-trained global model for several epochs with some clean data before employing it. We acquire the clean data by randomly sampling from the training set of each dataset and varying the fine-tuning epochs and the size of the clean data to investigate the impacting factors. When investigating the impact of the fine-tuning epochs, we fix the size of clean data to 2,000. When investigating the impact of the clean data size, we conduct experiments on CIFAR10 and fix the fine-tuning epochs to 30. Our results are depicted in Fig. 5, which demonstrates the effectiveness of fine-tuning. Furthermore, we summarize that more fine-tuning epochs and clean data help to decrease ASR and preserve ACC.

5.5 Abalation Studies

Model Architecture. In our default setting, we choose ResNet18 as the backbone of the SSL model. To demonstrate our UBA can generalize to various model architectures, we further consider ResNet34 and VGG19_bn as two other backbones and choose CIAFR10 for evaluation. Other configurations follow our default setting explicated in Sect. 5.1. The results are plotted in Fig. 6, which shows that UBA still can largely enhance the efficiency of SBA when the backbone is changed to ResNet34 or VGG19_bn. From Fig. 6, we can also notice that it is more challenging to backdoor VGG19_bn than backdooring ResNet34. This may be attributed to the lower ACC of the VGG backbone, which weakens its ability to build connections between the trigger and the target class. We deduce this is the reason why D-UBA only gets similar results with DBA on VGG19_bn.

Data Distribution. In this section, we investigate whether UBA is also effective against an FSSL service system in which clients' local training data are i.i.d distributed. To stimulate the i.i.d scenario, we construct each local client's training data by randomly sampling 2,000 images from each dataset's training set. We choose CIFAR10 and CIFAR100 for evaluations and present results in Fig. 7. From the results, we can observe that UBA remains highly effective in the i.i.d setting.

In conclusion, our ablations studies reveal that UBA generalizes well to various model architectures and data distributions.

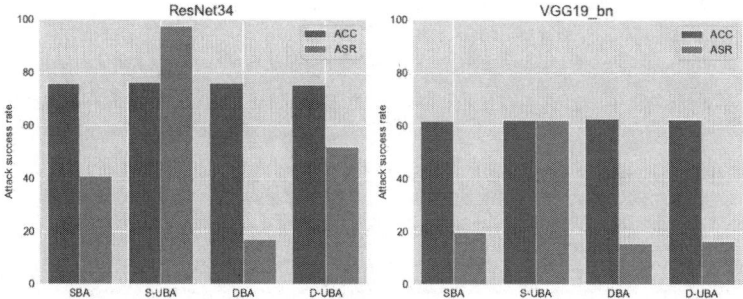

Fig. 6. Ablations on the model architectures, with CIFAR10 as the evaluation dataset.

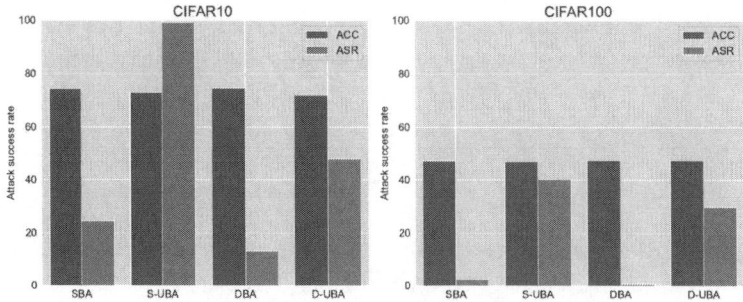

Fig. 7. The effectiveness of UBA in i.i.d data distribution setting.

6 Conclusion

In this paper, we have proposed UBA, a backdoor method that can achieve high efficiency against FSSL and generalize well to various model structures and data distributions. Next, we have demonstrated that existing defense algorithms are ineffective in defending against UBA. Furthermore, we have investigated the effect of fine-tuning as a backdoor mitigation approach as well as some impacting factors. Though fine-tuning is proven to be effective, we argue that the required clean data and computation resources may be unavailable in some scenes. Further defense algorithms requiring less external assistance should be explored.

References

1. Bagdasaryan, E., Veit, A., Hua, Y., Estrin, D., Shmatikov, V.: How to backdoor federated learning. In: International Conference on Artificial Intelligence and Statistics, pp. 2938–2948. PMLR (2020)
2. Bansal, H., Singhi, N., Yang, Y., Yin, F., Grover, A., Chang, K.W.: Cleanclip: mitigating data poisoning attacks in multimodal contrastive learning. arXiv preprint arXiv:2303.03323 (2023)
3. Blanchard, P., El Mhamdi, E.M., Guerraoui, R., Stainer, J.: Machine learning with adversaries: byzantine tolerant gradient descent. In: Advances in Neural Information Processing Systems, vol. 30 (2017)
4. Chen, T., Kornblith, S., Norouzi, M., Hinton, G.: A simple framework for contrastive learning of visual representations. In: International Conference on Machine Learning, pp. 1597–1607. PMLR (2020)
5. Coates, A., Ng, A., Lee, H.: An analysis of single-layer networks in unsupervised feature learning. In: Proceedings of the Fourteenth International Conference on Artificial Intelligence and Statistics, pp. 215–223. JMLR Workshop and Conference Proceedings (2011)
6. Feng, M., et al.: Federated self-supervised learning for acoustic event classification. In: ICASSP 2022-2022 IEEE International Conference on Acoustics, Speech and Signal Processing (ICASSP), pp. 481–485. IEEE (2022)
7. Feng, S., et al.: Detecting backdoors in pre-trained encoders. In: Proceedings of the IEEE/CVF Conference on Computer Vision and Pattern Recognition, pp. 16352–16362 (2023)
8. Fung, C., Yoon, C.J., Beschastnikh, I.: The limitations of federated learning in Sybil settings. In: 23rd International Symposium on Research in Attacks, Intrusions and Defenses (RAID 2020), pp. 301–316 (2020)
9. Grill, J.B., et al.: Bootstrap your own latent-a new approach to self-supervised learning. In: Advances in Neural Information Processing Systems, vol. 33, pp. 21271–21284 (2020)
10. He, C., Yang, Z., Mushtaq, E., Lee, S., Soltanolkotabi, M., Avestimehr, S.: SSFL: tackling label deficiency in federated learning via personalized self-supervision. arXiv preprint arXiv:2110.02470 (2021)
11. He, K., Fan, H., Wu, Y., Xie, S., Girshick, R.: Momentum contrast for unsupervised visual representation learning. In: Proceedings of the IEEE/CVF Conference on Computer Vision and Pattern Recognition, pp. 9729–9738 (2020)

12. He, K., Zhang, X., Ren, S., Sun, J.: Deep residual learning for image recognition. In: Proceedings of the IEEE Conference on Computer Vision and Pattern Recognition, pp. 770–778 (2016)
13. Jaiswal, A., Babu, A.R., Zadeh, M.Z., Banerjee, D., Makedon, F.: A survey on contrastive self-supervised learning. Technologies **9**(1), 2 (2020)
14. Jia, J., Liu, Y., Gong, N.Z.: Badencoder: backdoor attacks to pre-trained encoders in self-supervised learning. In: 2022 IEEE Symposium on Security and Privacy (SP), pp. 2043–2059. IEEE (2022)
15. Krizhevsky, A., Hinton, G., et al.: Learning multiple layers of features from tiny images (2009)
16. Krizhevsky, A., Nair, V., Hinton, G.: Cifar-10. Can. Inst. Adv. Res. **5**(4), 1 (2010). http://www.cs.toronto.edu/kriz/cifar.html
17. Li, C., et al.: An embarrassingly simple backdoor attack on self-supervised learning. In: Proceedings of the IEEE/CVF International Conference on Computer Vision, pp. 4367–4378 (2023)
18. Makhija, D., Ho, N., Ghosh, J.: Federated self-supervised learning for heterogeneous clients. arXiv preprint arXiv:2205.12493 (2022)
19. McMahan, B., Moore, E., Ramage, D., Hampson, S., Arcas, B.A.: Communication-efficient learning of deep networks from decentralized data. In: Artificial Intelligence and Statistics, pp. 1273–1282. PMLR (2017)
20. Nguyen, T.D., et al.: {FLAME}: Taming backdoors in federated learning. In: 31st USENIX Security Symposium (USENIX Security 22), pp. 1415–1432 (2022)
21. Rehman, Y.A.U., Gao, Y., Shen, J., de Gusmao, P.P.B., Lane, N.: Federated self-supervised learning for video understanding. In: Avidan, S., Brostow, G., Cissé, M., Farinella, G.M., Hassner, T. (eds.) ECCV 2022. Lecture Notes in Computer Science, vol. 13691, pp. 506–522. Springer, Cham (2022). https://doi.org/10.1007/978-3-031-19821-2_29
22. Rieger, P., Nguyen, T.D., Miettinen, M., Sadeghi, A.R.: Deepsight: mitigating backdoor attacks in federated learning through deep model inspection. arXiv preprint arXiv:2201.00763 (2022)
23. Saha, A., Tejankar, A., Koohpayegani, S.A., Pirsiavash, H.: Backdoor attacks on self-supervised learning. In: Proceedings of the IEEE/CVF Conference on Computer Vision and Pattern Recognition, pp. 13337–13346 (2022)
24. Shoham, N., et al.: Overcoming forgetting in federated learning on non-IID data. arXiv preprint arXiv:1910.07796 (2019)
25. Simonyan, K., Zisserman, A.: Very deep convolutional networks for large-scale image recognition. arXiv preprint arXiv:1409.1556 (2014)
26. Sun, Z., Kairouz, P., Suresh, A.T., McMahan, H.B.: Can you really backdoor federated learning? arXiv preprint arXiv:1911.07963 (2019)
27. Wang, B., et al.: Neural cleanse: identifying and mitigating backdoor attacks in neural networks. In: 2019 IEEE Symposium on Security and Privacy (SP), pp. 707–723. IEEE (2019)
28. Wang, H., et al.: Attack of the tails: yes, you really can backdoor federated learning. In: Advances in Neural Information Processing Systems, vol. 33, pp. 16070–16084 (2020)
29. Wu, C., Yang, X., Zhu, S., Mitra, P.: Mitigating backdoor attacks in federated learning. arXiv preprint arXiv:2011.01767 (2020)
30. Wu, Y., et al.: Federated self-supervised contrastive learning and masked autoencoder for dermatological disease diagnosis. arXiv preprint arXiv:2208.11278 (2022)

31. Wu, Z., Xiong, Y., Yu, S.X., Lin, D.: Unsupervised feature learning via nonparametric instance discrimination. In: Proceedings of the IEEE Conference on Computer Vision and Pattern Recognition, pp. 3733–3742 (2018)
32. Xie, C., Huang, K., Chen, P.Y., Li, B.: DBA: distributed backdoor attacks against federated learning. In: International Conference on Learning Representations (2019)
33. Yan, R., et al.: Label-efficient self-supervised federated learning for tackling data heterogeneity in medical imaging. IEEE Tran. Med. Imaging (2023)
34. Yin, D., Chen, Y., Kannan, R., Bartlett, P.: Byzantine-robust distributed learning: towards optimal statistical rates. In: International Conference on Machine Learning, pp. 5650–5659. PMLR (2018)
35. Zhuang, W., Wen, Y., Zhang, S.: Divergence-aware federated self-supervised learning. In: International Conference on Learning Representations (2022)

AMFiD: Attention Mechanism Based Deep Forgery Face Image Detection for Fintech Regulation

Shijing Hu[1], Hengqi Guo[1], Jing Liu[2(✉)], Mingyu Gu[3], Zhihui Lu[1], Jirui Yang[1], Yuan Deng[1], and Qiang Duan[4]

[1] School of Computer Science, Fudan University, Shanghai, China
{sjhu21,22110240063,yangjr23}@m.fudan.edu.cn, lzh@fudan.edu.cn
[2] Wangsu Science & Technology Co., Ltd., Shanghai, China
liuj@wangsu.com
[3] School of Foreign Studies, Shanghai University of Finance and Economics, Shanghai, China
2021110452@stu.sufe.edu.cn
[4] Information Sciences and Technology Department, Pennsylvania State University, Abington, USA
qduan@psu.edu

Abstract. With the rapid development of technologies such as big data and artificial intelligence, financial technology (fintech) has risen quickly, bringing development opportunities to the traditional financial industry. However, it also comes with fraud risks caused by deepfake faces in remote identity authentication based on biometrics. Existing methods for detecting deepfake faces have issues such as insufficient feature extraction, low recognition accuracy, and weak generalization capabilities in China's fintech regulation scenarios. To address these challenges, we propose AMFiD: a deepfake face detection method based on a multi-attention mechanism. AMFiD utilizes EfficientNet as the backbone network, incorporating shallow texture enhancement, multi-semantic space representation, and feature fusion modules to enhance the network's feature learning capabilities. Experimental results show that the classification accuracy and AUC of AMFiD reach 97.37% and 0.9943 respectively, outperforming mainstream detection methods. Additionally, to further validate the model's generalization in China's fintech regulation scenarios, we constructed a full-face generation dataset for the Asian face evaluation scenario based on a conditional diffusion model. On this dataset, the accuracy of AMFiD reaches 85.82%, a 0.8% improvement over the baseline model.

Keywords: deepfake face detection · attention mechanism · diffusion model · fintech regulation

1 Introduction

With the rapid development of the new generation of information technology such as big data and artificial intelligence, the rapid rise of financial technology(fintech) has brought great changes and opportunities to the traditional financial industry, but it is also accompanied by potential risks and challenges [4]. As the integration of financial business and information technology, fintech not only contains the risk of financial attributes, but also has a major hidden danger of technical risk transmission to the financial industry. Since financial risk prevention determines our country's high-quality economic development and security strategy layout, risk monitoring of financial technology products has great strategic significance and people's livelihood significance.

However, the current fintech innovation iteration is rapid, large scale, difficult to grasp the overall situation, so we focus on biometric-based remote identity authentication in this paper. This technology is widely used in mobile banking, authorization of large funds transactions, self-service equipment, e-commerce transaction payment, etc., bringing convenience to users but also introducing new technological risks. Specifically, attackers can use deep fake face technology to fake the identity of others, thereby bypassing biometric-based identity authentication systems for fraud, such as in 2019, Silicon Valley artificial intelligence company Kneron demonstrated how to use fake faces to bypass Alipay's face security authentication system. If the risk cannot be effectively monitored, it will inevitably bring a huge impact on financial security, and then affect the economic development and security layout of our country. Therefore, it is essential to conduct in-depth research on the related technologies of deep fake faces.

In order to reduce the harm caused by deep forged face technology, many scholars have devoted themselves to in-depth research on the detection of deep forged face images, and put forward a series of detection methods. Among them, the detection method based on deep learning relies on strong neural network to perform well and become the current mainstream solution. It is well known that Convolutional Neural Networks (CNN) are an important means to deal with various computer vision problems [7], and deep learning based deep forged face image detection is no exception. McCloskey et al. [1] used convolutional neural networks to extract image color cues as the detection basis. Li et al. [2] designed a special convolutional neural network to compare and detect the differences between the generated face region and its surrounding background, and so on. All in all, the current deep learning-based deep forged face image detection methods are mostly based on convolutional neural networks, combined with different discriminant features and advanced network structures. The detection effect of these methods may be very good when they are first proposed, but there are still some defects in the face of the ever-improving deepforged face image, so it is indispensable to continue to study the detection of deepforged face image.

To address these challenges, we focus on the detection methods based on deep learning, aiming to solve the challenges brought by the continuous maturity of the current deep forged face image generation technology and improve the existing detection methods, such as inadequate feature extraction, poor recognition accuracy and poor generalization ability. Based on this, we propose AMFiD: a detection method based on multi-attention mechanism to explore the deep forged face image detection field.

AMFiD aims to solve the problem of small and localized differences between the generated fake face image and the real face image. According to the characteristics of the problem, the deep forged face image detection task is defined as a special fine-grained classification problem. Then, the attention mechanism commonly used in the field of fine-grained classification was introduced into the deep forged face image detection task, and the network structure of the feature extractor EfficientNet was optimized according to the characteristics of the task itself, so as to improve the recognition rate of forged faces. Specifically, AMFiD uses EfficientNet as the backbone network, adding shallow texture enhancement, multi-semantic space representation, and feature fusion modules to further improve the feature learning ability of the network.

In order to verify the effectiveness of AMFiD, we designed and implemented multiple sets of ablation and comparison experiments, including validation of the effectiveness of different modules, selection of the number of attention maps, selection of texture feature enhancement layer and attention map generation layer, selection of counterfactual attention intervention strategies, comparison of mainstream models, and cross-dataset generalization test. In addition, we constructs a full-face generated fake face data set based on the diffusion model, and uses face type control conditions to make the data set more targeted to Asian faces, thus further verifying the model detection performance. Experimental results show that the classification accuracy and AUC of AMFiD can reach 97.37% and 0.9943 respectively on the open data set. On the self-built data set, the accuracy and AUC reach 85.82% and 0.9827, respectively, which are better than the mainstream models.

Specific contributions of this paper are as follows.

1. To address the fraud risk caused by deepfake faces in biometic-based remote authentication, we propose AMFiD, a fine-grained deepfake face image detection method based on multi-attention mechanism.
2. In AMFiD, we propose to combine shallow texture enhancement, multi-semantic space representation and feature fusion techniques to enhance the feature learning ability. The experimental results show that the classification accuracy and AUC of AMFiD reach 97.37% and 0.9943, respectively, which are better than the mainstream detection methods.
3. To meet the needs of China's fintech regulation, we also construct a full face generation dataset for the Asian face evaluation scene based on the conditional diffusion model. On this dataset, the accuracy of our method reaches 85.82%, which is 0.8% higher than the baseline model.

The rest of the paper is structured as follows. Section 2 explains the related work. The technical details of AMFiD are given in Sect. 3. Experimental results are presented in Sect. 4. Finally, we conclude the paper in Sect. 5.

2 Related Work

The research on face detection of deep forgery can be divided into two categories based on physiological features and deep learning according to different extraction perspectives. Next, these two types of detection methods are introduced.

2.1 Physiological Features Based Face Detection

Current deepfake face technology mainly focuses on improving the visual quality of face images, but does not pay enough attention to the physiological characteristics of the fake face in the image, such as head pose and eye color, which makes the generated fake image unable to be consistent with the real image. Therefore, detection methods based on physiological features have been proposed.

Yang et al. [3] used the difference in 3D head pose evaluation as a feature Vector to train a classifier based on Support Vector Machine (SVM) to distinguish original images from deepfake images. In addition, Yang et al. [5] also found that the forged face generated based on Generative Adversarial Network (GAN) was very realistic in the shape of the facial features, but the position of the facial features could not be as natural and coherent as the real face. Therefore, they first obtained facial key points through the face localization algorithm. Then, the normalized position coordinates of the key points are used as the feature vectors of the trained classifier. Finally, the trained classifier is used to recognize the real and fake face images. Matern et al. [6] pointed out that some deepfake faces have some problems in visual effects, such as obvious differences in the color of the eyes, shadows on both sides of the nose, and no geometric rules in the shape of the teeth. Based on this knowledge, they used the features of facial details to distinguish fake face images, and used logistic regression or small neural network with small parameter space to learn the difference between real and fake faces on this feature.

Most of the detection methods based on physiological features are designed for the defects of deepfake face technology at that time. However, with the continuous improvement of deepfake face technology, the defects of physiological features are gradually improved, which makes this kind of detection methods cannot be well applied to new deepfake faces. At the same time, this kind of method also has another shortcoming, that is, the detected face image needs to meet certain preconditions, such as opening eyes, exposing teeth, etc., if not satisfied, the corresponding detection accuracy will be reduced.

2.2 Deep Learning Based Face Detection

The detection methods based on deep learning mainly use deep neural networks to learn the feature differences between fake faces and real faces and use them as the detection basis for authentic and fake images. Afchar et al. [8] believe that the low-level features of images are easily affected by compression and other operations, while the high-level semantic features are difficult to distinguish. Therefore, they proposed to use the Mesoscopic Network (MesoNet) combined with the Inception [9] module to learn the mid-level features of face images to realize detection. Rossler et al. [10] directly used the Xception network [11] to train the classification of real and fake images, and found through experiments that the detection effect of the network trained on the cropped image with only face was better than that of the network trained on the whole image. Nguyen et al. [13] learned features for detection through two series of deep neural networks, that is, the VGG-19 network [14] was first used to extract potential features, and then the features were input into the capsule network to further extract spatial features such as facial pose.

In addition to the above simple use of deep neural network for feature learning, some scholars also consider the introduction of attention mechanism or other enhancement modules to make the deep neural network focus more on the forged regions in the image, so as to improve the detection effect. Dang et al. [15] designed a module based on the attention mechanism to process the feature maps in the backbone classification network. Wang et al. [16] pointed out that most deep learning-based detection methods pay too much attention to a small number of specific regions when learning the difference between real and fake face features. Therefore, they proposed an attention-based data augmentation framework to guide the network to mine previously ignored regions to obtain more representative feature information. Hsu et al. [17] introduced the training method of pair-wise learning to make the network pay more attention to the differences between real and fake images.

With the help of the powerful feature representation and learning ability of deep neural network, most detection methods based on deep learning provide better accuracy and robustness [12]. However, these methods have certain defects, such as poor generalization, and the features learned by the network are highly correlated with the training dataset, so they may not be able to detect deepfake faces that do not appear in the training set.

3 Proposed Method: AMFiD

3.1 Architecture Overview

The AMFiD model proposed in this section is a multi-attention mechanism network, and its overall model architecture is shown in Fig. 1. The input of the model is a face image of a certain size, and the output is the probability that the image is a fake face.

Firstly, the convolutional neural network EfficientNet is used as the backbone to extract the feature maps of the image. The shallow large feature maps contain detailed local fine texture information, while the deep smaller feature maps mainly describe the complex semantic content of the image. Secondly, the point convolutional attention mechanism and the densely connected convolutional layer DenseNet [18] are combined to enhance shallow texture features and prevent small local differences from being submerged by deep features. Thirdly,

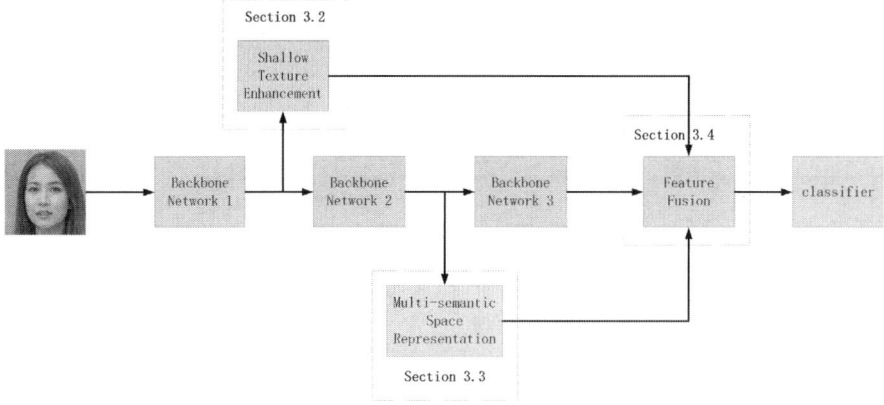

Fig. 1. Overview of AMFiD

the multi-head attention mechanism is introduced to capture the important features of different semantic Spaces, and the bilinear pooling is combined for information screening and fusion to alleviate the impact of global average pooling on salient feature regions. AMFiD improves the accuracy of classification through two stages. In the first stage, the attention mechanism is used to enhance and extract more discriminative local features, so that the model can more accurately capture the position of the object in the attention area. The second stage highly aggregates shallow fine-grained features and deep high-level semantic features as the representation of each local feature, so that the model pays more attention to the features that are beneficial to the learning target. In the following, the design and working principle of each module will be introduced in detail.

3.2 Shallow Texture Enhancement

In this section, the attention mechanism is used to replace the traditional convolutional layer as the texture feature extractor. The attention mechanism focuses on valuable features while inhibiting or filtering irrelevant information to improve the expression ability of features. The existing attention is generally obtained by 1×1 convolution layer, Batch Normalization (BN) layer and ReLU activation layer. Because the size of the convolution kernel limits the size of the receptive area, it is difficult to capture the comprehensive information of texture features. In this section, a new Global Convolutional Attention (GCA) mechanism is designed, which can cover the whole receptive field area of the image with low computational complexity through point convolution operation, and can enhance the contrast of information in shallow pixel space. At the same time, it can fully explore the sharing of effective features and the suppression of invalid information. The complete calculation process of GCA mainly consists of two stages, which perform point convolution operations in W and H dimensions respectively.

The input of the GCA module is the output feature map tensor $F \in R^{H \times W \times C}$ of a certain layer of the backbone network, where H and W are the height and width of the feature map, and C is the number of channels. In the first stage, $F^{(W)} \in R^{H \times C \times W}$ is obtained by transposing $F^{(W)}$ according to the dimension W, and then $Q^{(W)}$ is obtained by applying click convolution operation and ReLU activation to $F^{(w)}$. The calculation process is as follows:

$$Q^{(W)} = ReLU(Conv_{1 \times 1}(F^{(W)})) \tag{1}$$

In Eq. 1, $Q^{(W)} \in R^{H \times C \times W}$. Then, we transpose $Q^{(W)}$ to $P \in R^{H \times W \times C}$. For the feature map of the ith channel $Q_i \in R^{H \times W}$, the calculation process can be expressed as follows.

$$Q_i(h, u) = \sum_{w=0}^{W} F_i(h, w) K_u^W \tag{2}$$

In Eq. 2, $K_u^{(W)} \in R^W$ represents the convolution kernel output at the u-th channel in the 1×1 convolution. In the second stage, we take P as input, transpose $Q^{(H)} \in R^{C \times W \times H}$ according to H dimension, and apply the point convolution operation to $Q^{(H)}$ to get $G_H \in R^{C \times W \times H}$:

$$G^{(H)} = ReLU(Conv_{1 \times 1}(Q^{(H)})) \tag{3}$$

$$G_i(v, u) = \sum_{h=0}^{H-1} Q_i(h, u) K_v^H \tag{4}$$

In Eq. 4, G_i is the ith channel of the feature map G. After transposing G_H, $G \in R^{H \times W \times C}$ is obtained.

After the above two point convolutions, each element in G is related to all elements of the input feature map F, that is, G is the feature map of global attention, and the feature weight of each channel is expressed as follows

$$G_i(u, v) = \sum_{h=0}^{H-1} \sum_{w=0}^{W-1} F_i(h, w) K_u^{(W)}(w) K_v^{(H)}(h) \tag{5}$$

In Eq. 5, $i \in \{0, 1, 2, ..., C-1\}$, and each channel of Q_i is independent of each other. After the global convolutional attention weight is normalized by Softmax, the element multiplication is performed with the original input feature, and residual connection is introduced to obtain the final shallow global feature F_g:

$$F_g = Softmax(CGA(F)) \odot F + F \tag{6}$$

In Eq. 6, $\odot$ represents the multiplication of elements in corresponding positions. CGA is a simple and effective global attention operator, which can be used to extract a variety of contrast information in low level pixel space when it is applied to shallow texture feature extraction.

After the shallow global features are extracted, in order to retain more artifact trace information in the texture, the output tensor F of the shallow layer of the backbone network is convolved, batch normalized and activated by 3×3 convolution check, and the non-texture feature F_n is obtained. Then, similar to the texture representation of images in space, the texture information F_t is used as the pixel level residual, that is:

$$F_t = F_g - F_n \tag{7}$$

At this time, F_t contains most of the texture information of the image, and excludes the interference of other irrelevant features. Finally, the texture feature was passed through the enhancement module to improve the effect of the model in capturing forged features. The texture enhancement module is mainly composed of multiple densely connected convolutional blocks stacked. Compared with the residual connection, there are multiple information flow routes inside the densely connected convolutional block, and each layer can directly contact the gradient from the loss function and the feature map of all previous layers. The feature transfer and the influence of important features are strengthened with fewer parameters, which alleviate the problem of gradient disappearance and overfitting, and it is easier to train and converge the model.

3.3 Multi-semantic Space Representation

In the fine-grained classification of images, the introduction of the attention mechanism can strengthen the model to learn the local features related to the classification task in the image, reduce the interference of redundant information, and thus improve the computational efficiency and performance of the model. At present, related work has introduced the single attention mechanism into the deep face forgery detection task. However, the single-head attention mechanism usually only focuses on a certain local regional feature or a specific distribution in the image, and it is difficult to capture the complex associations and multi-level feature interactions in the image. However, there are many kinds of deepfake face methods, such as attribute editing, expression exchange, and full face generation. It is difficult for the detection model to distinguish all forgery cases by only one local feature. Therefore, a multi-attention mechanism is adopted in this section to map the deep feature maps to multiple different semantic Spaces to generate different attention maps. Each attention map corresponds to a specific face region, such as nose, eyes, mouth and other parts, which reduces the randomness of the attention mechanism and mines forgery discriminative features from multiple different Spaces, scales and levels, helping the detection model to understand and process images more accurately and improving the perception ability of the model.

The input of the multi-head attention mechanism is the feature map $F \in R^{H \times W \times C}$ extracted from the deeper layers of the backbone network, and the attention map $A \in R^{H \times W \times M}$ is calculated in parallel by multiple different GCA attention modules in Subsect. 3.3:

$$A_k = ReLU(BN(GCA(F))) \tag{8}$$

$$A = Concat([A_1, A_2, ..., A_k]) = \bigcup_{k=1}^{M} A_k \tag{9}$$

In Eq. 9, M represents the number of attention maps, $A_k \in R^{H \times W}$ is the attention object of a specific region of the face. After standardization and nonlinear transformation, the part with high response value (measuring the information richness of a certain region of the image) can be highlighted, and the part with low response value can be turned into zero, so as to achieve the purpose of information filtering and screening. In addition, the multi-head attention mechanism can dynamically adjust the distribution of attention, and the attention distribution of each head can be visualized, which makes the decisions of the model more interpretable.

3.4 Feature Fusion

After the feature map F and the multi-attention map A are obtained, they need to be fused. At present, the mainstream feature fusion methods mainly include splicing, addition, dot product, weight fusion and feature pyramid, etc. Although these methods are simple and effective in specific scenarios, they have the risk of dimension explosion, failing to deal with the complex relationship between features and increasing the computational cost of the model. In this section, we draw on the idea of Bilinear Attention Pooling (BAP) [19,20] to fuse multiple network flows, and apply it to the information aggregation of feature maps and multi-attention maps, which can help the model better understand various semantic features of images without adding additional parameters. On the one hand, the multi-attention map can be used to guide the feature map to select discriminative features related to the forgery face detection task. On the other hand, the second-order features of the feature map can be constructed to increase the expression ability of the model. First, the feature map is multiplied with each attention map element by element, and the calculation process is as follows:

$$F_k = A_k \odot F \tag{10}$$

In Eq. 10, $F_k \in R^{H \times W}$, $k = 1, 2, ..., M$. If the shapes of A_k and F are not consistent, they need to be interpolated or sampled to ensure that the operation proceeds normally. Then, the global average pooling or Max pooling operation is performed on F_k to obtain the final attention feature $f_k \in R^{1 \times N}$, where N is the number of channels in the feature map. Finally, the M attention features are stacked together to form the feature matrix Z, which is calculated as follows:

$$Z = \begin{bmatrix} g(A_1 \odot F) \\ g(A_2 \odot F) \\ ... \\ g(A_M \odot F) \end{bmatrix} = \begin{bmatrix} f_1 \\ f_2 \\ ... \\ f_M \end{bmatrix} \quad (11)$$

The function $g(...)$ represents a specific type of pooling operation. The essence of bilinear pooling is to use attention as a feature filter to replan the data of the original feature map and retain the high response value part. The bilinear pooling in this paper is applied to two parts: shallow texture enhancement features and deep semantic features.

4 Experiment

In this section, we conduct experimental tests on the AMFiD model and analyze the obtained results. We provide details on the dataset and experimental setup utilized for these tests. We perform various ablation experiments to investigate the individual contributions of each module towards the prediction results. Additionally, we conduct several comparison experiments to verify the superior performance of AMFiD over the majority of existing models.

4.1 Dataset

We utilized two well-known publicly available deep forgery face datasets, namely FaceForensics++ (FF++), and DeepFake Detection Challenge (DFDC) [21]. Since there is limited research on the detection task of full-face generation and acquiring full-face generation faked data is challenging, we additionally employed the state-of-the-art denoising diffusion model (DDPM) [22] to create a DDPM dataset, which helped in evaluating the performance of AMFiD. The majority of existing forged face datasets primarily consist of foreign videos, with a relatively small proportion of Asian yellow faces. This significant difference in data distribution can result in the model having insufficient exposure to and

Fig. 2. Example of Fake Face Data Based on Diffusion Modeling

learning of Asian faces, leading to reduced confidence in detecting them. To address this, we employed non-Asian faces from CelebA [23] and Asian faces from FFHQ [24] as training data. Additionally, we jointly trained the DDPM using face type cross-entropy loss and noise loss, incorporating the face type condition. Consequently, we generated 4,500 Asian and non-Asian faces each to construct the diffusion model forged face dataset (DDPM). In the example below, Fig. 2 demonstrates how both fake and real faces are nearly indistinguishable to the naked eye. To enhance the applicability of our self-built dataset DDPM for Asian face evaluation, we have employed a diffusion model with conditions to control the generation of face types, making it more inclined towards Asian faces. This modification ensures that the dataset contains a higher representation of Asian faces, thus improving its relevance for evaluating Asian face-related applications. Meanwhile, the DDPM dataset generates better quality and detects forgeries with higher difficulty, which provides a new reference index for existing detection techniques.

4.2 Experimental Setup

Our experiments were conducted on a Linux environment using Python version 3.8.3. The primary hardware used was an NVIDIA RTX3090 GPU graphics card. To initialize the backbone network parameters, we utilized the pre-trained model of EfficientNet-B4(EN) [25] on the ImageNet dataset. During the model training phase, we set the Batch Size to 16. We employed the Adam optimizer for gradient updating, with a learning rate of 0.001 and weight decay of 1e-6 per epoch. Additionally, we conducted experiments to determine the optimal parameters for conditions such as the number of attention maps and the extraction location of shallow and deep feature maps. Since the available public datasets primarily consist of videos, and our evaluation focused on images, we extracted frames from the videos at intervals of 5 frames to generate the dataset.

Table 1. Experimental results of evaluating models on the FF++ dataset.

Methods	CPCNN	FX	ELA	SPSL	TB	EN	AMFiD
AUC	–	0.8740	0.9480	0.9530	0.9870	0.9918	**0.9943**
ACC(%)	79.08	–	93.86	95.73	–	96.63	**97.37**

4.3 Performance Comparison

Comparison of Detection Results. We conducted a comparative test with several existing state-of-the-art methods, including CPCNN [26], Face X-ray (FX) [27], ELA [28], SPSL [29], Two Branch (TB) [30], and EN, on the well-known FF++ dataset. The test results are presented in Table 1. Additionally, we evaluated the Log loss on the challenging DFDC dataset. To ensure a fair comparison, we selected some detection methods that perform well on this dataset, including The Medics (TM), Selim Seferbekov (SS), Eighteen Years Old (EYO), WM, and NTechLab (NTL). The test results for these methods are presented in Table 2. Based on the results, AMFiD outperforms the majority of current mainstream detection methods, showcasing its superiority. To further highlight the advantages of AMFiD, we included a comparison with EN on our self-built DDPM dataset. In the self-constructed DDPM dataset, the AUC of EN is 0.9799, while AMFiD's is 0.9827. The ACC of EN is 85.07%, and AMFiD's is 85.82%. The multi-attention mechanism in AMFiD enables thorough extraction of sample features, facilitating differentiated feature learning and enhanced generalization. Even when faced with the challenges posed by the most difficult self-built DDPM dataset, AMFiD surpasses EN in terms of detection performance.

Table 2. Experimental results of evaluating models on the DFDC dataset.

Methods	TM	SS	EYO	WM	NTL	AMFiD
Log loss	0.157	0.1983	0.1882	0.1787	0.1703	**0.1669**

In order to further analyze the effectiveness of AMFiD, the FF++ dataset was divided into four categories based on forgery types, including DeepFakes, Neural Textures, Face2Face, and FaceSwap. Evaluating the model within each subcategory can verify the discriminative ability of the different types of forgery, providing a more comprehensive evaluation. 50 frames of each video in the dataset were sampled for evaluation, and the evaluation metrics calculated the AUC in the video dimension. The results are presented in Table 3.

Table 3. Experimental results for different forgery type sub-datasets of FF++.

Datasets	DeepFakes	NeuralTextures	Face2Face	FaceSwap	Avg
Xception	0.994	0.973	**0.995**	0.994	0.989
FX	0.998	0.989	0.993	0.996	0.994
AMFiD	**0.999**	**0.992**	0.993	**0.999**	**0.996**

Based on the results, it is evident that AMFiD attains optimal performance on the DeepFakes, FaceSwap, and Neural Textures sub-datasets, and is only marginally behind the Xception model on Face2Face. This indicates the model's capability to effectively distinguish between various forgery methods. Furthermore, the Neural Textures and Face2Face categories exhibit lower AUCs, primarily due to their minimal modification regions, closer resemblance to real images, and difficulty in visually capturing forgery features.

4.4 Ablation Experiment

We integrated the concept of fine-grained classification into the deep forgery face detection algorithm to enhance the existing algorithmic model based on the attention mechanism. We primarily introduced three strategic modules, namely the shallow texture enhancement(STE), multi-semantic space representation (MSR), and feature fusion (FF). To validate the effectiveness and contribution of these strategies, we conducted multiple sets of comparison experiments using the FF++ dataset. Each module was removed one at a time, and the ACC and AUC were calculated for evaluation, where ✓ indicates the presence of the module. The results are demonstrated in Table 4.

Table 4. Experimental results for different forgery type sub-datasets of FF++.

STE	MSR	FF	AUC	ACC (%)
✓	✓	✓	**0.9943**	**97.37**
–	✓	✓	0.9916	97.06
✓	–	✓	0.9940	97.27
✓	✓	–	0.9938	96.97

Each module has positively improved the model's effectiveness. Shallow texture enhancement plays a crucial role, as its removal decreases model performance by 0.2%–0.3%, making slight forgery traces more prominent and easily learned by the model. The multi-semantic space representation's removal leads to a decrease of less than 0.1% in AUC and ACC, suggesting overlap with other features. Eliminating the effect of feature fusion results in a flat AUC but decreased ACC, indicating its role in increasing differentiation for difficult-to-classify samples near the threshold and reducing data bias impact.

5 Conclusion

In recent years, the advancement of deep learning technology and increased computational resources have led to the maturity of Deepfake face image generation technology, posing a significant challenge to finTech regulation. To address this, we propose a novel deep forged face image detection method called AMFiD (Attention-based Multi-attention Mechanism for Deep Forgery). The AMFiD method approaches the deepfake face image detection task as a fine-grained classification problem, leveraging the distinctive characteristics that differentiate real and fake faces. AMFiD is achieved by incorporating the attention mechanism commonly used in fine-grained classification. The network optimization encompasses shallow texture enhancement, multi-semantic spatial representation, and the introduction of a feature fusion module. Through extensive comparison and ablation experiments, we demonstrate the effectiveness of our method and the rationale behind the module design. These experiments validate the superior performance of AMFiD in detecting deep forged face images.

Acknowledgement. This work was supported in part by the National Key Research and Development Program of China under Grant 2022YFC3302300 and Grant 2021YFC3300600, and in part by the Shanghai Science and Technology Project under Grant 22510761000.

References

1. McCloskey, S., Albright, M.: Detecting GAN-generated imagery using color cues. arXiv preprint arXiv:1812.08247 (2018)
2. Li, Y., Lyu, S.: Exposing deepfake videos by detecting face warping artifacts. arXiv preprint arXiv:1811.00656 (2018)
3. Yang, X., Li, Y., Lyu, S.: Exposing deep fakes using inconsistent head poses. In: ICASSP 2019-2019 IEEE International Conference on Acoustics, Speech and Signal Processing (ICASSP), pp. 8261–8265. IEEE (2019)
4. Hu, S., Lin, J., Du, X., et al.: ACSarF: a DRL-based adaptive consortium blockchain sharding framework for supply chain finance. Digit. Commun. Netw. (2023)
5. Yang, X., Li, Y., Qi, H., et al.: Exposing GAN-synthesized faces using landmark locations. In: Proceedings of the ACM Workshop on Information Hiding and Multimedia Security, pp. 113–118 (2019)
6. Matern, F., Riess, C., Stamminger, M.: Exploiting visual artifacts to expose deepfakes and face manipulations. In: Proceedings of 2019 IEEE Winter Applications of Computer Vision Workshops (WACVW), pp. 83–92. IEEE (2019)
7. Hu, S., Lin, J., Lu, Z., et al.: CoLLaRS: a cloud-edge-terminal collaborative lifelong learning framework for AIoT. Future Gener. Comput. Syst. (2024)
8. Afchar, D., Nozick, V., Yamagishi, J., et al.: Mesonet: a compact facial video forgery detection network. In: 2018 IEEE International Workshop on Information Forensics and Security (WIFS), pp. 1–7. IEEE (2018)
9. Szegedy, C., Liu, W., Jia, Y., et al.: Going deeper with convolutions. In: Proceedings of the IEEE Conference on Computer Vision and Pattern Recognition, pp. 1–9 (2015)
10. Rossler, A., Cozzolino, D., Verdoliva, L., et al.: Faceforensics++: learning to detect manipulated facial images. In: Proceedings of the IEEE/CVF International Conference on Computer Vision, pp. 1–11 (2019)
11. Chollet, F.: Xception: deep learning with depthwise separable convolutions. In: Proceedings of the IEEE Conference on Computer Vision and Pattern Recognition, pp. 1251–1258 (2017)
12. Hu, S., Deng, R., Du, X., et al.: LAECIPS: large vision model assisted adaptive edge-cloud collaboration for IoT-based perception system. arXiv preprint arXiv:2404.10498 (2024)
13. Nguyen, H.H., Yamagishi, J., Echizen, I.: Capsule-forensics: using capsule networks to detect forged images and videos. In: ICASSP 2019-2019 IEEE International Conference on Acoustics, Speech and Signal Processing (ICASSP), pp. 2307–2311. IEEE (2019)
14. Simonyan, K., Zisserman, A.: Very deep convolutional networks for large-scale image recognition. arXiv preprint arXiv:1409.1556 (2014)

15. Dang, H., Liu, F., Stehouwer, J., et al.: On the detection of digital face manipulation. In: Proceedings of the IEEE/CVF Conference on Computer Vision and Pattern recognition, pp. 5781–5790 (2020)
16. Wang, C., Deng, W.: Representative forgery mining for fake face detection. In: Proceedings of the IEEE/CVF Conference on Computer Vision and Pattern Recognition, pp. 14923–14932 (2021)
17. Hsu, C.C., Zhuang, Y.X., Lee, C.Y.: Deep fake image detection based on pairwise learning. Appl. Sci. **10**(1), 370 (2020)
18. Huang, G., Liu, Z., Van Der Maaten, L., et al.: Densely connected convolutional networks. In: Proceedings of the IEEE Conference on Computer Vision and Pattern Recognition, pp. 4700–4708 (2017)
19. Hu, T., Qi, H., Huang, Q., et al.: See better before looking closer: weakly supervised data augmentation network for fine-grained visual classification. arXiv preprint arXiv:1901.09891 (2019)
20. Lin, T.Y., RoyChowdhury, A., Maji, S.: Bilinear CNN models for fine-grained visual recognition. In: Proceedings of the IEEE International Conference on Computer Vision, pp. 1449–1457 (2015)
21. Dolhansky, B., Bitton, J., Pflaum, B., et al.: The deepfake detection challenge (DFDC) dataset. arXiv preprint arXiv:2006.07397 (2020)
22. Ho, J., Jain, A., Abbeel, P.: Denoising diffusion probabilistic models. In: Advances in Neural Information Processing Systems, vol. 33, pp. 6840–6851 (2020)
23. Liu, Z., Luo, P., Wang, X., et al.: Large-scale celebfaces attributes (celeba) dataset, **15**(2018), 11 (2018)
24. Karras T., Laine, S., Aila, T.: A style-based generator architecture for generative adversarial networks. In: Proceedings of the IEEE/CVF Conference on Computer Vision and Pattern Recognition, pp 4401–4410 (2019)
25. Tan, M., Le, Q.: Efficientnet: rethinking model scaling for convolutional neural networks. In: International Conference on Machine Learning, pp. 6105–6114. PMLR (2019)
26. Cozzolino, D., Poggi, G., Verdoliva, L.: Recasting residual-based local descriptors as convolutional neural networks: an application to image forgery detection. In: Proceedings of the 5th ACM Workshop on Information Hiding and Multimedia Security, pp. 159–164 (2017)
27. Li, L., Bao, J., Zhang, T., et al.: Face x-ray for more general face forgery detection. In: Proceedings of the IEEE/CVF Conference on Computer Vision and Pattern Recognition, pp. 5001–5010 (2020)
28. Gunawan, T.S., Hanafiah, S.A.M., Kartiwi, M., et al.: Development of photo forensics algorithm by detecting photoshop manipulation using error level analysis. Indones. J. Electr. Eng. Comput. Sci. **7**(1), 131–137 (2017)
29. Liu, H., Li, X., Zhou, W., et al.: Spatial-phase shallow learning: rethinking face forgery detection in frequency domain. In: Proceedings of the IEEE/CVF Conference on Computer Vision and Pattern Recognition, pp. 772–781 (2021)
30. Masi, I., Killekar, A., Mascarenhas, R.M., Gurudatt, S.P., AbdAlmageed, W.: Two-branch recurrent network for isolating deepfakes in videos. In: Vedaldi, A., Bischof, H., Brox, T., Frahm, J.-M. (eds) ECCV 2020. LNCS, vol. 12352, pp. 667–684. Springer, Cham (2020). https://doi.org/10.1007/978-3-030-58571-6_39

Service Application

Reservoir Flood Prediction Service Based on Seq2seq Model

Lincong Liu, Shijun Liu(✉), and Li Pan

School of Software Engineering, Shandong University, Jinan, China
{lsj,panli}@sdu.edu.cn

Abstract. Reliable reservoir flood prediction model is an indispensable part to improve the digital construction of small and medium-sized reservoirs. Flood flow, as one of the important bases for measuring flood prediction, its prediction accuracy directly affects the effectiveness of reservoir flood prevention and control. The traditional flood flow prediction model often can't get real-time and comprehensive data in time, which leads to the idealized prediction effect can't be realized, so for this situation, this paper proposes a reservoir flood flow prediction model based on Seq2seq model. Based on the Seq2seq model, this model not only integrates the LSTM network as a recurrent processing unit to facilitate the capture of temporal information and long-term dependencies in the data, but also uses the attention mechanism to reduce the loss of information in the transmission process and improve the model's generalization ability. At the same time, the model is compared with a variety of flood prediction machine learning models, and also compared with the prediction model based on the traditional flood flow statistics model, and then this paper further verifies the model's improvement in prediction accuracy by comprehensively comparing the results of five evaluation indexes. Finally, the modeling service has been applied in the real environment, which again proves the effectiveness of the present service.

Keywords: Flood flow prediction · Seq2seq model · LSTM model · Attention mechanism

1 Introduction

With the development of the times, the extreme weather events caused by global climate change are increasing, the rainfall pattern is more and more difficult to control, and the reservoir flood risk prevention and control becomes more and more important. Reservoir flood flow, as one of the important indicators to determine the level of flood risk [9], plays a crucial role in flood control downstream of the reservoir, which not only can guide the scheduling of the reservoir operators in principle, but also can provide decision-making support for the managers to deal with emergencies through the real-time prediction of the flood flow and improve the ability to deal with emergencies.

The prediction model based on the traditional flood flow statistics model is a prediction algorithm model with reservoirs and their catchment areas as the scope of study [7], and with the yield and sink model as the core of the prediction algorithm. To achieve real-time calculation of reservoir level rise due to heavy rainfall and ultimately realize real-time prediction of inflow and runoff, it is necessary to statistically discretize meteorological forecast data, incoming flow data, elevation topography data, vegetation soil data, and underwater topography data of the reservoir area. However, in real-world scenarios, the traditional algorithm often fails to acquire real-time, comprehensive data promptly. Consequently, the idealized reservoir flood forecasting model remains unrealized. As a result, emergency commanders must rely solely on typical flood prediction experience for scheduling, and the reasonableness and accuracy of their scheduling program depend on the decision maker's proficiency and on-the-spot adaptability. If all reservoirs are required to get comprehensive real-time data, most of them need to install all relevant equipment, which implies a high construction cost and is obviously not in line with the national strategy of high-quality development of water conservancy in the new period. Therefore, it is necessary to study a set of flood flow prediction models suitable for small and medium-sized reservoirs, which only need to be equipped with a small amount of relevant sensor data to realize accurate prediction.

With the development of artificial intelligence technology, Long Short-Term Memory (LSTM) and other machine learning algorithms have gradually made good progress in model prediction [4], which have achieved good results in practical applications. Sequence to sequence (Seq2seq) model is effective in the field of natural language translation [25], which can effectively deal with the relationship between the input and the output. Due to the similarity between natural language processing and time series prediction, researchers have begun to apply the Seq2seq model to the field of long time series processing. And LSTM, as a kind of recurrent neural network model, has a very good ability to process sequence data, and can capture the temporal information and long-term dependencies in the data. Meanwhile, attention mechanism improves the generalization ability of the model by providing a dynamic and gradually adjusted attention mechanism to reduce the loss of information in the transmission process [1], and these qualities are exactly the qualities needed for long-time sequence processing. So more and more people have applied these models to the field of time series prediction in recent years, in which good prediction results have been achieved. The fusion model, not only retains the original features, but also performs better in some aspects. So there seems to be some room for development in the use of a flood flow prediction model based on the Seq2seq model and the fusion of the use of the LSTM as a recurrent processing unit, as well as the introduction of attention mechanism to realize the prediction. Therefore, the main workshop of this paper proposes a flood prediction model based on the Seq2seq model, with the aim of hoping to improve the prediction accuracy of the model under limited conditions, providing early warning data support for reservoir maintainers, and improving the ability of reservoir risk prevention and control.

The main contributions of this study are as follows:

(a) The model can obtain more accurate flood flow predictions from a limited number of hydrological parameters, and the prediction results warn of emergencies in reservoir flood flows, which can help to prepare the relevant management and maintenance staff of the reservoir to cope with unfavorable situations. At the same time, the flood flow prediction results keep the staff alert and can increase the confidence to take control measures for the reservoir when needed.
(b) By using an LSTM model instead of a conventional RNN model as the loop processing unit, the fusion model can better capture the key information in the sequence, and the fusion model has a smaller error and higher stability compared to a single model.
(c) The attention mechanism can address one of the limitations of the standard Seq2seq model by moving away from just statically assigning the weights of the hidden states, and instead providing a dynamic, incrementally adjusted attention mechanism, in which appropriate weights are assigned to the hidden state outputs of each encoder and they are mapped to the output sequences, improving the accuracy of the model to a certain extent.

The rest of the paper is organized in the following manner: Sect. 2 presents related work on predictive models for flood flow prediction in related fields; Sect. 3 presents the design scheme of the Seq2seq model-based flood flow prediction model; Sect. 4 explains the experimental procedure of the proposed Seq2seq model-based flood flow prediction model; Sect. 5 gives the practical application of the model; and in Sect. 6, we discuss a conclusion and future research directions.

2 Related Work

Time series are a collection of data points or observations arranged in chronological order and are currently suitable for solving problems in a variety of fields, such as solving mathematical problems [21], which can be used to solve character recognition, solve finite element equation problems, and predict formula data or results [3]. They can also be involved in solving temperature prediction problems and rainfall prediction problems in meteorology with good results [14]. Good progress has also been made in the field of information control and medicine [16]. Time series have been found to be effective in predicting rainfall and evaluating autoregressive models [13], but the solution of nonlinear problems requires more sophisticated modeling calculations [12], such as the use of Artificial Neural Networks (ANNs) and their variants [8], the use of Convolutional Neural Networks (CNNs) and Recurrent Neural Networks (RNNs) [23], as well as other methods.

Closely related to the topic of this paper, time series forecasting studies have been applied in the field of flood forecasting. Mohammad Valipour conducted experiments using Auto-Regressive Moving Average Model (ARMA) and Autoregressive Integrated Moving Average Model (ARIMA) for reservoir inlet flows and the results showed that the ARIMA model gave better predictions and was more compatible with the requirements for making flood flow predictions [20]. Jeongwoo Lee and Jeong Eun Leede used artificial neural network and flow decomposition technique to estimate hourly flood process line from daily flow [10], which further improved the incoming flow prediction and promoted the development of flood flow prediction research. Tian and Pan proposed employing the structural deformer of the LSTM model to dynamically determine the optimal stopping time [19]. This approach amalgamated various parameter structures to establish a short- and medium-term prediction model conducive to decision-making. Through feature selection and genetic algorithms, they identified the optimal number of hidden layers and stopping time for the model. This comprehensive strategy aimed to thoroughly capture the characteristics of complex time series data, thereby enhancing prediction accuracy. Furthermore, in solving the problem of long time series prediction, Vuong and others used extreme gradient boosting as a means of solving the problem by transforming from high-dimensional data to low dimensions and retaining key features [22]. The model then utilized the selected features for inputting relevant data and leveraged the contextual data of the time series to achieve the prediction. Yutao Qi and Zhanao Zhou used an integrated learning model based on RNN networks for flood flow prediction [17], which further improved the accuracy of inlet flow prediction. Recently, Merin Skariah and others combined exponential smoothing, ARIMA and LSTM models for predicting reservoir inlet flow [18], which significantly improved the prediction accuracy.

Recently, in the field of natural language processing, methods based on the attention mechanism have achieved wide application [2], bringing the industry forward. Given the similar sequential nature of the principle steps of natural language processing and the time series processing steps, more and more attempts have been made to incorporate the mechanism into time series processing and good progress has been achieved [27]. For example, certain studies have proposed an innovative attention mechanism that attempts to use relevant time series data divided into different frequency domains as a way to achieve multifaceted predictions. On this basis, Lim and others [11]proposed a method called DSTP. RNN to solve the problem of long-term prediction by combining deep learning with topic modeling. In this method, the structure based on DSTP strengthens the spatio-temporal correlation between the exogenous sequences, and solves the problem of vanishing long-term dependence by focusing on the target sequence several times, through which an improvement in accuracy is obtained. Later, in order to solve the information bottleneck problem of the traditional Seq2seq model and improve the processing ability for long sequences, it is perfectly applied to text processing by combining with the attention mechanism [24], forming the rapid progress of natural language processing nowadays, and at the same time, laying the foundation for the introduction to the time series problem.

Therefore, based on the above study, it can be concluded that there seems to be some room for development in realizing flood flow prediction based on the

Seq2seq model, incorporating the use of LSTM model as a recurrent processing unit, and at the same time introducing the attention mechanism.

3 Model Design

In order to directly and succinctly solve the problem of prediction accuracy of a single model, this paper proposes a flood flow prediction model based on Seq2seq model. The model uses Seq2Seq model together with LSTM network and attention mechanism, and its general structure is shown in Fig. 1.

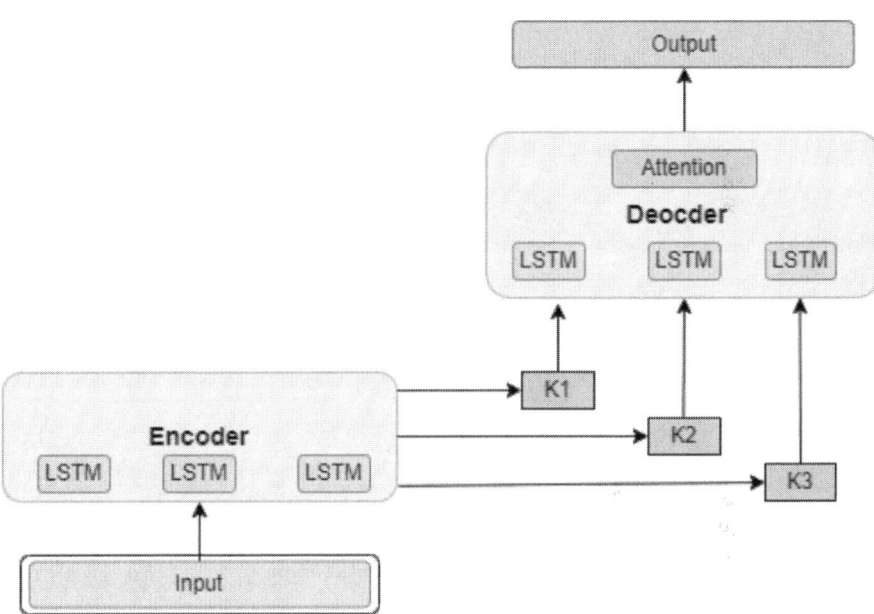

Fig. 1. Diagram of overall structure of fusion Model

Since the LSTM model is used as the input to the decoder, the construction of the LSTM model is introduced first, then the basic structure of the Seq2Seq model is introduced, and finally the implementation process of the model transformed by precipitation flooding is introduced.

3.1 LSTM Model

A typical LSTM network is composed of a series of LSTM cells. The next cell in the model receives and processes two states, a unitary state and a hidden state. The unit state is chained throughout the system from start to finish, and this is where the information is memorized. However, in order to add or remove

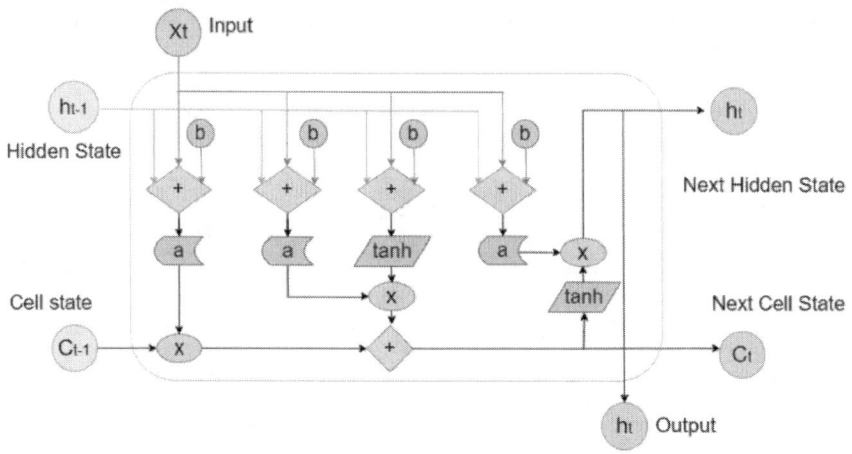

Fig. 2. Diagram of structure of of LSTM Model

information from the unitary state, the data can be optionally modified through sigmoid gates [5]. A typical LSTM structure is shown in Fig. 2 below.

Herein, h_{t-1} is the output of the previous moment, C_{t-1} is the hidden layer state of the previous layer, X_t is the input of this layer, h_t is the output of this moment, a stands for sigmoid function processing, b stands for bias, and $tanh$ stands for Tanh activation function.

The first step in building an LSTM network is to identify unwanted information and omit it from that cell. The process of identifying and eliminating data is determined by a sigmoid function that takes the output of the last LSTM unit(h_{t-1}) at time $t-1$ and the current input(X_t) at time t. This gate is called the forgetting gate (or f_t), where f_t is a vector taking values from 0 to 1 corresponding to each number in the cell state C_{t-1}.

The second step in constructing the LSTM network is to identify the value of the data and remove the invalid data from the cell. The function of identifying and removing the data is realized by the sigmoid function. The function takes the output value X_t of the last LSTM cell at the previous moment and the current input value h at the current moment, where f is a vector of values ranging from 0 to 1, corresponding to the numbers in the cell states.

$$f_t = \sigma(W_f[h_{t-1}, X_t] + b_f). \tag{1}$$

Here, σ is the sigma function and W and b_f are the weight matrix and bias of the acquisition gate, respectively.

The next step is to carry out the update of the unit state and select the appropriate feature data, which is realized by both the sigmoid layer and the tanhlayer layer. First, the sigmoid layer decides whether new information should be added to the new state or not; then, the $tanh$ function assigns different coefficient weights to the information to determine how much it affects the subsequent cell states. By combining these two values, the update of the cell state can be completed. The new information is then added to the old information to obtain the complete existing information C_t.

$$i_t = \sigma(W_t[h_{t-1}, X_t] + b_i). \tag{2}$$

$$N_t = \tanh(W_h[h_{t-1}, X_t] + b_n). \tag{3}$$

$$C_t = C_{t-1}f_t + N_t i_t. \tag{4}$$

Here, C_{t-1} and C are the cell states at time $t-1$ and t, respectively, and W and b are the weight matrix and bias, respectively, of the cell states.

Finally, it is again filtered by selection to output our unit state. A sigmoid function first determines those parts of the receiving unit state that are valuable, which is similar to the previous step. Then, after assigning a degree of influence to this value, the proportion of this value in the whole model and the output can finally be performed to obtain a brand new network sequence.

$$O_t = \sigma(W_o[h_{t-1}, X_t] + b_o). \tag{5}$$

$$h_t = O_t \tanh(C_t). \tag{6}$$

Here, W_o and b_o are the weight matrix and bias of the output gate, respectively.

3.2 Seq2seq Model

The Seq2seq model is a model that encodes input sequences into intermediate vectors and then decodes them into output sequences [26]. Its input and output sequences are free in length, and the basic framework consists of three parts: encoder, decoder and intermediate vectors. The encoder captures the regularity of the input sequence x and compresses x into an intermediate vector C of specified length, which then conveys the state of the last hidden layer or the transformation of all hidden layer states using the decoder to decode the output, so that the input sequence of any length is mapped to the output sequence of any length. The encoder and decoder of the Seq2seq model can be used according to the task using different Neural Network Models.

3.3 A Model for the Fusion of Seq2seq, LSTM, and Attention Mechanisms

The principle of the fusion model constructed in this study is to make the model constructed through the coupling between algorithms to have the advantages of a single model while overcoming the defects of a single model, so that the model is more complete. LSTM, with its long-term memory function facilitated by gating units, excels at learning hidden long-term information. This architecture ensures stability in gradient descent during training. However, it's important to note that each input generates a corresponding hidden state, and both input and output must align with the same time step. In this study, multivariate variables are required as inputs for medium- to long-term multi-step prediction. The Seq2seq model allows modeling at different input and output time steps and mitigates model forgetfulness through encoder-decoder information transfer, allowing the model to have a longer-term memory for long-sequence prediction, which is proved to be suitable for flood flow prediction. However, the fusion model based on both of them is unable to extract effective information in a targeted way due to the same weight assignment of the hidden layer during the transfer process, resulting in the failure to improve the prediction accuracy. To address this challenge, integrating the attention mechanism with the aforementioned model allows for assigning different weights to input values during model transfer. This enables the capture of effective information from each hidden layer, thereby enhancing model accuracy. This is favorable for the improvement of model accuracy. The final fusion model is shown in Fig. 3 below.

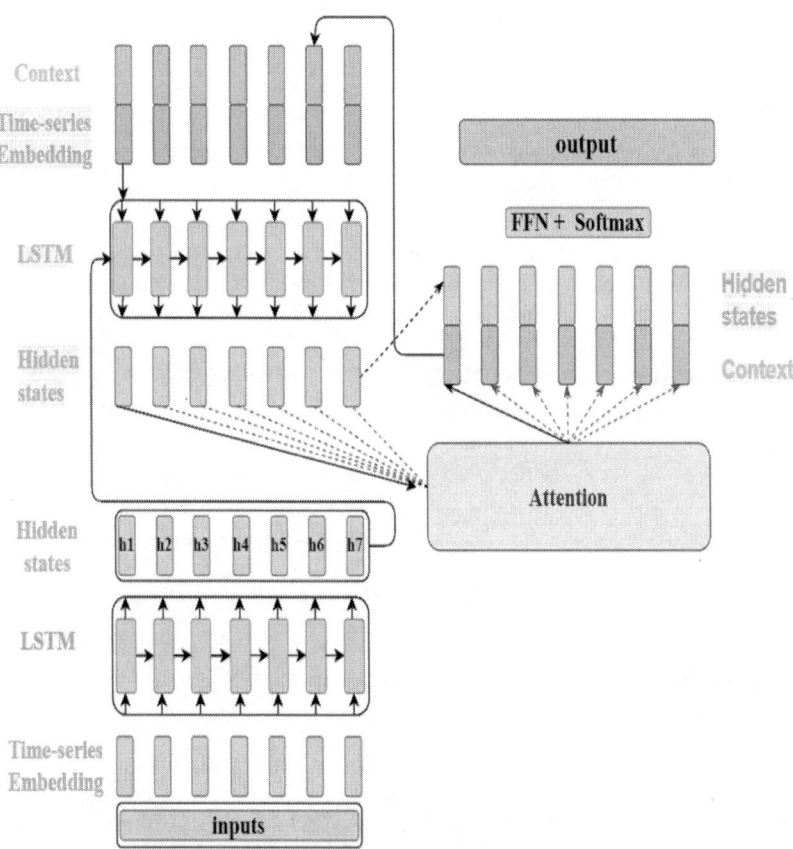

Fig. 3. Diagram of structure of fusion Model

In the Seq2Seq model, the attention layer will consider multiple layers of relationships. First, consider a set of encoder in which time series data is generated from the input sequence, the hidden state of the decoder is determined by a variety of neural network recursive architectures, here we choose the LSTM model for our experiments

The Encoder side of the model accepts each Time Series Embedding, and the hidden state of the previous point in time. The model outputs the hidden state of this point in time.

$$h_t = f(h_{t-1}, x_t) \tag{7}$$

Here, h_t is the hidden layer state and x_t is the input value.

The model Decoder side accepts the Time-series Embedding of the target time-series, and the last time point hidden state.

$$s_t = LSTM_{dec}(\hat{y_{t-1}}, s_{t-1}) \tag{8}$$

Here, s_{t-1} is the hidden layer state of the different layers on the Decoder side, $\hat{y_{t-1}}$ substituting the last output.

A score e_{kt} is computed by adding the hidden states of the decoder to the hidden states of the encoder to facilitate the next step.

$$e_{kt} = score(s_k, h_t) \tag{9}$$

The weights corresponding to the hidden states of each encoder are computed. The context vector is then used to compute the final output of the decoder and is defined as the weighted sum of the attention weights and the encoder's hidden states. Summing the sequence of hidden vectors by weights indicates that the allocation of attention is different when generating different outputs. a higher value of a_{tk} indicates that the kth output allocates more attention to the tth input, and is more influenced by the corresponding input when generating outputs.

$$a_{tk} = \frac{\exp(h_t, s_k)}{\sum_{k=1}^{K} \exp(h_t, s_k)} \tag{10}$$

c_k, which means the context vector, is a weighted average of the hidden states output by the encoder.

$$c_k = \sum_{j=1}^{n} a_{kt} h_t \tag{11}$$

The hidden layer state s_t is calculated again by combining the hidden state of the context vector and the decoder.

$$s_t = \tanh(W_c[c_t; s_t]) \tag{12}$$

Here, W_c is a weight matrix that connects the context vector to the hidden state and requires dimensional matching.

The next step is to calculate the final output probability.

$$p(y_t|y<t, x) = softmax(W_s S_t) \tag{13}$$

These steps are repeated until the end of the sequence. These parameters are updated at each epoch so that the model recognizes the most relevant parameters. The attention mechanism can be used as another way to improve the predictive performance of the model. It is very interesting when combined with preprocessing techniques.

4 Verification and Analysis of Algorithm Examples

4.1 Preconfigured Settings

This paper adopts the meteorological monitoring data of Mahe Reservoir between 2019–2022 as the data source. The meteorological monitoring data mainly includes solar radiation, gust wind, relative humidity, dew point temperature, wind direction and temperature. In addition, since this paper adopt the data of daily meteorology, if the selected features in the dataset are all 0 in the hour of the point of the data, it is settled that the study uses linear interpolation to solve the missing values. The raw data sets of hourly records is computed through preprocessing to get the daily meteorological data set. Then the training, validation and test sets are selected in the ratio of 6:3:1. In order to assess the predictive effectiveness of the model, this study uses five metrics to synthesize the predictive values. They are Root Mean Square Error (RMSE) [6], Mean Absolute Error (MAE), Median Absolute Error (MDAE), Coefficient of Determination (R^2), and Explained Variance Score (VAR) for the combined assessment. The specific assessment methods are shown below.

$$RMSE = \sqrt{\frac{1}{n}\sum_{i=1}^{n}(y_t - \hat{y}_t)^2} \qquad (14)$$

$$MAE = \frac{1}{n}\sum_{i=1}^{n}|y_i - \bar{y}_i| \qquad (15)$$

$$MDAE = medium(|y_1 - \hat{y}_1|, ..., |y_n - \hat{y}_n|) \qquad (16)$$

$$R^2 = 1 - \frac{\sum_{i=1}^{n}(\hat{y}_i - \bar{y}_i)^2}{\sum_{i=1}^{n}(y_i - \bar{y}_i)^2} \qquad (17)$$

$$VAR = 1 - \frac{Var\{Y - \hat{Y}\}}{Var\{Y\}} \qquad (18)$$

Here, y_t is the predicted value, $\hat{y}_t$ is the actual value, $\bar{y}$ is the mean, and Var is the variance.

Specifically, $RMSE$, MAE, and $MADE$ are used to measure prediction error: the smaller the value of prediction error, the better the prediction. R^2 and VAR calculate the correlation coefficient, which measures the ability of the prediction to represent the actual data: the larger the value, the better the prediction, and in the experiments, the difference between the two values is not significant.

4.2 Baseline

In order to verify the effectiveness of our proposed model, we have done several sets of comparative experiments, including the prediction model based on the traditional flood flow statistics model and other of its machine learning models, which are described as follows:

Prediction Model Based on Traditional Flood Flow Statistics Model. the model is based on rainfall prediction for traditional flood flow statistical model prediction to get the final experimental results.

Machine Learning Models. This study utilizes ARIMA, Multilayer Perceptron (MLP), Support Vector Regression (SVR), LSTM, Gradient Boosting Regression Tree (GBRT), and Extreme Gradient Boosting (XGBOOST) models to compare their evaluation metrics and validate the effectiveness of the fusion model.

4.3 Experimental Procedure of the Models

Setting appropriate parameters can help to get good model training results. In this experiment, the majority of the hyperparameters for the ARIMA model are determined through a smoothing test process. The optimal hyperparameters for the SVR model, specifically the penalty parameter C and the kernel coefficient *gamma*, are set to 20 and 0.01, respectively. For the GBRT model, the optimal hyperparameters include a learning rate of 0.07, 60 trees, and a maximum depth of 2. Similarly, for the XGBoost model, the optimal parameters consist of a learning rate of 0.03, 60 trees, and a maximum depth of 4.

The optimal parameters for MLP, LSTM, and Seq2Seq models are alike, focusing primarily on configuring the hidden unit settings [15]. In order to obtain the optimal prediction results, we design different hidden unit modules for comparison and obtain the optimal solution by comparing the loss values of the test set. The experimental results are shown in the following figure, the horizontal coordinate indicates the parameter settings of the hidden unit, and the vertical coordinate indicates the change of the loss value of the test set, which shows the loss results of different hidden unit settings. Fig. 4, Fig. 5 and Fig. 6 are the result diagrams of network models.

According to the three diagrams above, we can observe the performance of MLP, LSTM, and Seq2Seq models under different hyperparameter settings. The MLP model achieves optimal performance with a combination of hyperparameters: a hidden layer dimension of 64, 4 hidden layers, and a learning rate of 0.001. Conversely, the LSTM model demonstrates its best performance with a hidden layer dimension of 128, 3 recurrent networks, and a learning rate of 0.001. Regarding the Seq2Seq model, the highest performance is attained with a hidden layer dimension of 128 and a learning rate of 0.01.

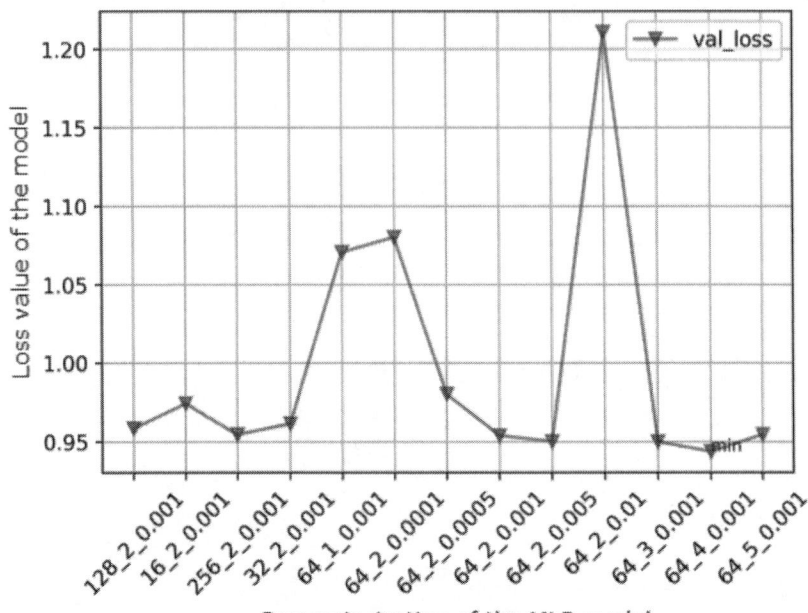

Fig. 4. Graph of parameter exploring results of MLP

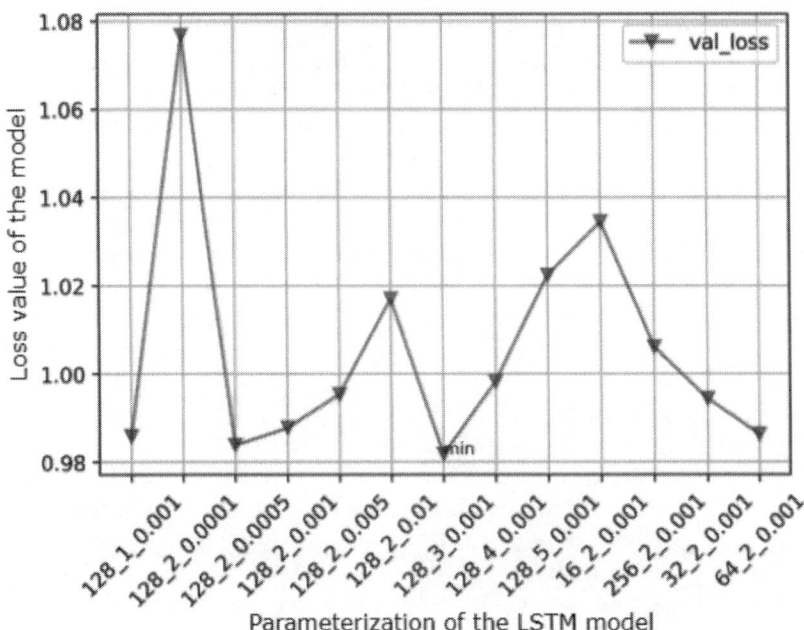

Fig. 5. Graph of parameter exploring results of LSTM

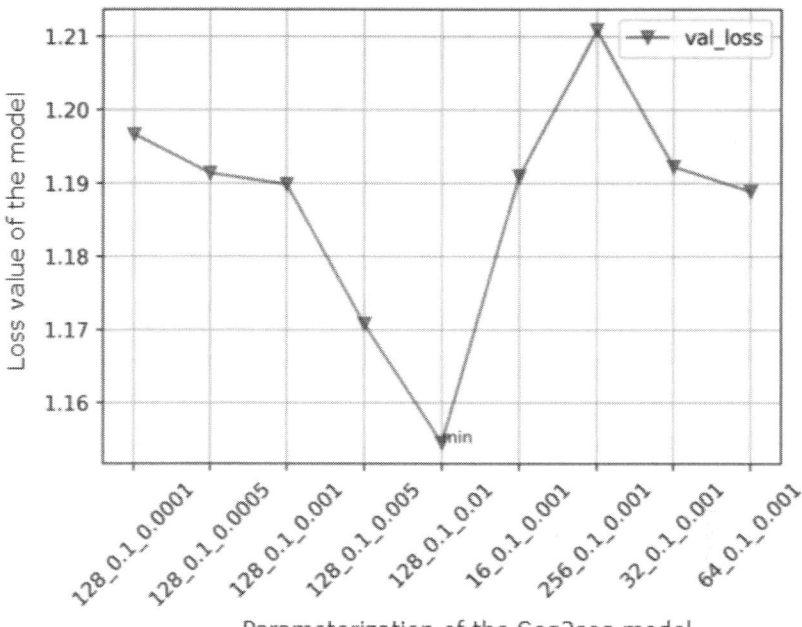

Fig. 6. Graph of parameter exploring results of Seq2seq

4.4 Model Result

The prediction result errors of the two types of experimental schemes are compared and the results of the evaluation indicators of the model are shown in Fig. 7 and Fig. 8 below.

Overall, the prediction results of the seq2seq network are better in several metrics, and the fusion model based on the seq2seq model also better captures the characteristics of the flood flow. The results of the five metrics evaluated in the dataset are presented in the figure, and the prediction results do not vary much with the dataset in a comprehensive view. For example, in the prediction task, the RMSEs of Seq2seq and LSTM decrease by 25% and 24% respectively compared to the ARIMA model, and the r2 score reaches close to 0.3, the RMSE of seq2seq and LSTM decrease by 9.5% and 9.5% respectively compared to the SVR model, and the r2 scores improve by close to 80%. seq2seq and LSTM decrease by 2.2% and 9.5% respectively compared to the GBRT model, and the r2_score improves by 2.2%. The RMSE of seq2seq and LSTM decrease by 2.2% and 2.1% respectively compared to the GBRT model, and the r2 score increases by 18% and 14%. Therefore, in the end, the results of Seq2seq are 4% higher than the LSTM model in terms of r2_score improvement, which proves that the model effectiveness is improved, while the other evaluation indexes are not much different. Therefore the combined prediction of the fusion model is the

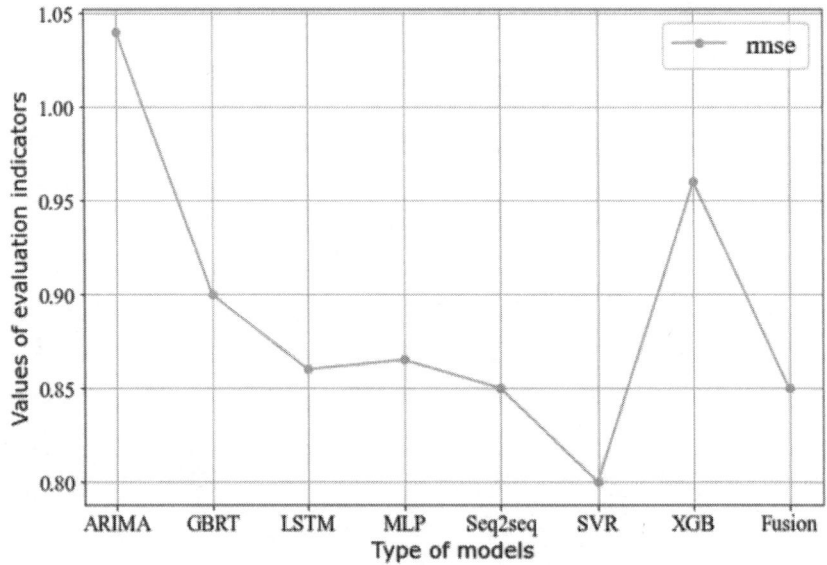

Fig. 7. Graph of the results for the evaluation metric RMSE of the model

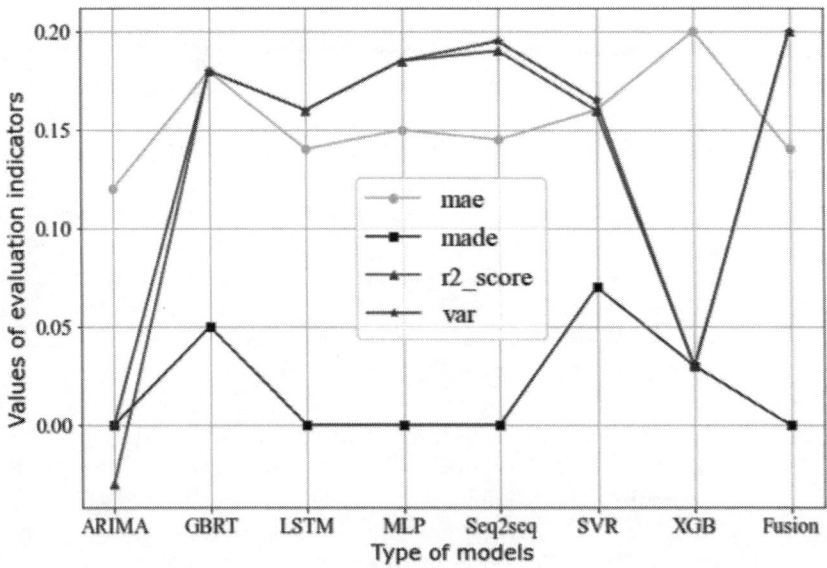

Fig. 8. Graph of the results of other evaluation indicators of the model

best compared to other machine learning models and the flood flow prediction map obtained based on this model is shown in Fig. 9 below.

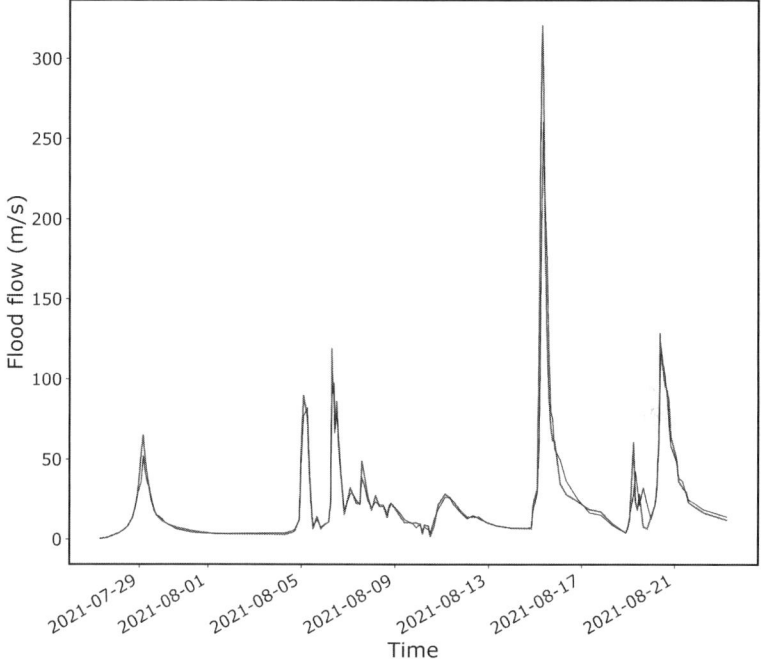

Fig. 9. Graph of the model result based on Seq2seq model

Based on the aforementioned data analysis, the flood prediction model can effectively discern the general trend of the flood process during flood occurrences. Furthermore, it can accurately identify the trajectory of flood flow escalation during sharp increases. This capability provides sufficient grounds for issuing timely warning notices to reservoir managers in accordance with the early warning program. At the same time, the flood prediction model can seldom judge that there are floods when there are no floods, and it has a certain generalization ability, which is in line with the ideal effect on the whole.

4.5 Prediction Model Based on Traditional Flood Flow Statistical Models

The prediction model based on the traditional flood flow statistical model relies on the physical statistical model recorded in relevant hydrological data. The main steps of this model involve utilizing data from the rainfall prediction model to calculate the average rainfall in the watershed. This process entails employing a fusion model based on the Seq2seq model for rainfall prediction, including data preprocessing, feature selection, and model parameter setting. Subsequently, the corresponding net rainfall depth is calculated based on the "rainstorm runoff relationship map of Shandong Province". Then, the maximum flood flow is determined using relevant parameters from the "flood flow map of catchment area of Shandong Province". This maximum flood flow is obtained based on the flood flow determined in the previous step. The total amount of floodwater is estimated based on the maximum flood flow obtained earlier. The duration of water rise is calculated based on the maximum flood flow. Finally, the final flood flow process curve is derived according to the "flood generalization process line table", thus completing the final flood flow prediction.

Fisrt of all, rainfall is predicted using the same fusion model and the rainfall results obtained are shown in Fig. 10 below.

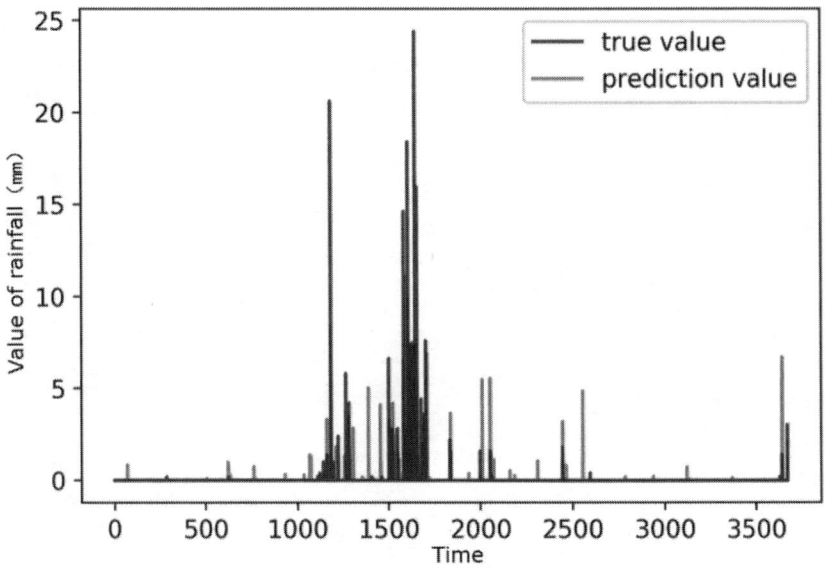

Fig. 10. Graph of the rainfall model results of Seq2seq model

The equations associated with the statistical flood flow prediction model are shown below.

$$H_t = H_{24} * K. \tag{19}$$

$$Q_m = K F^{0.62} H_t^{0.55} R_T^{0.60}. \tag{20}$$

$$W = 1000\phi R^t F. \tag{21}$$

$$t_p = \frac{\phi R_t F}{1.8 Q_m}. \tag{22}$$

Here, F is the basin area, K is the average precipitation coefficient, h_{24} is the rainfall in the past 24 h, R_t is the net rainfall depth; Q_m is the maximum flood flow; W is the total amount of flood (cubic meters), the coefficient represents the empirical coefficient of comparison of the main flood flow process with the instantaneous unit line according to the design rainfall type; t_p represents the rise of water over the calendar time.

The table of flood generalization process for the standard area obtained at the same time is shown in Table 1 below.

Table 1. Table of generalized process lines

t'	0.30	0.50	0.70	0.80	0.70	0.90
Q'	0	0.010	0.125	0.554	0.795	0.952
t'	1.00	1.10	1.20	1.30	1.50	1.70
Q'	1.000	0.960	0.872	0.743	0.515	0.343
t'	2.0	2.5	3.0	4.0	5.0	
Q'	0.184	0.072	0.032	0.009	0.003	

Finally the data in the generalized process line table we obtained above can be used to obtain the final flood process flow curve of the simulation by multiplying the horizontal and vertical coordinates by the upwelling calendar time and the flood flow, respectively. The result of predictive model based on traditional flood flow statistical models is shown in Fig. 11 below.

Combined with the above data analysis can be obtained, the traditional flood flow prediction model can predict the general trend characteristics of the flood flow, but in the face of a small probability of large-scale flood flow changes, the model is difficult to predict very accurately.

4.6 Evaluation and Analysis of Results

The prediction result errors of the two types of experimental schemes are compared and the results are shown in Table 2 below:

Table 2. Table of evaluations of modeling programs

model	rmse	mae	mde	r2_score	var
Fusion model	0.85	0.14	0	0.2	0.2
Statistic model	1.02	0.42	0.23	0.12	0.08

In general, from the five error analyses, the flood flow prediction model based on Seq2seq model has smaller errors on MAE, RMSE, MADE, and higher scores on r2_score and Var, so the fusion model based on Seq2seq model is superior to the traditional flood flow prediction model, which improves the prediction accuracy to some extent. Therefore, we adopt the flood flow prediction model based on Seq2seq model as the flood flow prediction model of the system.

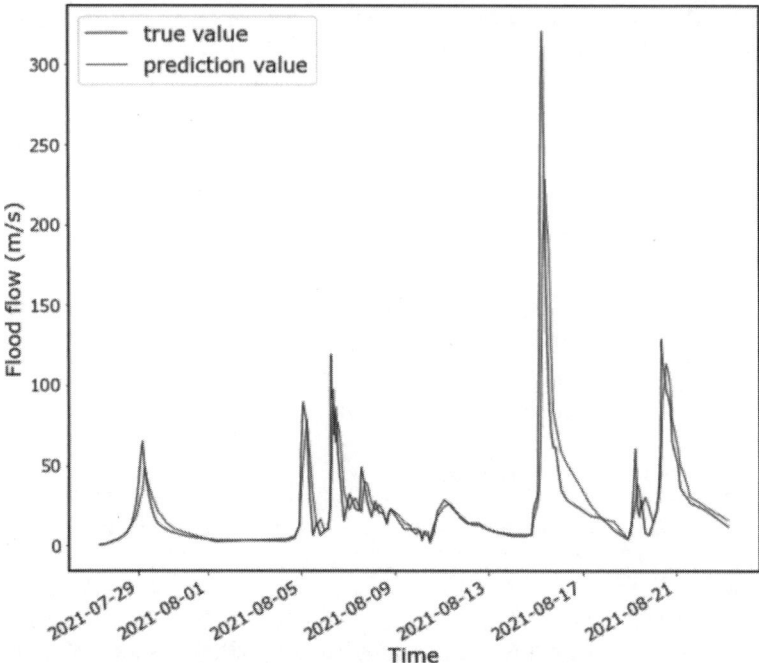

Fig. 11. Graph of model prediction result based on traditional models

5 Practical Application

In addition to the success of the reservoir flood forecasting modeling service on the experimental environment, meanwhile, in the production environment, the reservoir flood forecasting model has been extracted as a service and integrated into the reservoir flood monitoring and forecasting system. In the system, managers can make timely preventive measures on flood forecasting through this platform. The system can obtain real-time precipitation data in the Mahe reservoir basin, collect data through sensors and process and store the data, and complete the precipitation prediction and flood forecasting through the model service, as well as provide early warning notification services. The reservoir flood monitoring and prediction system includes six major functions, including user information management, data source information management, network communication connection management, data visualization and analysis, early warning notification management, and flood process prediction, which basically meets the needs of the digital system of Mahe Reservoir.

This modeling service has been validated for implementation in a production environment and has effectively improved the accuracy and performance of the reservoir flood forecasting system and greatly improved the efficiency of the modeling service.

6 Conclusion

Aiming at the problem that the traditional flood flow prediction model cannot get real-time and comprehensive data in time, which makes the idealized prediction effect unattainable, this paper proposes a reservoir flood flow prediction model based on Seq2seq model. The fusion model is based on the Seq2seq model, and the fusion uses the Long Short-Term Memory Network (LSTM) as the recurrent processing unit, and introduces the attention mechanism to realize the construction of the overall model, which not only makes the constructed model have the advantages of a single model, but also overcomes the shortcomings of a single model, and improves the accuracy of the model prediction. In this study, the monitoring data related to the flood flow of Mahe Reservoir is used for training and testing. During the experiment, the fusion model is compared not only with a single machine learning model, but also with a prediction model based on a traditional flood flow statistical model. Finally, the study verifies the effectiveness of the model by using five evaluation metrics such as RMSE for model evaluation. Meanwhile, the modeling service has been applied in the real environment, which confirms the effectiveness of the modeling service again.

However, the present model still has some problems that need to be solved. For example, when the obtained monitoring data may be intermittent, the accuracy of the prediction decreases substantially and the intrinsic pattern of change cannot be accurately captured. These problems need to be further studied, and we need to make further improvements and corrections on this work in the follow-up work[1].

Acknowledgement. The authors would like to acknowledge the support provided by the National Key R&D Program of China under Grant 2023YFC3304904, the Shandong Provincial Natural Science Foundation of China under Grant ZR2023LZH016, the "New 20 Regulations for Universities" funding program of Jinan (202228089), and the TaiShan Industrial Experts Programme (tscx202312128).

References

1. Abbasimehr, H., Paki, R.: Improving time series forecasting using LSTM and attention models. J. Ambient Intell. Humaniz. Comput. **13**(1), 673–691 (2022)
2. Bahdanau, D., Cho, K., Bengio, Y.: Neural machine translation by jointly learning to align and translate. arXiv preprint arXiv:1409.0473 (2014)
3. Chen, S.M., Hwang, J.R.: Temperature prediction using fuzzy time series. IEEE Trans. Syst. Man Cybern. Part B (Cybern.) **30**(2), 263–275 (2000)
4. Fang, Z., Wang, Y., Peng, L., Hong, H.: Predicting flood susceptibility using LSTM neural networks. J. Hydrol. **594**, 125734 (2021)
5. Farzad, A., Mashayekhi, H., Hassanpour, H.: A comparative performance analysis of different activation functions in LSTM networks for classification. Neural Comput. Appl. **31**, 2507–2521 (2019)

---

[1] If EquinOCS, our proceedings submission system, is used, then the disclaimer can be provided directly in the system.

6. Hodson, T.O.: Root mean square error (RMSE) or mean absolute error (MAE): when to use them or not. Geosci. Model Dev. Discuss. **2022**, 1–10 (2022)
7. Kong, X., Li, Z., Liu, Z., et al.: Flood prediction in ungauged basins by physical-based topkapi model. Adv. Meteorolo. **2019** (2019)
8. Koprinska, I., Wu, D., Wang, Z.: Convolutional neural networks for energy time series forecasting. In: 2018 International Joint Conference on Neural Networks (IJCNN), pp. 1–8. IEEE (2018)
9. Kundzewicz, Z.W., Su, B., Wang, Y., Xia, J., Huang, J., Jiang, T.: Flood risk and its reduction in China. Adv. Water Resour. **130**, 37–45 (2019)
10. Lee, J., Lee, J.E., Kim, N.W.: Estimation of hourly flood hydrograph from daily flows using artificial neural network and flow disaggregation technique. Water **13**(1), 30 (2020)
11. Liu, Y., Gong, C., Yang, L., Chen, Y.: DSTP-RNN: a dual-stage two-phase attention-based recurrent neural network for long-term and multivariate time series prediction. Expert Syst. Appl. **143**, 113082 (2020)
12. McClanahan, T., Sala, E., Mumby, P., Jones, S.: Phosphorus and nitrogen enrichment do not enhance brown frondose" macroalgae". Mar. Pollut. Bull. **48**(1), 196–199 (2004)
13. Mehrmolaei, S., Keyvanpour, M.R.: Time series forecasting using improved Arima. In: 2016 Artificial Intelligence and Robotics (IRANOPEN), pp. 92–97. IEEE (2016)
14. Mishra, N., Soni, H.K., Sharma, S., Upadhyay, A.: A comprehensive survey of data mining techniques on time series data for rainfall prediction. J. ICT Res. Appl. **11**(2) (2017)
15. Orrù, P.F., Zoccheddu, A., Sassu, L., Mattia, C., Cozza, R., Arena, S.: Machine learning approach using MLP and SVM algorithms for the fault prediction of a centrifugal pump in the oil and gas industry. Sustainability **12**(11), 4776 (2020)
16. Pollock, D.S.G., Green, R.C., Nguyen, T.: Handbook of Time Series Analysis, Signal Processing, and Dynamics. Elsevier, Amsterdam (1999)
17. Qi, Y., Zhou, Z., Yang, L., Quan, Y., Miao, Q.: A decomposition-ensemble learning model based on LSTM neural network for daily reservoir inflow forecasting. Water Resour. Manag. **33**, 4123–4139 (2019)
18. Skariah, M., Suriyakala, C.D.: Forecasting reservoir inflow combining exponential smoothing, Arima, and LSTM models. Arab. J. Geosci. **15**(14), 1292 (2022)
19. Tian, Y., Pan, L.: Predicting short-term traffic flow by long short-term memory recurrent neural network. In: 2015 IEEE international conference on smart city/SocialCom/SustainCom (SmartCity), pp. 153–158. IEEE (2015)
20. Valipour, M., Banihabib, M.E., Behbahani, S.M.R.: Comparison of the Arma, Arima, and the autoregressive artificial neural network models in forecasting the monthly inflow of DEZ dam reservoir. J. Hydrol. **476**, 433–441 (2013)
21. Velasquez, C.E., Zocatelli, M., Estanislau, F.B., Castro, V.F.: Analysis of time series models for Brazilian electricity demand forecasting. Energy **247**, 123483 (2022)
22. Vuong, P.H., Dat, T.T., Mai, T.K., Uyen, P.H., et al.: Stock-price forecasting based on Boost and LSTM. Comput. Syst. Scie. Eng. **40**(1) (2022)
23. Waheeb, W., Ghazali, R.: A novel error-output recurrent neural network model for time series forecasting. Neural Comput. Appl. **32**(13), 9621–9647 (2020)
24. Xiao, Y., Li, Y., Yuan, J., Guo, S., Xiao, Y., Li, Z.: History-based attention in seq2seq model for multi-label text classification. Knowl.-Based Syst. **224**, 107094 (2021)

25. Xu, J., Wang, K., Lin, C., Xiao, L., Huang, X., Zhang, Y.: FM-GRU: a time series prediction method for water quality based on seq2seq framework. Water **13**(8), 1031 (2021)
26. Zhang, Y., Li, D., Wang, Y., Fang, Y., Xiao, W.: Abstract text summarization with a convolutional seq2seq model. Appl. Sci. **9**(8), 1665 (2019)
27. Zhou, K., Wang, W., Hu, T., Deng, K.: Time series forecasting and classification models based on recurrent with attention mechanism and generative adversarial networks. Sensors **20**(24), 7211 (2020)

Optimization Algorithm for Emission Reduction Schemes Based on Carbon Footprint Prediction

Hongliang Sun[1(✉)], Feifei Wang[2], Meng Wang[2], Jinlan Liu[1], and Qiao Guan[1]

[1] Harbin Institute of Technology, Weihai, China
{21B903094,2021211961,21S030194}@stu.hit.edu.cn
[2] Weichai Power Co., Ltd., Weifang, China
wangfeif@weichai.com, wangmeng01@weichaihm.com

Abstract. Greenhouse gas emissions, especially carbon dioxide, play a critical role in intensifying climate change, a challenge exacerbated by the carbon-intensive operations of businesses and organizations worldwide. As a result, the urgent need to reduce carbon emissions has become a shared priority for corporations and policymakers alike. The research community has shown a growing interest in the precise quantification of emissions, detailed carbon footprint assessments, and the development of effective strategies to mitigate carbon emissions. Yet, the practical execution of these strategies is hampered by significant challenges, including the difficulty of accurately measuring emissions, the impracticality of short-term carbon footprint forecasting, and the inherent uncertainty in the effectiveness of mitigation efforts. Furthermore, existing strategies often fail to balance the need for production efficiency with economic realities, which are crucial for achieving sustainable carbon management. To address these problems, this paper presents a novel research on algorithms that optimize emission reduction plans based on carbon footprint predictions. Our approach is centered on three main components: enhancing carbon emission data completeness, improving carbon footprint predictions, and refining emission reduction strategies through the application of deep learning and optimization techniques. To overcome data granularity and gaps, we introduce a deep learning algorithm that completes carbon emission data sets, utilizing prior physical knowledge to generate training samples and predict missing values. We then propose a deep learning model for carbon footprint prediction that integrates spatial and temporal features, guided by physical knowledge for enhanced accuracy. This model is further refined with transformation modules grounded in physical principles, ensuring a comprehensive consideration of spatial, temporal, and physical insights. Culminating in an optimization algorithm, our approach delivers the most effective emission reduction plans that align with current production efficiency and economic interests. Our experimental findings validate the algorithm's effectiveness in optimizing emission reduction strategies while incorporating both efficiency and economic perspectives.

Keywords: Carbon emissions · Emission reduction · Carbon footprint prediction · Deep learning

1 Introduction

Carbon dioxide emissions are inextricably linked to a spectrum of pressing concerns, ranging from economic impacts to health risks and environmental degradation. As global climate change and environmental pollution escalate in severity, the imperative to curb carbon emissions has emerged as a challenge that transcends borders. Carbon emissions stand out as a principal catalyst for climate change, with the operations of businesses and organizations contributing significantly to the global carbon footprint. In light of these developments, the quest to diminish carbon emissions has risen to the forefront as a vital mission for both the corporate sector and public policy.

Traditional approaches to emission reduction often focus on a single aspect and fail to account for a multitude of factors that contribute to carbon emissions, such as energy use, logistics, and production processes. Consequently, the challenge lies in devising strategies that effectively reduce carbon emissions without compromising production efficiency and economic viability, striking a balance that is both environmentally responsible and economically sustainable.

A carbon footprint represents the cumulative carbon emissions that result from the entire production activities of an organization or individual, and it is often used interchangeably with the term 'carbon emissions' [10]. The nuanced difference between the two concepts is that carbon emissions are indeed a component of the broader carbon footprint. When our analysis focuses on a single production method, the carbon emissions from that method are synonymous with the carbon footprint. Yet, in scenarios where multiple production methods are under consideration, the carbon footprint is defined as the aggregate of carbon emissions from each distinct method.

To assess the impact of carbon emissions effectively, this paper necessitates temporal data to track carbon emissions over a defined period. Furthermore, spatial data is crucial for analyzing the spatial effects of carbon emissions and for attributing responsibility for these emissions. However, the process of calculating the carbon footprint and devising emission reduction strategies faces three principal challenges: (1)Data Accuracy: While capable businesses can accurately measure carbon emissions through relevant indicators, less resourced enterprises must rely on emission factor formulas for estimation. Individual carbon footprints are frequently overlooked or simplified to electricity usage emissions due to practical limitations. (2)Plan Lag: Emission reduction plans are typically crafted using carbon footprint data from previous periods, with their effectiveness only assessable at the end of the current calculation period, leading to a temporal lag in strategy optimization. (3)Plan Effectiveness: The strategies developed may lead to varied outcomes. One scenario involves minimal adjustments to resource use, with a focus on stable electricity supply and secondary emphasis on emission reduction, potentially requiring carbon offset purchases if targets are exceeded. The alternative scenario involves substantial shifts in resource allocation, prioritizing carbon reduction over electricity supply. This approach, while allowing for the sale of surplus emission quotas in the trading market, risks incurring costs during power shortages and facing penalties for overage. These challenges underscore the complexity of balancing emission reduction goals with the practical considerations of resource management and economic viability.

Therefore, crafting an effective emission reduction plan that is grounded in accurate carbon footprint data is crucial for effectively mitigating carbon emissions. Ensuring the precision of carbon footprint data and clearly delineating the measurement boundaries is equally significant. Above all, it is essential to pinpoint emission reduction strategies that maintain a balance, minimizing disruptions to economic interests and production efficiency without compromising their environmental effectiveness.

In light of the discussed challenges, this paper presents a predictive approach for businesses to forecast their carbon footprints over a defined time frame, considering key influencing factors. These forecasts are instrumental in formulating tailored emission reduction plans that aim to reduce any negative effects on economic and production efficiency. The paper refines these plans to achieve a precise and effective emission reduction strategy. Post-implementation, the plans can be reassessed using updated carbon footprint predictions. This iterative cycle not only monitors the execution of the plans but also allows for agile modifications in response to their actual performance.

This paper delves into an analysis of meteorological data sourced from monitoring stations, with experimental findings indicating that our approach outperforms existing benchmarks. The contributions of this work are as follows:

– To address the prevalent challenges of data granularity and gaps within carbon emission datasets, we introduce an innovative algorithm that employs deep learning for carbon emission data imputation.
– We present a deep learning algorithm for the prediction of carbon footprints, which adeptly incorporates spatial and temporal elements and is informed by prior physical knowledge to enhance the training process. This culminates in a model that effectively integrates spatial-temporal analysis with foundational physical principles.
– In tackling the complexities of emission reduction strategies, we propose an optimization algorithm tailored for emission reduction planning. This algorithm utilizes carbon footprint predictions, along with current operational status and permissible fluctuation margins, to devise the most effective plan for reducing emissions under prevailing conditions. It is designed to optimize both production efficiency and economic outcomes.

2 Related Work

2.1 Factors Influencing Carbon Footprint

Factor decomposition analysis of carbon emissions is a research focus in different countries and regions seeking effective ways to mitigate carbon emissions. Within the factor decomposition analysis, Structural Decomposition Analysis (SDA) and Index Decomposition Analysis (IDA) are two primary analytical techniques. For instance, Zhu et al. and Su et al. employ SDA to address energy emission issues [28,29,39], and numerous researchers have used SDA to explore the major factors influencing national carbon dioxide emissions [7,32,34,36]. Wang et al. [31] compared IDA and SDA, indicating that SDA is typically used to study production techniques, demand-side effects, and trade-related issues, while IDA is generally applied to analyze changes in energy usage, emissions, and driving forces. Compared to SDA, IDA decomposition analysis has advantages in handling residual, negative, and zero values. IDA is used in various studies to decompose carbon emissions from different sectors or industries, such as manufacturing, transportation, tourism, and the power sector [1,3,33]. The Logarithmic Mean Divisia Index (LMDI) decomposition model is an important branch of IDA and has found extensive application in carbon emission factor decomposition. Gonzalez et al. [14] employ LMDI to track EU carbon dioxide emissions and categorize factors into population, per capita output, fuel composition, carbonization, and energy intensity. Moutinho et al. [22] use Kaya's identity and LMDI to analyze factors influencing changes in carbon dioxide emissions levels in four groups of European countries (East, West, North, and South). Given that the power sector is a major carbon emitter in many countries and regions, factor decomposition of carbon emissions in the power industry has garnered significant attention worldwide, especially in countries heavily reliant on coal-fired power generation. Karmellos et al. [17] analyze changes in carbon emissions from the power sector in the EU-28 countries using the LMDI-I method, considering five driving factors: activity level, power intensity, power trade, power efficiency generation, and fuel mix. Diakoulaki et al. [25] quantify the driving factors of carbon emissions generated by electricity production in Greece using LMDI, with a primary focus on factors such as economic growth, economic power intensity, power trade, fuel composition, and power generation efficiency. However, when it comes to the issue of data sources for carbon emissions, many scholars opt to bypass data completion and instead focus on studying and analyzing other factors that may influence carbon emissions. Only a minority of scholars [6,11] choose to confront the problem of missing carbon emissions data directly. Currently, there is a lack of a more precise method to complete carbon emissions data that is partially missing.

2.2 Carbon Footprint Predictions

In recent years, scholars have explored factors directly influencing carbon footprints to construct and validate machine learning models. Ahmed et al. [2] utilized Long Short-Term Memory (LSTM) to assess the impact of energy consumption, financial development, GDP, population, and renewable energy on carbon footprints, predicting emission trends in China and India. Li et al. [18] combined ride-sharing data with the COPERT model to estimate carbon emissions from carpooling and cycling in Chengdu. Milczarski et al. [20] applied various machine learning algorithms to optimize the food processing industry, thereby reducing carbon footprints. Aryai et al. [4] introduced a PSO-ERT model for predicting emission intensity in the Australian electricity market, using meteorological data for pre-processing. Chen et al. [9] investigated the effect of residential density on office building carbon footprints using an LSTM model. Mu et al. [23] developed a regional carbon emissions prediction method, integrating dynamic vehicle and static building models to forecast emissions. Despite these advances, research still falls short in predicting the spatial dynamics of carbon footprints, with a dearth of models informed by physical priors, leading to an incomplete understanding of their spatial characteristics.

2.3 Emission Reduction Options

Some countries have initiated targeted emission reduction policies, sparking scholarly interest in evaluating the efficacy of these measures. Marchand et al. [19] analyzed the "Green Deal" proposed by the UK and observed that public understanding and awareness of the initiative were lower than anticipated, not aligning with their expectations. Zheng et al. [38] examined China's policy aimed at fostering renewable energy adoption to reshape the energy sector and found that the expansion of renewable sources serves to curb carbon emissions. Concurrently, researchers have turned their attention to production-side emission reduction strategies. Chen et al. [8] advocate for the commercialization of CO_2 reduction technologies. Zhang et al. [37] are exploring the potential to transform carbon dioxide into fuel through photovoltaic conversion, focusing on the development of high-performance photocatalysts with strong light absorption, robust redox potential, efficient charge separation, and superior durability. Wang et al. [35] have investigated the thermochemical reduction of carbon dioxide, while Sun and colleagues have delved into the electrocatalytic reduction of CO_2 using multiphase molecular catalysts [30]. Miller's team [21] has examined the impact of emission reduction efforts on CO_2 emissions in cement production. However, the current design of emission reduction strategies does not directly correlate with carbon footprint assessments. This disconnect arises because prevailing carbon footprint predictions are based on long-term data and projections at the industry or national level. Consequently, these footprints offer only broad guidance for policy development, without ensuring that the balance between production efficiency and economic gains is maintained. The field is in need of an optimization approach that integrates production efficiency, economic benefits, and emission reduction outcomes to inform the nuanced development of effective emission reduction plans.

3 Methodology

3.1 Carbon Emission Data Completion

This paper uses data from meteorological monitoring stations as a foundation and supplements it with additional data, as shown in Fig. 1, with data measured by meteorological monitoring stations in a specific region at a particular time point.

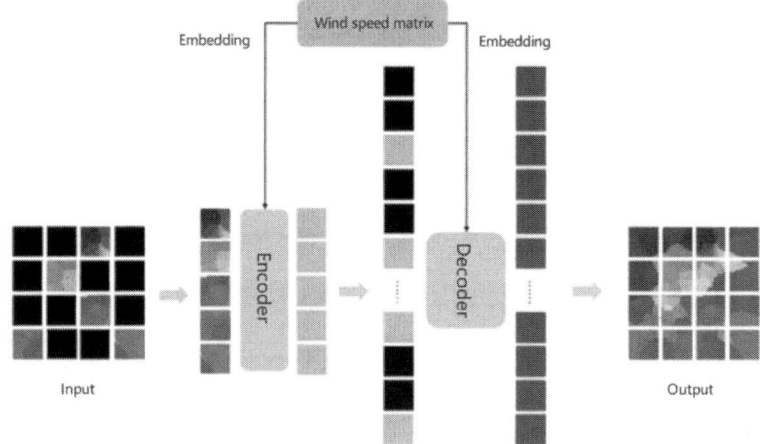

Fig. 1. Carbon emission data complete model structure.

Existing meteorological data contains gaps reaching up to 70%, which account for 80% of the total dataset. Of the remaining 20%, 5% consist of entries with a single data point or no data points at all. To address this issue, this paper introduces a deep learning model based on Masked Autoencoders (MAE) for data imputation [16].

For an input image, it is initially divided into equally-sized smaller images. On the encoder side, a portion of each small image, along with its positional information within the context of the larger image, is encoded into a vector and fed into the encoder. The other parts of the image that are not visible to the model only have their positional information encoded, which is then utilized for decoding. The visible portion of the image after passing through the encoder and the positional information directly encoded for the unseen parts are combined. This combined information is then input into the decoder. The decoder processes this input to output a long vector, which is used to reconstruct the image through a series of deformation operations.

The specific model structure is depicted in Fig. 1. As shown in the figure, it illustrates the structure of the MAE model. This paper introduces certain modifications to the MAE model structure by incorporating the two wind speed matrices, one aligned with the x-direction and the other with the y-direction, into both the encoder and decoder. Since the MAE is based on the Vision Transformer (ViT) [13], the encoder and decoder have been adapted from those of ViT, which are part of the Transformer model architecture. Consequently, the paper positions these embeddings prior to the multi-head attention mechanism.

To preserve the semantic information of the original image, the embedding weights are intentionally kept low with a ratio of 1:10. This approach ensures that the model retains the majority of the encoded positional information from the image. This is crucial because the paper not only needs to specify the location information of the images but also requires a higher degree of positional accuracy than the original task. Additionally, the decoder incorporates the wind speed matrix as input, further ensuring that the necessary information is preserved. The model's parameter selection has been tailored to account for the differences in input data between this study and the standard MAE. For instance, the paper opts for a 64-pixel image size and a single input channel, while other parameters are maintained as per the MAE. Consequently, the resulting model is capable of effectively imputing missing data.

3.2 Carbon Footprint Predictions

Since all datasets selected for this paper necessitate imputation, employing the data imputation model discussed in above section for predictions presents two primary issues. The first is that the generative model effectively functions as another prediction model, leading to an evaluation on the training dataset, which compromises the generalizability of the results. The second issue is the model's performance; while it excels on fixed datasets, it necessitates retraining when applied to data of varying scales. This paper aspires to train a deep learning model that has grasped the principles of advection-diffusion equations, and it is clear that a data imputation model falls short of meeting the paper's requirements.

We first introduce a footprint prediction model based on Convolutional LSTM (ConvLSTM) [27]. This generative model takes carbon concentration maps at successive time points as input and produces carbon concentration estimates at future time points, enabling the prediction of carbon dioxide movement trajectories.

Compared to the formulas in [27], this paper refines the formulas by omitting elements less pertinent to this study's objectives. The specific formulas are shown in the following equations.

$$i_t = Sigmoid(Conv(x_t; w_{xi}) + Conv(h_{t-1}; w_{hi}) + b_i) \quad (1)$$

$$f_t = Sigmoid(Conv(x_t; w_{xf}) + Conv(h_{t-1}; w_{hf}) + b_f) \quad (2)$$

$$o_t = Sigmoid(Conv(x_t; w_{wo}) + Conv(h_{t-1}; w_{ho}) + b_o) \quad (3)$$

$$g_t = \tanh(Conv(x_t; w_{xg}) + Conv(h_{t-1}; w_{hg}) + b_g) \quad (4)$$

$$c_t = f_t \odot c_{t-1} + i_t \odot g_t \quad (5)$$

$$h_t = o_t \odot \tanh(c_t) \quad (6)$$

The motion prediction module consists of three layers of ConvLSTM, each using the ConvLSTM cells described earlier. The first layer has a hidden layer dimension of 64, the second layer also features 64 units, and the third layer is configured with two output channels, aligning with the input and output specifications of the subsequent comparative motion field generation module.

In the matrices associated with the motion fields discussed above, this paper employs a clever implementation strategy. It concatenates the input and hidden

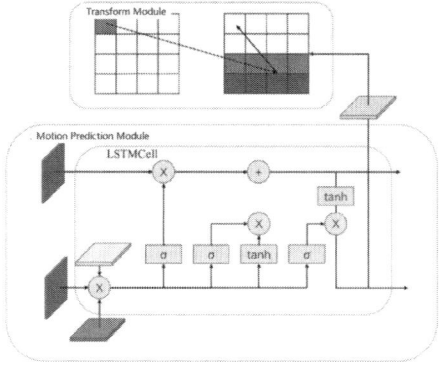

Fig. 2. An overview of the model structure.

layers and then applies a convolution operation to the resulting concatenated matrix. The number of input channels for the convolution is the sum of the input channel count and the output channel count of the preceding hidden layer. The output channels are set to four times the channel count of the current hidden layer. By doing so, the paper efficiently partitions this dimension into four tensor blocks of identical size, each designated for use by a respective gate.

The second part of the process involves transforming each point in the carbon concentration map produced by the generative model. This transformation is based on a formula derived from a convection-diffusion equation. The formula corrects the final positions of each pixel, as illustrated in Fig. 2. Specifically, this component discretizes the solution of the convection-diffusion equation, substituting integration with summation. It utilizes the initial image tI as the starting condition to devise a method for calculating subsequent images based on the estimated motion fields. The paper [12] demonstrates the equivalence of this transformation to the physical equation. Moreover, the deformation scheme is fully differentiable, enabling error signals to be backpropagated to the motion field estimation module, which lays the groundwork for integrating and optimizing both modules.

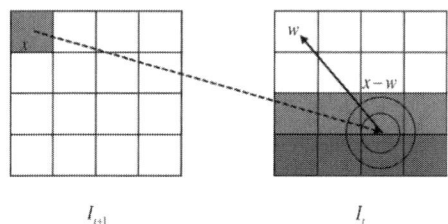

Fig. 3. Transform module.

In addition, for the comparative motion prediction models, all except the GAN (Generative Adversarial Networks) model [15] utilize this transformation module to further refine the motion prediction results post-model output. The final outcome is subsequently presented as the output of the comprehensive carbon footprint prediction model. The structure diagram of the transformation module is depicted in Fig. 3. To compute the pixel value of I_{t+1} at position x, the paper first calculates its previous position at time I_t, which is denoted as $x - w$. Then, at that position, a centered Gaussian is applied based on the distance from $x - w$, obtaining weight values for each pixel in it and computing the weighted average of the pixel values in I_t. This weighted average will correspond to the new pixel value at position x in I_{t+1}, as shown in the following equation:

$$\hat{I}_{t+1}(x) = \sum_{y \in \Omega} k(x - \hat{w}(x), y) I_t(y) \tag{7}$$

where the definition of $k(x - \hat{w}(x), y)$ is given by

$$k(x - \hat{w}(x), y) = \frac{1}{4\pi SD\Delta t} e^{-\frac{1}{4SD\Delta t}\|x - \hat{w} - y\|^2} \tag{8}$$

For training, supervision is provided at the output of the transformation module. This involves minimizing the difference between the warped image $\hat{I}t + 1$ and the target image $It + 1$. The loss is measured using differentiable functions, and gradients are backpropagated through the transformation function to adjust the parameters of the module responsible for generating the motion vector field.

3.3 Optimization Algorithm of Emission Reduction Scheme

This section primarily addresses two key issues. The first issue concerns the lag in emission reduction plans, which are currently designed based on the carbon footprint data from the previous calculation period. Consequently, the effectiveness of these plans can only be assessed after the conclusion of the current calculation period. The second issue pertains to the effectiveness of the emission reduction plans themselves, which often prioritize electricity generation over emission reduction. When the emission reduction targets are not met during the final accounting period, any excess emissions must be offset by purchasing carbon credits through carbon emission trading markets.

Given the aforementioned issues, the problem in this section can be formulated as an optimization objective described by

$$\min m\left(M_f, M_n, M_h, M_b\right) \tag{9}$$

where $m(x, y, z)$ represents the total monetary cost under the conditions altered to x, y, z. M_f denotes the expenditure associated with transitioning from non-clean energy to fuel-based electricity generation, M_n signifies the cost of clean energy electricity generation, M_h accounts for miscellaneous expenses (e.g., labor costs), and M_b reflects the expenses incurred in the carbon trading market.

Given the constraints in this paper that involve variables from integer or natural number sets, the solution space is inherently discontinuous. To streamline the problem-solving process, a two-step external penalty function method is implemented. The outer penalty function is tailored to address integer value constraints, ensuring that the final solution is within the discrete solution space outlined in this paper. Concurrently, the inner penalty function manages constraints related to continuous values, ensuring that these variables, which are subject to specific ranges, conform to the defined solution space. For the inner-level optimization, a variable scaling method is applied. Initially, various constraint conditions are standardized to formulate the inner-level constraints, as detailed in the subsequent equations

$$s_c(\lambda_c, \lambda_n) = C_{\text{total}} - C_f - C_n - C_h \geq 0 \tag{10}$$

$$s_{el}(\lambda_c, \lambda_n) = E_f + E_n - E_{\text{total}} + \varepsilon \geq 0 \tag{11}$$

$$s_{ea}(\lambda_c, \lambda_n) = E_{\text{total}} + \varepsilon - E_f - E_n \geq 0 \tag{12}$$

where the calculation method here introduces additional equality constraints, which will not be discussed in detail in this paper. Instead, only the carbon emissions described in the carbon trajectory prediction section are used for calculation.

4 Experiments

4.1 Experimental Setup

Datasets. In this paper, meteorological data from monitoring stations, covering the latitude range of 34–41 and the longitude range of 112–119, from January 1, 2016, to December 31, 2020, were selected. Following an 80:20 split, data from January 1, 2016, to December 31, 2019, were utilized for training the carbon footprint prediction model. The data from January 1, 2020, to December 31, 2020, were then used to assess the model for overfitting and to compare its performance with other models. The dataset is sourced from the National Meteorological Science Data Center.

Baselines. This paper compared the performance of four other models as motion prediction models

- U-net [26]. Each convolutional module is constructed with a single convolutional layer of 3×3 kernel, a padding of 1, and a stride of 2, followed by a Batch Normalization layer and then a ReLU activation layer. This structure reduces the output dimensions in both width and height by half.
- U^2-net [24]. The second model for comparison is an advanced version of the $U - net$ called $U^2 - net$. The idea of choosing $U^2 - net$ stemmed from its superior performance in tasks compared to the $U - net$, hence we replicated $U^2 - net$ as the second model for comparison.

Table 1. Main experiment results.

Model	MSE result
U-net	2.609192133
U^2-net	3.807606697
ACNN	9.821571112
GAN	13.410935402
Our model	**2.140608132**

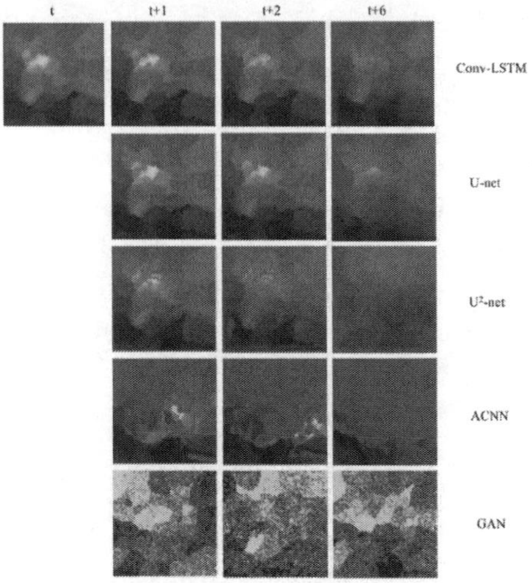

Fig. 4. Experiment heat map.

- *ACNN* [5]. ACNN consists of two modules. The upper module applies a 1×1 convolution layer with a stride of 1 to the input, followed by Batch Normalization and activated by LeakyReLU with a parameter of 0.01. The result is added to the input and multiplied by the output of multiple convolution modules below. Finally, it passes through a 1×1 convolution layer with a stride of 1, inputting 4 channels and outputting 2 channels to produce the model's final output.
- *GAN* [15]. The GAN generates 4×100 data from a Gaussian normal distribution as input to the generator. The first module consists of a Linear layer that maps 100 to 128, followed by a LeakyReLU activation layer with a parameter of 0.2. The next three layers are composed of a Linear layer followed by Batch Normalization with a parameter of 0.8 and another LeakyReLU activation layer with a parameter of 0.2, producing the final output.

Evaluation Protoclos. As this chapter's task, when simplified, can be seen as predicting the similarity between the predicted images and reference images, mean square error is adopted as the evaluation metric for each model in this chapter. The specific calculation method is as follows:

$$MSE = \frac{1}{n} \sum_{(x,y) \in \Omega} \left(\hat{I}_{(x,y)} - I_{(x,y)} \right)^2 \qquad (13)$$

4.2 Performance Comparison

In the previous sections, we introduced the carbon footprint prediction model employed in this paper, as well as the motion prediction models, and we will compare their performance. Table 1 presents the MSE metrics for various motion prediction models on the test set. As observed from the table, the Conv-LSTM model outperforms the others overall. We will now illustrate the predictions of different motion estimation modules for the upcoming six time steps, given an input at a fixed time point, and showcase the final carbon footprint prediction post-deformation. Notably, the number of output channels is increased to 6 for testing, up from the 2 used during training.

Figure 4 displays the predictions of various motion prediction modules for the next three time steps, with each subsequent time step being one, two, and six hours apart, respectively. The top row presents the improved ConvLSTM module utilized in this paper. The second row shows the output of the U-net following processing by the transformation module. The third row corresponds to the U^2-net, also after transformation. The fourth row displays the output of ACNN post-transformation. The bottom row illustrates the GAN's prediction as the carbon footprint module.

5 Conclusion

This paper begins by examining the prevalent practical demands for emission reduction, analyzing the reasons why existing emission reduction plans may not be sufficiently effective, and proposes a new method tailored to address specific user concerns based on these insights. In response to these issues and market demand, the paper introduces three novel algorithms focused on carbon emission data completion, carbon footprint prediction, and emission reduction plan optimization, effectively bridging a gap in the current research field.

References

1. Achour, H., Belloumi, M.: Decomposing the influencing factors of energy consumption in Tunisian transportation sector using the LMDI method. Transp. Policy **52**, 64–71 (2016)
2. Ahmed, M., Shuai, C., Ahmed, M.: Influencing factors of carbon emissions and their trends in China and India: a machine learning method. Environ. Sci. Pollut. Res. **29**(32), 48424–48437 (2022)
3. Akbostancı, E., Tunç, G.İ, Türüt-Aşık, S.: CO2 emissions of Turkish manufacturing industry: a decomposition analysis. Appl. Energy **88**(6), 2273–2278 (2011)
4. Aryai, V., Goldsworthy, M.: Day ahead carbon emission forecasting of the regional national electricity market using machine learning methods. Eng. Appl. Artif. Intell. **123**, 106314 (2023)
5. Binkowski, M., Marti, G., Donnat, P.: Autoregressive convolutional neural networks for asynchronous time series. In: International Conference on Machine Learning, pp. 580–589. PMLR (2018)
6. Brandt, A.R., Sun, Y., Vafi, K.: Uncertainty in regional-average petroleum GHG intensities: countering information gaps with targeted data gathering. Environ. Sci. Technol. **49**(1), 679–686 (2015)

7. Cansino, J.M., Román, R., Ordonez, M.: Main drivers of changes in CO2 emissions in the Spanish economy: a structural decomposition analysis. Energy Policy **89**, 150–159 (2016)
8. Chen, C., Kotyk, J.F.K., Sheehan, S.W.: Progress toward commercial application of electrochemical carbon dioxide reduction. Chem **4**(11), 2571–2586 (2018)
9. Chen, C.Y., Chai, K.K., Lau, E.: Ai-assisted approach for building energy and carbon footprint modeling. Energy AI **5**, 100091 (2021)
10. Creswell, A., White, T., Dumoulin, V., Arulkumaran, K., Sengupta, B., Bharath, A.A.: Generative adversarial networks: an overview. IEEE Signal Process. Mag. **35**(1), 53–65 (2018)
11. Cui, C., Li, S., Zhao, W., Liu, B., Shan, Y., Guan, D.: Energy-related CO2 emission accounts and datasets for 40 emerging economies in 2010–2019. Earth Syst. Sci. Data Discuss. **2022**, 1–20 (2022)
12. De Bézenac, E., Pajot, A., Gallinari, P.: Deep learning for physical processes: incorporating prior scientific knowledge. J. Stat. Mech: Theory Exp. **2019**(12), 124009 (2019)
13. Dosovitskiy, A., et al.: An image is worth 16x16 words: transformers for image recognition at scale. arXiv preprint arXiv:2010.11929 (2020)
14. González, P.F., Landajo, M., Presno, M.J.: Tracking European union CO2 emissions through LMDI (logarithmic-mean divisia index) decomposition. The activity revaluation approach. Energy **73**, 741–750 (2014)
15. Goodfellow, I., et al.: Generative adversarial networks. Commun. ACM **63**(11), 139–144 (2020)
16. He, K., Chen, X., Xie, S., Li, Y., Dollár, P., Girshick, R.: Masked autoencoders are scalable vision learners. In: Proceedings of the IEEE/CVF Conference on Computer Vision and Pattern Recognition, pp. 16000–16009 (2022)
17. Karmellos, M., Kopidou, D., Diakoulaki, D.: A decomposition analysis of the driving factors of CO2 (carbon dioxide) emissions from the power sector in the European union countries. Energy **94**, 680–692 (2016)
18. Li, W., Li, Y., Pu, Z., Cheng, L., Wang, L., Yang, L.: Revealing the real-world CO2 emission reduction of ridesplitting and its determinants based on machine learning. arXiv e-prints pp. arXiv-2204 (2022)
19. Marchand, R.D., Koh, S.L., Morris, J.C.: Delivering energy efficiency and carbon reduction schemes in England: lessons from green deal pioneer places. Energy Policy **84**, 96–106 (2015)
20. Milczarski, P., Zieliński, B., Stawska, Z., Hłobaż, A., Maślanka, P., Kosiński, P.: Machine learning application in energy consumption calculation and assessment in food processing industry. In: Rutkowski, L., Scherer, R., Korytkowski, M., Pedrycz, W., Tadeusiewicz, R., Zurada, J.M. (eds.) ICAISC 2020. LNCS (LNAI), vol. 12416, pp. 369–379. Springer, Cham (2020). https://doi.org/10.1007/978-3-030-61534-5_33
21. Miller, S.A., John, V.M., Pacca, S.A., Horvath, A.: Carbon dioxide reduction potential in the global cement industry by 2050. Cem. Concr. Res. **114**, 115–124 (2018)
22. Moutinho, V., Moreira, A.C., Silva, P.M.: The driving forces of change in energy-related CO2 emissions in eastern, western, northern and southern Europe: the LMDI approach to decomposition analysis. Renew. Sustain. Energy Rev. **50**, 1485–1499 (2015)
23. Mu, Y., Gao, K., Du, R.: Prediction of regional carbon emissions using deep learning and mathematical–statistical model. J. Ambient Intell. Smart Environ. 1–17 (2023)

24. Qin, X., Zhang, Z., Huang, C., Dehghan, M., Zaiane, O.R., Jagersand, M.: U2-net: going deeper with nested u-structure for salient object detection. Pattern Recogn. **106**, 107404 (2020)
25. Robaina-Alves, M., Moutinho, V., Costa, R.: Change in energy-related CO2 (carbon dioxide) emissions in Portuguese tourism: a decomposition analysis from 2000 to 2008. J. Clean. Prod. **111**, 520–528 (2016)
26. Ronneberger, O., Fischer, P., Brox, T.: U-Net: convolutional networks for biomedical image segmentation. In: Navab, N., Hornegger, J., Wells, W.M., Frangi, A.F. (eds.) MICCAI 2015, Part III. LNCS, vol. 9351, pp. 234–241. Springer, Cham (2015). https://doi.org/10.1007/978-3-319-24574-4_28
27. Shi, X., Chen, Z., Wang, H., Yeung, D.Y., Wong, W.K., Woo, W.C.: Convolutional LSTM network: a machine learning approach for precipitation nowcasting. In: Advances in Neural Information Processing Systems, vol. 28 (2015)
28. Su, B., Ang, B.: Multiplicative structural decomposition analysis of aggregate embodied energy and emission intensities. Energy Econ. **65**, 137–147 (2017)
29. Su, B., Ang, B., Li, Y.: Input-output and structural decomposition analysis of Singapore's carbon emissions. Energy Policy **105**, 484–492 (2017)
30. Sun, L., Reddu, V., Fisher, A.C., Wang, X.: Electrocatalytic reduction of carbon dioxide: opportunities with heterogeneous molecular catalysts. Energy Environ. Sci. **13**(2), 374–403 (2020)
31. Wang, H., Ang, B.W., Su, B.: Assessing drivers of economy-wide energy use and emissions: IDA versus SDA. Energy Policy **107**, 585–599 (2017)
32. Wang, S., Zhu, X., Song, D., Wen, Z., Chen, B., Feng, K.: Drivers of CO2 emissions from power generation in China based on modified structural decomposition analysis. J. Clean. Prod. **220**, 1143–1155 (2019)
33. Wang, W., Zhang, M., Zhou, M.: Using LMDI method to analyze transport sector CO2 emissions in China. Energy **36**(10), 5909–5915 (2011)
34. Wang, Y., Zhao, H., Li, L., Liu, Z., Liang, S.: Carbon dioxide emission drivers for a typical metropolis using input-output structural decomposition analysis. Energy Policy **58**, 312–318 (2013)
35. Wang, Z.J., Song, H., Liu, H., Ye, J.: Coupling of solar energy and thermal energy for carbon dioxide reduction: status and prospects. Angewandte Chemie Int. Ed. **59**(21), 8016–8035 (2020)
36. Wei, J., Huang, K., Yang, S., Li, Y., Hu, T., Zhang, Y.: Driving forces analysis of energy-related carbon dioxide (CO2) emissions in Beijing: an input-output structural decomposition analysis. J. Clean. Prod. **163**, 58–68 (2017)
37. Zhang, W., Mohamed, A.R., Ong, W.J.: Z-scheme photocatalytic systems for carbon dioxide reduction: where are we now? Angew. Chem. Int. Ed. **59**(51), 22894–22915 (2020)
38. Zheng, H., Song, M., Shen, Z.: The evolution of renewable energy and its impact on carbon reduction in China. Energy **237**, 121639 (2021)
39. Zhu, B., Su, B., Li, Y.: Input-output and structural decomposition analysis of India's carbon emissions and intensity, 2007/08-2013/14. Appl. Energy **230**, 1545–1556 (2018)

CCRisk: Automated Risk Detection on Heterogeneous Consortium Chains for Supply Chain Finance

Junxiong Lin[1], Ruijun Deng[1], Mingyu Gu[2], Jing Liu[3(✉)], Zhihui Lu[1], Yubing Bao[1], Sheng Mao[1], and Qiang Duan[4]

[1] Fudan University, Shanghai 200433, China
{jxlin18,rjdeng18,lzh}@fudan.edu.cn,
{ybbao23,21210240281}@m.fudan.edu.cn
[2] School of Foreign Studies, Shanghai University of Finance and Economics, Shanghai, China
2021110452@stu.sufe.edu.cn
[3] Wangsu Science & Technology Co., Ltd., Shanghai, China
liuj@wangsu.com
[4] Information Sciences and Technology Department, Pennsylvania State University, Abington, PA, USA
qduan@psu.edu

Abstract. The consortium blockchain aims to provide a secure and trusted digital platform for data sharing among multiple organizations, in which, participants are typically groups with common interests and are allowed to manage the network, reach consensus, and share data. However, a prominent issue is the lack of evaluation metrics and assessment methods for consortium blockchains. Accurately measuring consortium blockchains' performance, security, and consistency is still challenging. This paper proposes an automated risk detection tool for heterogeneous consortium blockchains, namely CCRisk, which can be adapted to multiple consortium blockchain–based services such as Supply Chain Finance, enabling full-process automation of detection. It begins by constructing risk indicators for various heterogeneous consortium blockchain technologies. A chaos engineering-based risk indicator detection method and an abstract syntax tree–based smart contract risk detection method are proposed based on these indicators. We implement this tool to examine three widely adopted consortium blockchains—Hyperledger Fabric, Fisco-bcos, and Chainmaker. Experiment results demonstrate its ability to accurately detect risks in different consortium blockchain networks.

Keywords: Consortium blockchain · Risk detection · Chaos engineering · Abstract syntax tree · Smart contract · Fintech

1 Introduction

In the era of Web 3.0, blockchain technology plays a crucial role as an infrastructure, leveraging its distributed, decentralized, and immutable characteristics to ensure secure and transparent data storage [1]. This technology empowers users to have ownership of their data, control access to it, and participate in data sharing and exchange, thereby unlocking the true value and significance of data. Beyond its initial role in cryptocurrency, blockchain has evolved to drive exploration and innovation across various domains. For instance, blockchain enables faster, more convenient, transparent, and trustworthy cross-border payments in finance, while decentralized financial ecosystems (DEFIs) are reshaping traditional financial systems. In supply chain management, blockchain ensures unprecedented security and transparency in logistics tracking, traceability, and quality assurance [2].

Different types of blockchain networks have emerged to meet diverse needs. Public, private, and consortium chains are common classifications. Public chains like Bitcoin and Ethereum [3] are open and decentralized, allowing any user to create an account and participate in transactions. Private chains, used within enterprises, restrict participants and enable secure internal data sharing. Consortium chains have entry barriers and joining restrictions, facilitating cooperation and information sharing among multiple organizations or entities. Compared to public blockchains, consortium chains emphasize privacy and control. Participants can share data while maintaining privacy. Consortium chains also offer higher throughput and faster transaction confirmation and execution speeds due to the limited number of participants, enabling efficient consensus. This makes consortium chains widely applicable in supply chain management.

Despite the rapid development of consortium chain technology, it is important to recognize that the corresponding detection mechanisms are not yet fully established. The consortium chain's components, including the consensus algorithm and smart contract, are vulnerable and can potentially disrupt critical supply chain finance services [4–6]. While individual enterprises and units utilizing consortium chains may have conducted internal technical risk assessments and tests, there is a lack of universal testing guidelines and detection tools. Specifically, in the context of the consortium chain, there is currently a lack of appropriate technical risk indicators and detection tools.

This paper aims to address this gap by constructing practical risk indicators, as well as developing a comprehensive automated technology risk detection tool, CCRisk (Consortium Chain Risk detection tool), that can be adapted to various heterogeneous consortium chains. It establishes rational risk indicators for heterogeneous consortium blockchains. Then, detection methods are suggested for these indicators, where network and system indicators utilize chaos engineering for collective detection and smart contracts employ lexical and syntax analysis to construct an abstract syntax tree (AST) structure, enabling the identification of potential risks. **Specific contributions of this paper are as follows:**

- We comprehensively analyze risk indicators for consortium blockchain systems and propose a risk detection tool (CCRisk) for them, which assesses important indicators such as consortium blockchain network metrics, consensus algorithms, encryption algorithms, data security, privacy, and smart contracts.

- For blockchain network metrics and consensus algorithms, a risk detection method is introduced based on chaos engineering for heterogeneous consortium blockchains.
- Regarding smart contract indicators, a static code detection method based on abstract syntax trees (AST) is proposed, which is compatible with different smart contract versions and includes fuzzy testing to assess interface robustness.

2 Related Work

Recent works have shown that chaos engineering [7] can be a practical blockchain detection tool, enabling the simulation of abnormal conditions for improved detection outcomes. Sondhi et al. [8] utilized chaos engineering to evaluate consensus algorithm performance in a consortium blockchain, considering various loads, Byzantine faults, and communication failures. They assessed three consensus algorithms (PBFT, Clique, Raft) and their respective blockchain platforms using chaos engineering. Zhang et al. [9] introduced CHAOSETH, a chaos engineering tool for the elastic evaluation of Ethereum clients. They examined 22 system call errors and evaluated their impact on Ethereum clients using 15 application-level metrics. Ayham et al. [10] presented C2B2, a benchmark test suite combining blockchain with the ChaosMesh chaos engineering tool to assess the performance and robustness of blockchain systems under fault scenarios. Huang et al. [11] proposed an anomaly detection method for consortium blockchains based on machine learning classification algorithms. They employed machine learning techniques to classify data and identify potential anomalies, along with suggesting appropriate strategies.

Smart contracts are crucial for the interaction between blockchains and external entities. They play an integral role in blockchain operations. Detecting technical risks in consortium blockchains requires examining smart contracts. Qian et al. [12] proposed a cross-modal mutual learning approach to enhance vulnerability detection of bytecode generated from smart contract development. By combining source code and bytecode information, and utilizing feature extraction and similarity loss, they identified potential risks and vulnerabilities in Ethereum smart contracts. Yamashita et al. [13] introduced a Chaincode Analyzer (CA) to detect potential risks and factors in smart contracts. They used abstract syntax trees for analysis. Building on CA, Lv et al. [14] proposed an enhanced detection system called CAII, which incorporated additional metrics and described its design and implementation. Liu et al. [15] presented a method that combines Graph Neural Networks (GNN) and expert knowledge for smart contract vulnerability detection. They aimed to improve the effectiveness and accuracy of testing by integrating deep learning with expert knowledge. Liao et al. [16] introduced "SmartDagger," a bytecode-based static analysis method that detects cross-contract vulnerabilities using detailed bytecode analysis and data flow tracing techniques. Huang et al. [17] proposed a novel blockchain platform called "Highsimb", which uses virtualization technology to simulate multiple blockchain nodes. It provides realistic simulations of Ethereum and Fabric platforms, along with real-time monitoring, statistical information, and visualization, supporting effective smart contract vulnerability detection.

In conclusion, the current focus of blockchain detection is primarily on public blockchains, with limited attention given to consortium blockchains. Chaos engineering can assist in assessing network and other metrics related to blockchain. For smart contract detection, the common approach involves parsing and analyzing static bytecode. Bytecode is the binary code obtained from compiling smart contract source code and serves as an intermediate representation. Thus, static code analysis is a feasible approach for examining smart contracts in consortium blockchains.

3 Risk Detection Tool for Consortium Chain

3.1 Construction of Technical Risk Indicators

This paper analyzes, selects, and optimizes various security indicators in blockchain, specifically focusing on consortium blockchains characterized by small scale, high efficiency, and entry barriers. The study identifies and explains the indicators to be detected within consortium blockchains.

Reliability: Blockchain reliability refers to its ability to ensure stable, secure, and efficient operation. It includes network reliability and ledger reliability. Only the first two indicators will be tested in this study.

a) Blockchain network reliability: Evaluate the blockchain network's stability during node changes, including load testing.
b) Ledger reliability: Assess consistency and integrity of the ledger among nodes during node changes and recovery.

Cryptography Algorithms: The foundation of blockchain technology, including encryption algorithm detection and verification.

a) Encryption algorithm verification: Test and verify the blockchain's encryption algorithms.

Consensus Algorithms: Ensure unanimous agreement among participants. Consistency testing examines data consistency among consensus nodes. Consensus algorithm verification checks if the algorithm meets requirements in different scenarios.

Smart Contracts: Test language-related risks (e.g., Golang syntax uncertainties), external access risks (e.g., calling external libraries), privacy data security risks (e.g., cross-channel contract access), logical security risks (e.g., write-after-read vulnerabilities), other logical risks (e.g., unhandled function parameters), and data persistence, contract interface idempotence, and robustness.

Others: Optional detection items, including support for trusted timestamps [18], cross-chain transactions, encryption and desensitization of on-chain privacy data, and support for microservice architecture [19].

3.2 Risk Indicator Detection Using Chaos Engineering

This section presents a specific detection scheme for risk indicators in heterogeneous consortium blockchains using chaos engineering.

Reliability Detection. For the reliability of consortium blockchains, similar to blockchain reliability, it is essential to test whether the consortium blockchain network can operate normally and stably in various scenarios, without service interruptions, unresponsiveness, or network crashes. Therefore, the benchmark test involves completing write and query operations on all nodes and verifying data consistency. Additionally, benchmark tests are conducted by adding, removing, modifying, stopping, and starting node services, and adjusting the load conditions of each node, including CPU, IO, memory, and network loads. The reliability detection is shown in Algorithm 1.

Algorithm 1. Reliability detection algorithm f_1

Input: Node set C, submission operation *invoke*, query operation *query*, inject fault operation *blade* (as a list, including various fault injection commands), stop node operation *stop*, start node operation *start*.
Output: Output result $True/False$.
1: Initialize input parameters and variable information.
2: When the network is working normally, take any node in the node set C and perform a submission *invoke* and *query* operation, and record it as result 1.
3: **for** *node* in C **do**
4:    Turn off node service *stop node*
5:    Execute the *query* and submission operations *invoke*, and check if they are normal. Record the result as 2
6:    Enable node service *start node*
7:    Execute the *query* and submission operations *invoke*, and check if they are normal. Record the result as 3
8:    Verify whether the results 1, 2, and 3 are consistent and correct
9:    **for** *operation* in *blade* **do**
10:       Execute the fault injection *operation* and set the time to 30-60 seconds
11:       Execute the *query* and submission operations *invoke*, and check if they are normal. Record the result as 2
12:       sleep 60 waiting for operation *invoke* to end
13:       Execute the *query* and submission operations *invoke*, and check if they are normal. Record the result as 3
14:       Verify whether the results 1, 2, and 3 are consistent and correct
15:    **end for**
16:    Summarize all results and confirm that the node block information in set C is consistent and up-to-date
17: **end for**
18: **if** all results are normal and consistent **then**
19:    **return** True
20: **else**
21:    **return** False
22: **end if**

Cryptography Algorithm Detection. Cryptography algorithms form a crucial foundation for data protection in blockchain technology. They ensure the privacy, confidentiality, and integrity of data within a blockchain, providing reliable security for consortium blockchain networks. Cryptography algorithm testing focuses on verifying blockchain node communication and the encryption and hashing algorithms employed.

The testing tool utilizes OpenSSL, a widely adopted open-source Cryptography library. OpenSSL offers a comprehensive range of cryptography functions and security tools, supporting encryption, decryption, digital signatures, SSL/TLS protocol, and certificate management. With its support for multiple encryption algorithms and protocols, OpenSSL guarantees data confidentiality, integrity, and identity verification. It finds extensive application in computer systems, servers, and software, providing robust support for network communication and data protection. The cryptography algorithm detection is shown in Algorithm 2.

Algorithm 2. Cryptography Algorithm Detection Algorithm f_2

Input: Node certificate key path *pathList*.
Output: Encryption algorithm results.
1: Initialize input parameters and variable information.
2: **for** *path* in *pathList* **do**
3:    **for** *v* in 'ls path' **do**
4:       **if** *v* is the directory **then**
5:          recursive call detection function f_2
6:       **else if** *v* is the certificate/key file format **then**
7:          (At this point, *v* is the file.)
8:          Use OpenSSL tool to detect the file, obtain the encryption algorithm, and extract it.
9:       **end if**
10:    **end for**
11: **end for**
12: Summarize all results, sort, and deduplicate.
13: **return**

The specific steps are as follows:

a) Install OpenSSL tool on the testing environment. b) Use OpenSSL tool to scan relevant key files of consortium blockchain nodes (file directories loaded during initialization). c) Apply "sed +'regular expressions to filter the encryption algorithms used. d) Determine the field type and directly match common encryption algorithms (e.g., ECC, AES). If the encryption algorithm is displayed as an OID (unique OIDs are assigned to all encryption algorithms in China, e.g., SM2 corresponds to OID 1.2.156.10197.1.301), cross-reference and determine the corresponding encryption+hash algorithm (e.g., SM2+SM3). e) Filter, refine, and eliminate duplicates from the results of all encryption algorithms to obtain the final result.

Consensus Algorithm Detection. Consensus algorithms are mechanisms that address the challenge of achieving agreement among distributed system nodes regarding state and transaction content. They ensure consensus on transaction validity, order, and final state in decentralized consortium blockchain networks. Consensus algorithms are vital for network security, reliability, and consistency, constituting an integral part of blockchain technology.

The primary focus is to test ledger data consistency among current consensus nodes. In some consortium blockchain technologies like Fabric, consensus, and accounting nodes are separate entities, while others combine these functions into node nodes. Node nodes record transactions, synchronize blocks, and maintain distributed consistency through consensus algorithms. It is crucial to verify the feasibility and effectiveness of the employed consensus algorithm. For example, the widely used Raft consensus algorithm in consortium blockchains will be tested for exceptional scenarios it can tolerate and those it cannot. This ensures compliance with the Raft protocol by all consensus nodes.

Algorithm 3. Consensus Algorithm Validation Algorithm f_3

Input: Node set C, submission operation *invoke*, query operation *query*, stop node operation *stop*, start node operation *start*, successful consensus requires closing node set *nodeList1*, failed consensus requires closing node set *nodeList2*
Output: Output result *True/False*.
1: Initialize input parameters and variable information
2: When the network is working normally, take any *node* in node set C and perform a submission *invoke* and *query* operation, and record it as result 1
3: Success scenarios for setting consensus protocols:
4: Close multiple node services stop *nodeList1*
5: Execute the *query* and submission operations *invoke* and check if they are normal. Record the result as 2
6: Enable multiple node services start *nodeList1*
7: Execute the query and submission operations *invoke* and check if they are normal. Record the result as 3
8: Verify whether the results 1, 2, and 3 are consistent and correct, and verify whether the blocks are consistent and synchronized through log verification
9: Scenario of failure in setting consensus protocol:
10: Close multiple node services stop *nodeList2*
11: Execute the *query* and verify whether the results 1, 2, and 3 on the blockchain are consistent and correct. Verify whether the blocks are consistent and synchronized through logs, and determine if they are normal. Record as result 2
12: Verify if result 2 has failed and is inconsistent with 1
13: Start multiple node services *nodeList2* and restore the site
14: Summarize all results and confirm if all operations are as expected
15: **if** all results are as expected, i.e. $future == expected$ **then**
16:     **return** True
17: **else**
18:     **return** False
19: **end if**

Algorithm 3 supports common consensus algorithms such as Raft, PBFT, TBFT, MBFT, etc. Future extensions can be accommodated by selecting the corresponding testing scenarios.

Other Trivial Risks Detection. In addition to the aforementioned important indicators such as reliability, cryptography algorithms, and consensus algorithms, other indicators reflect the risks in current consortium blockchain technology. These include privacy, smart contracts, and interface security. The following testing procedures are straightforward and independent, and are collectively explained in this subsection:

a) Determine if the consortium blockchain is deployed as microservices by querying and filtering container image names.
b) Verify if block data is encrypted by capturing and analyzing block data from different consortium blockchains.
c) Check for support of trusted timestamps and cross-chain transactions by testing corresponding smart contract interfaces.
d) Assess data persistence, contract interface idempotence, and robustness by comparing query results and conducting fuzzy testing on smart contract interfaces.

These indicators provide insights into the risks associated with consortium blockchains.

3.3 Static Code Analysis Based on AST

This section provides an overview of the testing process for detailed metrics related to smart contracts. The specific test metrics include language-related risks, external access risks, privacy data security risks, logical security risks, and other logical risks.

As shown in Fig. 1, the Golang AST library offers various node types. For instance, importSpec represents package import information, Ident denotes identifiers such as variable names and function names, Decl represents declarations and can be further classified into GenDecl for general variable declarations and FuncDecl for function declarations. Stmt represents common operation statements, including ExprStmt for expression statements and AssignStmt for assignment statements. FuncType represents function types, among others. After constructing the abstract syntax tree (AST), the Inspect function can be used to traverse the entire tree structure. By analyzing different node types and their data, various detection metrics can be evaluated.

It is worth noting that smart contract versions and the third-party blockchain contract libraries they reference are continuously updated and upgraded over time. This evolution leads to changes in the corresponding APIs. For example, in the case of Fabric, versions prior to 1.4 supported the Shim package, while versions from 2.0 onwards added support for the Contractapi library while maintaining compatibility with the Shim package. Therefore, the proposed testing approach in this section is compatible with various smart contract-related

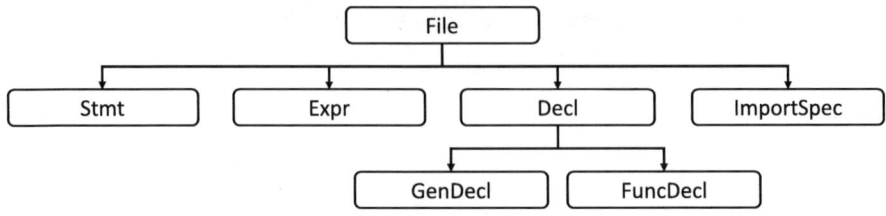

Fig. 1. AST node simple type diagram.

libraries used in different versions of consortium blockchains. This compatibility avoids potential detection anomalies caused by differences in smart contract versions across all currently released versions.

The general detection process, as depicted in Fig. 2, begins with providing a smart contract file for testing. The file undergoes static code analysis using Golang's built-in lexical analyzer token[1] and parser[2] for preprocessing, resulting in the corresponding abstract syntax tree (AST). The AST is then traversed to detect various metrics, with the results, reasons, locations, and recommendations for each metric encapsulated in a map. Finally, the results of all metrics in the map are consolidated, checked, and printed as output.

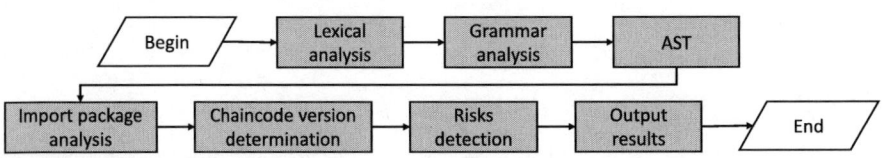

Fig. 2. Smart Contract Detection Flowchart.

In compilers, the Intermediate Representation (IR) serves as an abstract and intermediate-level representation used for conversion and analysis between source and target code. It can be a high-level representation similar to the source code or a lower-level representation closer to machine code. At different stages of the compiler, the IR can be transformed, modified, and optimized to improve code quality and performance. One form of IR is Static Single Assignment (SSA), which ensures that each variable in the program is assigned only once and is not modified before its usage. This constraint helps the compiler optimize the code more easily by accurately tracking the value of each variable. In SSA, each variable has a version number, and a new version is created with each assignment. This feature makes it easier to perform optimizations such as data flow analysis, code elimination, and constant propagation.

During the detection process, the first step involves analyzing all the imported packages in the code to determine their dependencies. This step involves converting all AST nodes obtained into the Intermediate Representation (IR). From

---

[1] Go-token[EB/OL]. https://pkg.go.dev/go/token.
[2] Go-parser[EB/OL]. https://pkg.go.dev/go/parser.

the IR, the names and paths of top-level packages are extracted and used as input for parsing functions to read the import statements in the specified package and obtain the list of dependent packages. The process further traverses the list of dependent packages and recursively calls the corresponding detection functions to obtain dependency lists at each level. When reading the dependency lists recursively from the IR, up to three levels of the standard Golang library can be read, resulting in the package dependency relationship of the chaincode. The detection results include basic libraries such as fmt, strconv, encoding/json, the blockchain smart contract-related libraries imported (e.g., github/hyperledger/fabric/core/shim), and potential risky external libraries, such as encryption-related libraries like crypto/md5.

During the examination and scanning of package dependencies, certain risks can be identified, such as external library usage and data encryption (which can only be achieved if encryption-related libraries are imported). Additionally, the current version of the smart contract being used can be determined, which provides a solid foundation for further metric detection.

Next, potential risks can be identified by traversing the abstract syntax tree (AST) nodes. The analysis focuses on external access risks of smart contracts, including calling external websites, third-party libraries, system commands, and accessing external files. Each operation corresponds to specific commands and function calls. Language-related risks and privacy data security risks include the use of map iterators, local random number generation, system timestamps, object addresses, program concurrency, cross-channel chaincode invocations, and unused privacy data mechanisms. Specifically, the first five categories are influenced by the deployment and invocation environments of the smart contract, as multiple function calls cannot guarantee consistent results, violating the idempotence principle of interfaces and potentially causing unforeseen harm in practical use. Cross-channel chaincode invocations may modify data in other channels' smart contracts, potentially compromising the security of other smart contracts and leading to data inconsistency. Querying data may also be affected by the uncertain runtime state of other smart contracts, so it is not advisable to call smart contracts from other channels within a specific smart contract. Additionally, for a specific smart contract, by detecting whether it uses private data collections, developers can be warned to use privacy data protection mechanisms such as private data collections to enhance the protection level of important and sensitive data, thereby improving the security of the smart contract and data.

Logical security risk detection is based on the internal function call relationships within the smart contract. This module specifically examines range queries and read-after-write risks. Range query risks involve identifying range-based query functions such as GetPrivateDataQueryResult or GetQueryResult in the code. Read-after-write risks occur when a write operation is followed by a read operation within the same smart contract function. Due to the current use of the MVCC mechanism in smart contracts, regular reads are snapshot reads instead of current reads, meaning they can only access the view corresponding to the snapshot. Therefore, write operations in the same function do not affect the subsequent read operation, and the read operation will not be affected by the previous write operation, potentially leading to unknown logical risks.

Additionally, when analyzing a function's AST nodes (FuncDecl), the usage of its passed parameters and the utilization of return values for any Stmt nodes are recorded. After traversing all nodes, the occurrences of unused function parameters and unused return values are counted to analyze and detect these two types of potential technical risks.

Once all the metric detections are completed, the results are consolidated, including any anomalies, their locations, reasons, and other relevant details, and presented as a unified output.

4 Experiments

4.1 Setups

The experimental hardware configuration for the academic paper included two Dell servers: Dell R730xd and Dell R730. The Dell R730xd server had 4 memory modules of 32GB each and a 3.6TB hard drive. The Dell R730 server had 4 memory modules of 32GB each, along with two 500GB hard drives and one 1.2TB hard drive.

We built three types of consortium blockchains and deployed smart contracts to simulate a simplified testing environment in this experiment:

- *Hyperledger Fabric (Fabric)*. The Fabric network test environment comprises three organizations, each with a peer node named peer0. These organizations have installed the basic chaincode for testing, and the smart contracts are deployed in containerized form. The network includes three orderer nodes for endorsement, and all peer and orderer nodes have joined the "mychannel" channel in the Fabric consortium blockchain cluster.
- *Chainmaker*. The Chainmaker comprises four node nodes named cm-node1 to cm-node4. These nodes serve dual roles as accounting nodes (peers) and consensus nodes (orderers), facilitating block synchronization and ensuring data consistency. The nodes are equipped with the smart contract contract_tinygo, deployed using the CMC binary tool, which supports essential operations such as registration, storage, query, and revocation.
- *Fisco*. The Fisco-bcos (Fisco) comprises four node nodes, denoted as [directory string]+[node]1 to [directory string]+[node]4. These nodes serve as both accounting nodes (peers) and consensus nodes (orderers), ensuring block synchronization and data consistency. The console control panel is utilized to deploy a HelloWorld smart contract for testing purposes, offering fundamental save and query functions.

4.2 Reliability

Using the Fisco as an example, the initial network state is normal. Query and invoke operations are performed, and multiple nodes execute consistent query operations. On-chain operations proceed smoothly, confirming the integrity of the initial data. Fault injection tests for high CPU, disk IO, and memory loads are conducted, and query operations remain unaffected. After shutting down node0, other nodes successfully execute on-chain operations. Upon restarting node0 and ensuring its recovery, querying all nodes reveals consistent and complete block data, with each node having the latest block number of 28. This indicates successful data synchronization and demonstrates the network's overall high availability and reliability during partial node failures.

Correctness Validation: executing on-chain and query operations within each node container is successful in the test environment. The synchronization and consistency of block information, confirmed through log analysis, further validate the reliability of the testing network.

4.3 Cryptography Algorithm

Taking Chainmaker as an example, the network employs the ECDSA (Elliptic Curve Digital Signature Algorithm) as the encryption algorithm and SHA256 as the hash algorithm. To perform the detection, the tool traverses all subdirectories within the directory containing the key and certificate files. It continues traversal for folders encountered and performs OpenSSL-based detection for files with the ".pem" or ".crt" extension.

In terms of correctness validation, Chainmaker defaults to using ECDSA as the encryption algorithm Additionally, the hash algorithm is set to SHA256.

4.4 Consensus Algorithm

Taking the Fabric network as an example, the test network consists of three consensus nodes that utilize the Raft protocol. The testing process involves initial query operations, recorded as Result 1. Subsequently, consensus node orderer2 is shut down, and query and on-chain operations are conducted. The query results match Result 1, and the on-chain operations succeed. Upon restarting consensus node orderer2, the data consistency and integrity among all consensus nodes are verified. The latest block is 24, with a Raft ID of 28. Thus, the network satisfies the Raft protocol, and the consensus nodes demonstrate consistency.

Correctness Validation: In a network with three consensus nodes, shutting down one node does not hinder the successful execution of queries and on-chain operations on the remaining two nodes. Upon restoring the previously shutdown node, all nodes exhibit consistent and synchronized block data, including the node that was shut down during the on-chain operation.

4.5 Smart Contracts

This section focuses on testing and validating the technical risks associated with smart contracts in consortium blockchain technology.

200 open-source smart contracts from GitHub were collected and subjected to risk detection. The accuracy of the detection results for these contracts was

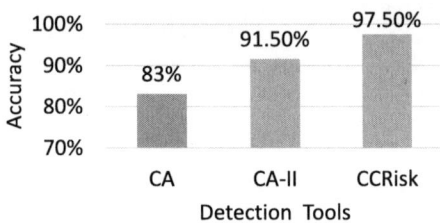

Fig. 3. Comparison of smart contract detection accuracy.

compared with other tools, such as Chancode Analyzer (CA) [13] and CA-II [14]. Figure 3 shows that the detection tool used in this study achieved a slightly higher accuracy in detecting smart contract risks compared to the other tools.

Table 1. Comparison of smart contract indicators coverage among various tools.

Risk Indicator	CA	CA-II	CCRisk (Ours)
Map Iterator	✓	✓	✓
Local Random Number Generation	✓	✓	✓
System Timestamp	✓	✓	✓
Program Concurrency	✓	✓	✓
Concrete Object Address	✓	✓	✓
External Library Invocation		✓	✓
External Network Invocation		✓	✓
System Command Invocation	✓	✓	✓
External File Access		✓	✓
Cross-Channel Contract Access	✓	✓	✓
Unencrypted/Sensitive Data		✓	✓
Lack of Private Data Collection Mechanism		✓	✓
Write-After-Read Risk		✓	✓
Unhandled Function Parameters			✓
Unhandled Exception Handling			✓
Contract Interface Idempotence			✓
Contract Interface Robustness			✓

Our detection tool also expands the coverage of detection indicators, as shown in Table 1. In addition to supporting a broader range of chaincode versions, it includes additional detection for unhandled function parameters and exception handling. Furthermore, it optimizes the detection methods and processes for other indicators, improving overall accuracy.

5 Conclusion

This paper addresses the lack of risk indicators and weak detection in consortium blockchain technology. Extensive research establishes rational risk indicators for heterogeneous consortium blockchains. Detection methods are proposed, utilizing chaos engineering and lexical/syntax analysis for network/system indicators and smart contracts, respectively. All functionalities are integrated into a scalable, maintainable, and user-friendly tool. However, further exploration is needed to expand technical risk indicators, adapt to more consortium blockchains, and explore efficient risk examination methods.

Acknowledgments. This work was supported in part by the National Key Research and Development Program of China under Grant 2022YFC3302300; in part by the Natural Science Foundation of China under Grant 92046024, Grant 92146002, and Grant 61873309; in part by the Shanghai Science and Technology Project under Grant 22510761000; and in part by the Intel Sponsored Research Agreement under Grant 89533661.

References

1. Guan, C., Ding, D., Guo, J., Teng, Y.: An ecosystem approach to web3.0: a systematic review and research agenda. J. Electron. Bus. Digit. Econ. **2**(1), 139–156 (2023)
2. Rehan, M., Javed, A.R., Kryvinska, N., Gadekallu, T.R., Srivastava, G., Jalil, Z.: Supply chain management using an industrial internet of things hyperledger fabric network. Hum.-Centric Comput. Inf. Sci. **13** (2023)
3. Buterin, V., et al.: A next-generation smart contract and decentralized application platform. White Paper, vol. 3, no. 37, pp. 2–1 (2014)
4. Zheng, P., Zheng, Z., Luo, X.: Park: accelerating smart contract vulnerability detection via parallel-fork symbolic execution. In: Proceedings of the 31st ACM SIGSOFT International Symposium on Software Testing and Analysis, pp. 740–751 (2022)
5. Li, Z., Wang, Y., Wen, S., Ding, Y.: Evil chaincode: APT attacks based on smart contract. In: Xu, G., Liang, K., Su, C. (eds.) FCS 2020. CCIS, vol. 1286, pp. 178–196. Springer, Singapore (2020). https://doi.org/10.1007/978-981-15-9739-8_15
6. La Salle, A., Kumar, A., Jevtić, P., Boscovic, D.: Joint modeling of hyperledger fabric and sybil attack: petri net approach. Simul. Model. Pract. Theory **122**, 102674 (2023)
7. Basiri, A., et al.: Chaos engineering. IEEE Softw. **33**(3), 35–41 (2016)
8. Sondhi, S., Saad, S., Shi, K., Mamun, M., Traore, I.: Chaos engineering for understanding consensus algorithms performance in permissioned blockchains. In: 2021 IEEE International Conference on Dependable, Autonomic and Secure Computing, International Conference on Pervasive Intelligence and Computing, International Conference on Cloud and Big Data Computing, International Conference on Cyber Science and Technology Congress (DASC/PiCom/CBDCom/CyberSciTech), pp. 51–59. IEEE (2021)
9. Zhang, L., Ron, J., Baudry, B., Monperrus, M.: Chaos engineering of ethereum blockchain clients. Distrib. Ledger Technol. Res. Pract. **2**(3), 1–18 (2023)

10. Kassab, A., Rivière, E., Rosinosky, G., Sadre, R., Tran, V.H.: C2B2: a cloud-native chaos benchmarking suite for the hyperledger fabric blockchain. In: 2022 18th European Dependable Computing Conference (EDCC), pp. 89–96. IEEE (2022)
11. Huang, D., Chen, B., Li, L., Ding, Y.: Anomaly detection for consortium blockchains based on machine learning classification algorithm. In: Chellappan, S., Choo, K.-K.R., Phan, N.H. (eds.) CSoNet 2020. LNCS, vol. 12575, pp. 307–318. Springer, Cham (2020). https://doi.org/10.1007/978-3-030-66046-8_25
12. Qian, P., Liu, Z., Yin, Y., He, Q.: Cross-modality mutual learning for enhancing smart contract vulnerability detection on bytecode. In: Proceedings of the ACM Web Conference 2023, pp. 2220–2229 (2023)
13. Yamashita, K., Nomura, Y., Zhou, E., Pi, B., Jun, S.: Potential risks of hyperledger fabric smart contracts. In: 2019 IEEE International Workshop on Blockchain Oriented Software Engineering (IWBOSE), pp. 1–10. IEEE (2019)
14. Lv, P., Wang, Y., Wang, Y., Zhou, Q.: Potential risk detection system of hyperledger fabric smart contract based on static analysis. In: 2021 IEEE Symposium on Computers and Communications (ISCC), pp. 1–7. IEEE (2021)
15. Liu, Z., Qian, P., Wang, X., Zhuang, Y., Qiu, L., Wang, X.: Combining graph neural networks with expert knowledge for smart contract vulnerability detection. IEEE Trans. Knowl. Data Eng. **35**(2), 1296–1310 (2021)
16. Liao, Z., Zheng, Z., Chen, X., Nan, Y.: Smartdagger: a bytecode-based static analysis approach for detecting cross-contract vulnerability. In: Proceedings of the 31st ACM SIGSOFT International Symposium on Software Testing and Analysis, pp. 752–764 (2022)
17. Huang, P., et al.: Highsimb: a concrete blockchain high simulation with contract vulnerability detection for ethereum and hyperledger fabric. In: Xu, Y., Yan, H., Teng, H., Cai, J., Li, J. (eds.) ML4CS 2022. LNCS, vol. 13656, pp. 455–468. Springer, Cham (2022). https://doi.org/10.1007/978-3-031-20099-1_39
18. Forouzan, B.A.: Cryptography & Network Security. McGraw-Hill, Inc., New York (2007)
19. Newman, S.: Building Microservices. O'Reilly Media, Inc., Sebastopol (2021)

Wiki2GH: A Recommendation Service to Link Software Engineering Knowledge to Practical Development

Yuqi Zhou[3], Yanchun Sun[1,2(✉)], Jiawei Wu[1,2], Jiaqi Zhang[1,2], and Gang Huang[1,2,4]

[1] Key Laboratory of High Confidence Software Technologies, Ministry of Education, Beijing, China
{sunyc,jw_wu,zhangjq17,hg}@pku.edu.cn
[2] School of Computer Science, Peking University, Beijing, People's Republic of China
[3] School of Software and Microelectronics, Peking University, Beijing, People's Republic of China
yqzhou@pku.edu.cn
[4] National Key Laboratory of Data Space Technology and System, Beijing, China

Abstract. High-quality software applications are built on the knowledge and best practices of software engineering. However, there is a huge gap between the theoretical knowledge of software engineering and its practical implementation for software developers, especially beginners of software development. This paper proposes an innovative recommendation service named Wiki2GH to link Wikipedia software engineering knowledge to GitHub frameworks and libraries, aiming to help software developers systematically learn knowledge and apply it into practice.

To implement the Wiki2GH recommendation service, this paper first uses the public data of Wikipedia to build a hierarchy software development knowledge catalog as the entrance of the service. Next, we propose a deep learning method to identify frameworks and libraries and construct a knowledge graph of open source software repositories based on dependency graph. Then, we propose a combined application recommendation service of frameworks and libraries in the development practice. The methods proposed in this paper are all evaluated, including the repository type classification method, the recommendation method, and the knowledge graph construction method. Experimental results show the effectiveness of the recommendation service proposed in this paper.

Keywords: Recommendation service · Open source community · Knowledge graph · Deep learning

1 Introduction

The development of high-quality software applications relies on a solid knowledge base and best practices of software engineering. However, there is a large gap between the theoretical software engineering knowledge and its practical implementation in real projects. Although software developers can acquire rich of knowledge from internet platforms such as online encyclopedias, it is difficult to systematically learn software development knowledge and effectively apply the them into practical developments, especially for beginners in software development.

Although there are Wikis and open source communities on the Internet, they cannot combine systematic software development knowledge learning with software development practice. The existing communities have following problems:

1) Existing software development communities lack a combination of software development knowledge with open source software repositories., i.e. lack a combination of theory and practice. Although software developers can learn knowledge points on Wiki websites, they don't know how to apply them in the actual development practice.
2) It is difficult for software development beginners to use the open source software community to systematically learn software development knowledge, especially for beginners. Take GitHub as an example, the website hosts more than 100 million software repositories. Massive open source software repositories lack systematic software development knowledge organization, which is unfriendly and difficult for software development beginners to learn.
3) For existing knowledge learning encyclopedic community such as "Wikipedia", software development beginners can only learn isolated software development knowledge. But in software development practice, a software often requires the use of multi-domain frameworks and libraries. Taking Web development as an example, developers need to be proficient in front-end development, back-end development, database development, and other related fields.

To address this challenge, this paper proposes a recommendation service named Wiki2GH to bridging the gap between software engineering knowledge and practical development. The service consists of five parts: a) constructing a software development knowledge catalog from Wikipedia, b) predicting the types of open source software repositories from GitHub, c) constructing knowledge graphs of open source software repositories, and d) recommending frameworks and libraries for software developers in practical development, e) Web service interface.

To construct a software development knowledge catalog, we utilize public data from Wikipedia. In the part of predicting the types of open source software repositories, we propose a BERT based deep learning approach that achieves high accuracy in repository topic prediction. In the part of constructing the knowledge graphs, we construct the knowledge graphs of open source software repositories according to dependency graphs and repository types. Therefore, we can link the systematic software development knowledge with the open source software project through the link relationship between the software knowledge catalog and the knowledge graph of open source software repositories. Finally, we propose a recommendation method based on a knowledge graph translation model, to recommend top k frameworks and libraries combined to help software developers link software development knowledge with practical applications.

We conduct several experiments to evaluate each method in Wiki2GH service. To evaluate the repository type prediction model, we use precision, recall, and F1 score. To evaluate the effectiveness of combinations recommendation method, we use hit ratio and precision. Furthermore, we analyze the impact of knowledge graph construction methods on recommendation results. Experimental results show that the methods adopted in this paper are effective and reasonable.

The contributions of this paper are as follows:

1) To the best of our knowledge, the recommendation service proposed in this paper is the first to recommend combined application of framework and library repositories in software development practice.
2) As far as we know, this paper constructs a knowledge graph for open source repositories based on dependency graphs. Compared with previous works, our knowledge graph is easier to recommend repositories based on dependency relationships.
3) This paper proposes a prediction model based on Bidirectional Encoder Representations from Transformers (BERT) to predict the framework and library type of a repository, which can achieve high accuracy in repository topic prediction.

2 Related Work

This section reviews the existing literature in three research areas, including knowledge graph construction in open source software communities, recommendation methods on GitHub, and GitHub repository mining.

2.1 Knowledge Graph in Open Source Software Community

In the education research field, Novak et al. further verify the effectiveness of the tool by studying the principles of the "Concept Map" tool [1]. With the development of the Internet, the numbers of online education platforms, online courses are also growing rapidly [2], and the demand for online learning platforms is high. Wang et al. apply the "concept map" tool to online learning and achieve great results [3]. According to the definition, "concept map" is an example under the definition of knowledge graph.

Nowadays, there are many researchers focusing on constructing knowledge graph in knowledge communities such as Wikipedia, Stack Overflow and GitHub. Liang et al. propose the RefD method, which uses machine learning technology to extract the pre-order relationship of concepts from Wikipedia to build a knowledge graph [4]. Wang et al. propose the "XLore" method, which uses the technology of cross-lingual knowledge linking to discover cross-lingual links between entities, and utilizes a larger heterogeneous online wiki to enrich Chinese knowledge [5]. Huang et al. propose the EMRCM knowledge graph framework, which can construct a knowledge graph using various data sources including Wikipedia, textbook corpus, and so on [6]. Yin et al. construct an API knowledge graph by mining discussion posts in Stack Overflow, and provide solutions to the problems faced by API learners [7]. Yin et al. use the GitHub open source repository to propose an open source software knowledge graph based on the internal information of open source software projects [8].

In short, it can be seen that knowledge graph technology plays an important role in both traditional and online education fields, and it can also help software developers especially beginners to better understand the correlation of software development knowledge.

2.2 GitHub Repository Mining

There are many related studies on mining GitHub software repositories, and developer behavior is often considered as a feature. Freira et al. analyze the impact of "Pull Request" activities on software developer sentiment [9]. Rastogi et al. analyze the relationship between the "Pull Request" success rate and the developer's geographic location [10]. Kikas et al. build a model to predict whether an issue will be closed within a given calendar period at different time in the issue life cycle [11] Liao et al. investigate some features of issues to facilitate issue management and software management [12] Some studies have performed repository mining by studying GitHub Commit behaviors. Sinha analyzes the sentiment of software developers through Commit logs [13]. Guzman et al. analyze the sentiment expressed in the commitment reviews of different open source projects based on lexical sentiment analysis techniques [14]. Vasilescu et al. study the interaction between Stack Overflow activity and the development process as reflected in code changes submitted to GitHub [15]. Researchers also analyze other behaviors, including Star, Fork, and Watch, to gain insights into the mining of GitHub repositories [16–18].

Repository README files and source code are also frequently used to mine GitHub repositories. McMillan et al. propose a method based on API usage patterns, named CLAN, for detecting similar software applications [19]. Santos et al. propose a method to identify library experts based on their knowledge generated on GitHub [20]. Zhang et al. propose RepoPal, which detects similar software repositories based on repository README files and GitHub Star et al. [21]. Prana et al. annotate sections in the README file and implement a section-level multi-classifier [22]. Soll et al. propose an ensemble learning algorithm based on software repository README files, languages, file names, etc. [23]. C Sas et al. annotate source code files in a software project by using a weak labelling approach and a subsequent hierarchical aggregation [24].

From the related work, it can be seen that the researches on GitHub repositories mining often take developers' behavior and repositories' information as important features. There is seldom support for the unexperienced software development beginners.

2.3 GitHub Recommendation Methods

The current related work of GitHub recommendation methods mainly focuses on two parts, one of which is to provide recommendation services around software developers by focusing on the development activities of software repositories. H. Kagdi et al. [25], M. Linares-Vasquez et al. [26] and Xia et al. [27] recommend new bug reports to developers for review via their GitHub public information. Yu et al. [28] and Rahman et al. [29] help the development of open source projects by mining the technical capabilities of software developers and recommending suitable Pull Request reviewers to developers. N. Nalini et al. build a recommendation system that suggests relevant repositories for users to contribute to on Github by utilizing the user's past activity [30].

Another part of the GitHub recommendation service research focuses on mining the characteristics of software developers and providing them with project-level recommendation services for open source software projects. Sharma et al. [31] propose a user collaborative filtering algorithm that uses developer attributes (including company, location, etc.) to recommend software repositories. Pearson correlation coefficient and cosine similarity are applied to GitHub data to identify and cross-check similar users on GitHub. Liu et al. extract 9 features from developer information, build a neural network-based recommender system named NNLRank to rank candidate software items [32]. Xu et al. propose a method for recommending related software projects on the GitHub platform by considering developer behavior as well as software project characteristics (extracted from description documents and source code) [33]. Zhou et al. use GitHub's themes to generate a latent vector of software developers' development preferences, and recommend GitHub's trending open source software projects for software developers [34]. Xiao et al. propose RecGFI to recommend of good first issues in GitHub to newcomers [35].

At present, the project-level recommendation service for open source software projects aims at software developers with development experience, so it is difficult to help beginners who lack of software development knowledge and experience.

3 Overview of Recommendation Service

Figure 1 shows the architecture of the Wiki2GH service proposed in this paper. It consists of following parts: a) constructing a software development knowledge catalog, b) predicting the types of open source software repositories, c) constructing knowledge graphs of open source software repositories, d) recommending combined application of frameworks and libraries for developers, e) Web service interface.

3.1 Constructing a Software Development Knowledge Catalog

To help software developers, especially beginners, systematically learn software development knowledge and apply them in practice, we can first utilize the systematic software knowledge in online encyclopedias. In this part, we construct a software development knowledge catalog from the online encyclopedia Wikipedia. The construction process consists of two parts: 1) Data collection; 2) Catalog Construction.

Data Collection: Considering that the online encyclopedias provide rich and structured software development knowledge content, Wikipedia is the largest online encyclopedias with more than 10 million knowledge entries and 100 million daily views. Therefore, in this paper, we utilize the public data available on Wikipedia's "Contents" page to construct a software development knowledge catalog. On the "Contents" page, Wikipedia organizes knowledge by subject categories for users to browse. For items on the "Contents" page, there are usually two types of subsidiaries: categories and pages. Page type items usually correspond to specific software knowledge. Category type items usually correspond to more general software development knowledge that contains other category items and page items (Fig. 2).

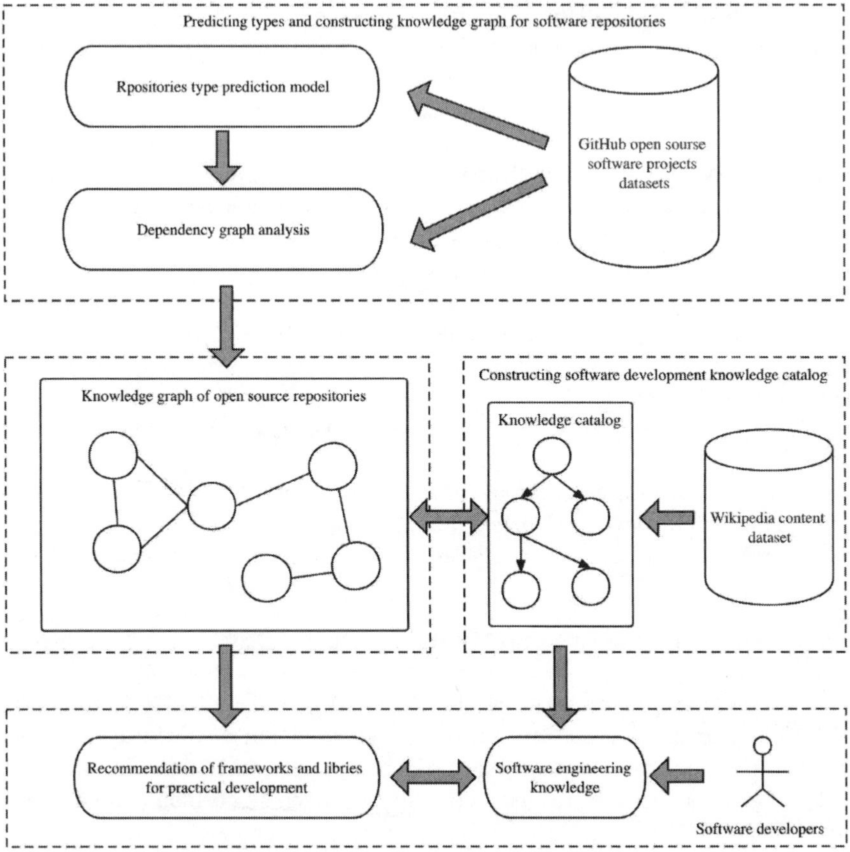

Fig. 1. The architecture of the Wiki2GH service.

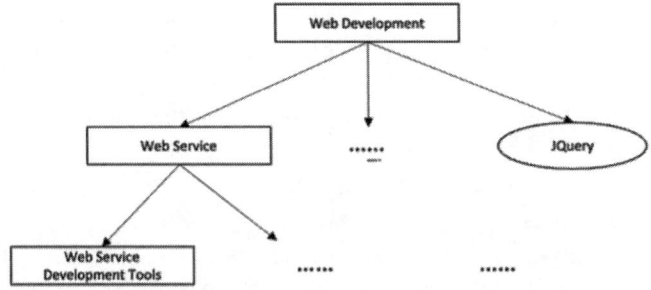

Fig. 2. An example of software engineering knowledge catalog.

Catalog Construction: In the "Contents" page of Wikipedia, knowledge is organized according to subject categories. By analyzing the URL links contained in the "Contents" page of "Software Engineering" subject, a software development knowledge catalog with natural tree structure can be constructed. In this tree-structure catalog, each leaf node represents a specific software development knowledge point and each non-leaf node represents a sub-category under "Software Engineering" subject.

Because of a large amount of knowledge items under the category are irrelevant to software development, this paper prunes the tree-structured software development knowledge catalog by manual selection. Finally, this paper builds a software development knowledge catalog containing 50,000 nodes, including 5,000 categories nodes and 45,000 knowledge nodes.

3.2 Predicting Types for Open Source Software Repositories

One goal of this paper is to provide the combined application recommendation service of frameworks and libraries for software developers, especially beginners. Therefore, this paper proposes a prediction model based on BERT to predict whether a repository is framework and library or not. The prediction process includes three parts:

Data Collection: Considering that almost all open source software repositories in GitHub contain descriptive text and "README" text, this paper uses the descriptive text to label the repositories, and uses the "README" text to train the model.

This paper automatically labels the dataset based on the keywords in the description text of the open source software repositories. For example, once the description text of a repository contains keywords like "Library" or "Framework", that repository will be labeled as the type of framework and library. However, the automatically labeling process may have errors, so manual verification is also adopted.

Finally, this paper collects all public event records from January 2020 to June 2020 through GH Archive and GitHub Rest API tools, and 14,000 labeled datasets are finally obtained for subsequent model training.

Data Preprocessing: Before model training, we preprocess the "Readme" text of repositories in the labeled datasets. Since the Markdown format in the "Readme" text is difficult to remove, this paper uses the "markdown" library in Python to convert the Markdown format into HTML format. Then, this paper uses "BeautifulSoup" library to identify and remove HTML format. Next, this paper removes URL links based on regular expression and finally uses "NTLK" tool to remove stop words in "Readme".

Framework and Library Prediction Model: After data preprocessing, the "Readme" text of GitHub open source software repository is inputted into the prediction model for training. The architecture of the prediction model is shown in Fig. 3.

In order to generate a document-level vector representation, this paper first inputs the "Readme" text into the model. For every input text, this paper adds character '[CLS]' to the head and character '[SEP]' to the tail. After BERT embedding layer, we get a set of token-level vector, and this paper regards the vector of first character '[CLS]' as the representation of the repository. Then we put that vector into fully-connected layer and sigmoid layer for the classification task.

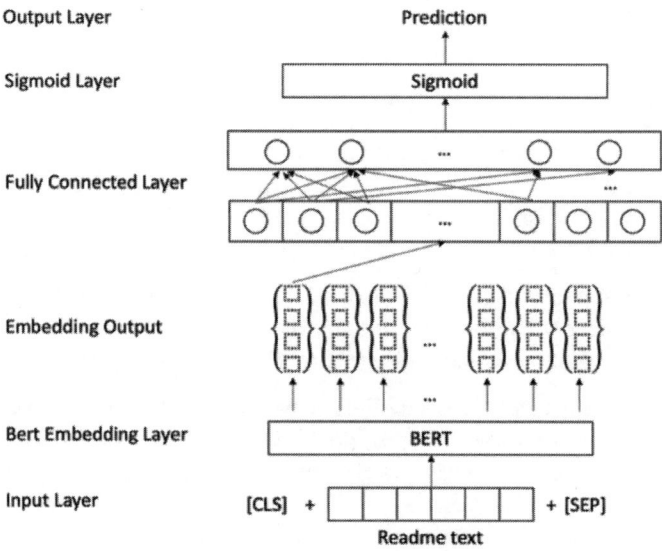

Fig. 3. The architecture of predicting model.

3.3 Constructing Knowledge Graph of Open Source Software Repositories

In the Wiki2GH service proposed in this paper, the premise of providing recommendation method for developers in software development is to construct a knowledge graph of open source software repositories. The construction process includes two parts:

Scheme Definition: This paper designs two types of entities and four types of relationships. The first type of entities is "framework/library project", meaning a repository that acts as a development framework or library. The other is "other project", meaning repositories that are not frameworks or libraries. The relationship types are introduced in Table 1.

Knowledge Graph Construction: This paper builds a new GitHub repository dataset to construct knowledge graphs. The size of the dataset depends on the software development knowledge catalog to better express the knowledge embedding vectors of open source software repositories in subsequent training.

Table 1. Relation Types of the Knowledge Graph.

Relation types	Type meanings
Dependent_OF	A *project* repository depends on a *framework/library* repository
Dependent_FF	A *framework/library* repository depends on a *framework/library* repository
Dependent_FO	A *framework/library* repository depends on a *project* repository
Dependent_OO	A *project* repository depends on a *project* repository

GitHub generates dependency graphs for open source software repositories. According to the official document description, GitHub obtains the *Dependency Repositories* and *Dependent Repositories* through the manifest files, lock file and some other files in a specific open source software repository. For example, as for Flask, "kapi2410/twitter-bot" is a dependent repository and "pallets/jin" is exposed as a dependency.

In order to explain the construction of the open source project knowledge graph and subsequent experiments, this paper defines repositories as follows:

- *Direct Repository*: a repository that can directly link to the software development knowledge catalog.
- *Dependent Repository*: a repository depends on one or more *Direct Repository*.
- *Dependency Repository*: a repository that is depended by a *Direct Repository* or a *Dependent Repository*.

In the construction of knowledge graph, for each *Direct Repository*, this paper selects all the *Dependency Repositories* and a part of *Dependent Repositories* as the entities. The reason why *Dependent Repositories* are not all selected is because a *Direct Repository* of frameworks and libraries may be depended on by millions of *Dependent Repositories*, it is impractical to obtain all of them to construct the knowledge graph. This paper selects a certain number of *Dependent Repositories* to construct the knowledge graph by sampling them from each *Direct Repository* and sorting them through the stars. After selecting the, this paper builds the relationship according to the dependencies between the open source software repositories, and finally completes the construction.

3.4 A Recommendation Method Based on TransD

When new libraries or frameworks are introduced to software developers through the software development knowledge catalog, combined recommendation of libraries and frameworks commonly used in practical development will be generated. This recommendation process is consistent with the overall goal of our paper, which is to bridge the gap between software engineering knowledge and practical development.

The TransD model is implemented on an open source software knowledge graph to generate knowledge embeddings for each repository. By training a knowledge graph, the dependency relations between repositories can be captured to identify frameworks and libraries that are easier to combine in practice. An offline computing method is used in the knowledge graph, and the knowledge embedding vector of each entity and relation is retrained whenever the knowledge graph is updated.

After calculating the knowledge embedding vectors of the open source software repositories, a suitable measurement method is needed to calculate the similarity between them. In this paper, Pearson correlation coefficient is used for experiments, it can be used to measure the similarity between users in recommendation systems. The calculation formula is as follows:

$$Pearson\ similarity = \frac{\sum_{i=1}^{n}(x_i - \bar{x})(y - \bar{y})}{\sqrt{\sum_{i=1}^{n}(x_i - \bar{x})^2 \sum_{i=1}^{n}(y_i - \bar{y})^2}} \qquad (1)$$

After selecting the similarity calculation method, the frameworks and libraries in dependence repositories in the knowledge graph can be reordered by the similarity ranking of knowledge embedding. This paper will recommend top-k frameworks and libraries for software developers.

3.5 Web Service Interface

After implementing the methods above, this paper designs and implements the Wiki2GH service as a Web service. The Web service contains two pages: knowledge catalog page and development recommendation page. The knowledge catalog page is shown in Fig. 4(a). When enter the knowledge catalog page, software developers can systematically learn software development knowledge from the root node of the knowledge catalog by clicking the "Explore" button. When developers select a specific node of the interested software development knowledge and click the "Details" button, users can get combined recommendation of libraries and framework commonly used in practical development in the recommendation results page which is shown in Fig. 4(b).

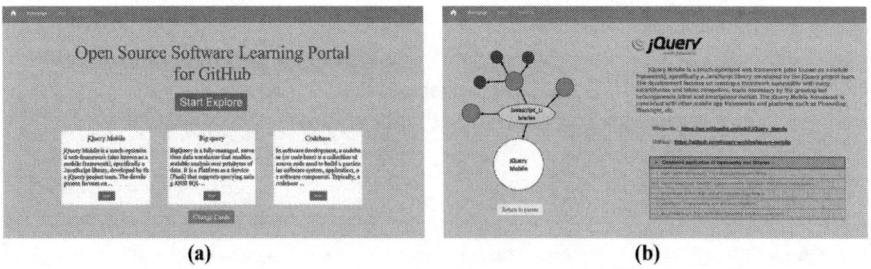

Fig. 4. (a) The software engineering knowledge catalog entrance page of the recommendation system. (b) The recommendation result page of frameworks and libraries for software developers.

4 Evaluations

This section mainly evaluates the effectiveness of the Wiki2GH recommendation service proposed in this paper. Considering Wikipedia naturally involves the systematic and comprehensive knowledge of software development, we only need to evaluate the effectiveness of the recommendation method and the construction process of the recommendation method. The evaluation process includes three parts: 1) evaluation of the repository prediction model, 2) evaluation of the TransD-based recommendation method, and 3) evaluation of the knowledge graph construction method.

4.1 Evaluation of the Repository Prediction Model

The evaluation of the type prediction model consists of the following three parts.

Design of Comparative Experiments: In this paper, 13472 open-source software repositories with labels are prepared for training and validating the prediction model. The dataset is divided into training set and testing set according to the ratio of 9:1. In order to verify the effectiveness of the prediction model in this paper, five traditional machine learning models are selected to predict the type of the software repositories.

Experimental Implementation: In the software project type identification model based on deep learning, the pretraining model of the BERT layer uses the "bert-base-uncased" model in the Transformers toolkit provided by Hugging Face.

In the comparative experiment, this paper uses the TF-IDF method to generate document vectors for the "README" text of repositories, and then uses the Singular Value Decomposition (SVD) method to reduce the dimensions of the document vectors.

Results & Analysis: Precision, recall and F1 score are used to evaluate the prediction model. Table 2 shows the experimental results that the BERT-based deep learning open source software project type identification model can accurately predict whether a repository is a framework and library type. Compared with the traditional machine learning models, the BERT-based model has significant performance in terms of precision, recall and F1 scores.

Table 2. Results of type prediction model.

	Precision	Recall	F1
Decision Tree	0.744	0.683	0.712
Random Forest	0.653	0.590	0.620
AdaBoost	0.803	0.765	0.784
GBDY	0.819	0.829	0.824
XGBoost	0.825	0.799	0.812
BERT	**0.906**	**0.938**	**0.922**

4.2 Evaluation of TransD-Based Recommendation Method

The evaluation of the recommendation method includes following five parts.

Evaluation Method: In order to evaluate the effectiveness of the TransD-based recommendation, this paper designs an evaluation method with Ground-Truth.

Based on the knowledge graph construction method in this paper, the knowledge graph of open source software repositories is constructed using 35 *Dependent Repositories* and all *Dependency Repositories* of each *Direct Repository*.

The selected *Dependent Repositories* are divided into a training set and a test set in a ratio of 4:1. After the training, this paper recommends Top-K frameworks and libraries with the highest ranking of knowledge embedding similarity. In the test set, each *Dependent Repository* has at least one *Direct Repository*, we can think those *Dependent Repository* as the open source software projects that software developers can develop. Therefore, the effectiveness of the recommendation method can be evaluated by comparing combined application of frameworks and libraries for each *Direct Repositories* to the *Dependency Repository* of each *Dependent Repository* in the test set.

Comparative Experiments: The comparative experiment consists of two parts: comparative experiment of different similarity calculations and the comparative experiment of different knowledge embedding models of the recommendation method.

In the comparative experiment of different similarity calculation methods, this paper chooses the similarity calculations methods by comparing the results of the TransD-based recommendation methods. Similarity calculations include cosine similarity, Euclidean distance and Pearson correlation coefficient.

In the comparative experiment of different recommendation methods, we compare the results when using different knowledge embedding models, including TransE, TransH, TransR and TransD. Since there is no previous research work on combined application recommendation of frameworks and libraries, in addition to comparing random recommendation, this paper designs a heuristic method as a baseline. The heuristic method considers the description text of a repository, which involves semantic information about the functionality and usage of the repository. Therefore, this paper adopts the unsupervised algorithm doc2vec as a baseline to train knowledge embeddings of software repositories.

Experimental Implementation: For the knowledge embedding training, this paper uses the open source knowledge embedding framework OpenKE to train the TransE model, TransH model, TransR model and TransD model. In the heuristic experiment, this paper uses the gensim library of Python for the implementation of doc2vec.

Metric Selection: We choose precision and hit rate as an evaluation metric. Hit rate is a common metric to measure the recall rate of Top-K recommendations. For the test set R, the formula for calculating the hit rate is as follows:

$$HR@K = \frac{\sum_{r \in R} I(TP)}{|R|} \qquad (2)$$

In the formula, the I function is set as the indicator function. When TP is greater than 0, it takes 1, and when TP is 0, it takes 0.

Results & Analysis: Table 3 shows the results of the recommendation method using different similarity calculation methods. The results show that cosine similarity and Pearson correlation coefficient are much better than Euclidean similarity. Considering that the Pearson correlation coefficient is slightly better than the cosine similarity, this paper will use the Pearson correlation coefficient as the similarity calculation method.

The precision and hit ratio results of the recommendation method comparison experiment are shown in Table 4 and Table 5. The experimental results show that the recommendation method on TransD based works best. The performance of heuristic is better than that of random recommendation method, which verifies the effectiveness of this heuristic method. Therefore, this paper chooses TransD as the knowledge embedding model, and finally implements it on the recommendation method of the service proposed in this paper.

Table 3. Results of different similarity measurements

	Cosine		Euclidean		Pearson	
	Hit Ratio	Precision	Hit Ratio	Precision	Hit Ratio	Precision
Top 3	0.658	0.409	0.562	0.316	**0.665**	**0.419**
Top 5	0.730	0.380	0.609	0.283	**0.770**	**0.402**
Top 8	0.773	**0.366**	0.630	0.263	**0.792**	0.359
Top 10	0.791	**0.363**	0.643	0.254	**0.798**	0.356
Top 12	0.804	**0.357**	0.652	0.240	**0.813**	0.340
Top 15	0.811	**0.338**	0.655	0.220	**0.822**	0.324

Table 4. Precision of different similarity calculation methods

	TransE	TransH	TransR	TransD	Doc2Vec	Random
Top 3	0.419	0.391	0.387	**0.419**	0.076	0.005
Top 5	0.382	0.381	0.378	**0.402**	0.054	0.005
Top 8	0.357	0.361	**0.364**	0.359	0.035	0.005
Top 10	0.350	0.341	0.347	**0.356**	0.032	0.004
Top 12	0.337	0.335	0.332	**0.340**	0.028	0.003
Top 15	0.323	0.322	0.322	**0.324**	0.026	0.003

Table 5. Hit ratio of different similarity calculation methods

	TransE	TransH	TransR	TransD	Doc2Vec	Random
Top 3	0.645	0.636	0.646	**0.665**	0.186	0.015
Top 5	0.735	0.733	0.736	**0.770**	0.196	0.025
Top 8	0.774	**0.795**	0.789	0.792	0.202	0.040
Top 10	0.787	0.798	0.791	**0.798**	0.217	0.040
Top 12	0.796	0.811	0.798	**0.813**	0.243	0.040
Top 15	0.807	0.813	0.807	**0.822**	0.258	0.050

4.3 Evaluation of Knowledge Graph Constructing Method

The evaluation of knowledge graph constructing method includes three parts:

Comparative Experiments: The construction of the knowledge graph is mainly affected by the selection number of *Dependent Repositories* for each *Direct Repository*. As the number of *Dependent Repositories* changes, the total number of *Dependency Repositories* in the knowledge graph changes. This paper first compares the recommendation method results based on different numbers of *Dependent Repositories* selected. Then polynomial regression is used to analyze the change function and speed function of the total number of *Dependency Repositories* in the knowledge graph. The result shows the rationality of the choice of the number of *Dependent Repositories*.

Experimental Implementation: This paper uses OpenKE framework to construct a knowledge graph and train the knowledge embedding of entities, uses Python's scipy toolkit in function fitting, and uses Python's sympy toolkit for derivation calculation.

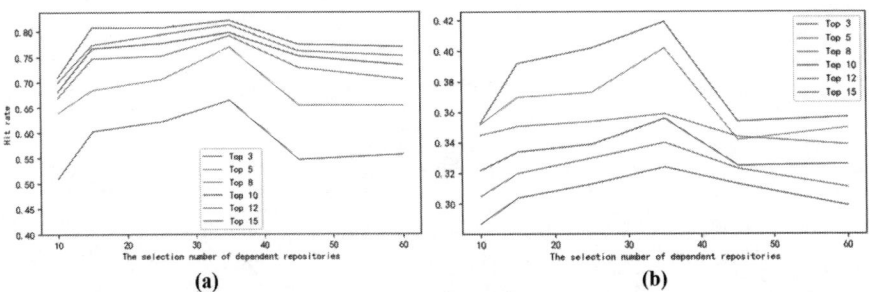

Fig. 5. (a) Hit rate of recommendation service when selecting different number of *Dependent Repositories*. (b) Precision of recommendation service when selecting different number of *Dependent Repositories*

Results & Analysis: The evaluation experiment firstly compares the recommendation results when selecting different number of *Dependent Repositories*. The results of hit rate and precision are shown in Fig. 5(a) and Fig. 5(b) respectively. It shows that the recommendation method achieves the best performance when 35 *Dependent Repositories* are selected for each *Direct Repository*. With the number of *Dependent Repositories* increases, the hit rate and precision of the recommendation method first rises, then falls.

In the evaluation experiment of polynomial regression, this paper first collects the changes of the *Dependency Repositories* in knowledge graph when selecting different number of *Dependent Repositories*. In the following, this paper defines the selection number of *Dependent Repositories* for each *Direct Repository* as x, the change function of the total number of *Dependency Repositories* in the knowledge graph as y(x), and the speed function of the total number of Dependency Repositories in the knowledge graph as v(x). In order to better analyze the function of y(x), this paper uses a fourth-order polynomial to fit the function. The formula of the polynomial is as follows:

$$y(x) = a*x^4 + b*x^3 + c*x^2 + d*x + e \tag{3}$$

Through fitting, this paper finally obtains a fitting function with parameter a of -0.002, parameter b of 0.345, parameter c of -20.035, parameter d of 755.922, parameter e of 3918.13. The original function and fitted function are shown in Fig. 6.

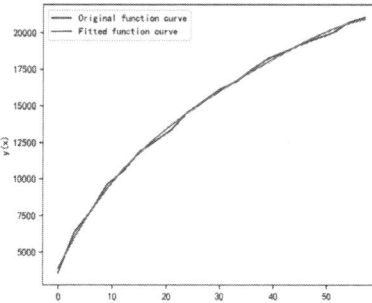

Fig. 6. The change function y(x) of the total number of Dependency Repositories

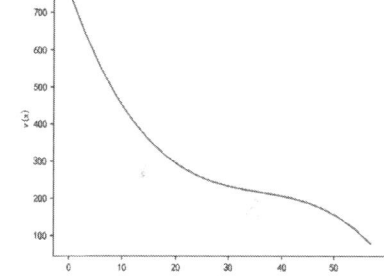

Fig. 7. The speed function v(x) of the total number of Dependency Repositories

This paper obtains the speed function $v(x)$ by calculating derivation of $y(x)$. The function curve of $v(x)$ is shown in Fig. 7. By analyzing the $v(x)$ function, it can be known that the function has an inflection point. By calculating, $x = 35.8$ is the inflection point of the function $v(x)$. According to the definition of the inflection point, when x takes the value of the inflection point, the change speed of $v(x)$ is the most stable.

By analyzing the concave-convexity of the $v(x)$, when $x < 35.8$, selection number for each *Direct Repository* is less than the inflection point, so the decreasing trend of $v(x)$ decreases, indicates that there are additional *Dependency Repository* increments, but the increments are getting smaller gradually. When $x > 35.8$, the selection number for each *Direct Repository* is greater than the inflection point of $v(x)$, the decreasing trend of $v(x)$ increases at this time, indicating that there are almost no additional increments of *Dependency Repositories* in the knowledge graph.

Combined with the above results, we can see that the recommendation service matches the expectation of polynomial analysis experiment. The recommendation service has the best results when selecting approximately 35 of *Dependent Repositories*. The polynomial regression experiment provides theoretical support for the construction method of knowledge graph of open source software projects in this paper.

5 Conclusion and Future Work

In conclusion, this paper proposes a new Wiki2GH service to address the challenge of systematically learn software development knowledge and effectively applying software engineering knowledge in practical developments. By using software engineering knowledge from Wikipedia and practical examples from GitHub repositories, the proposed recommendation service offers a promising avenue for software developers especially beginners, to enhance their capabilities and achieve better results in their software development projects.

In order to better improve the Wiki2GH service proposed in this paper, we plan to do improvements in the future: 1) optimize the recommendation method to improve the performance of the recommendation method for the combined application of framework and library repositories; 2) extend the entity and relationship types of open source software projects to provide more recommendation types for developers in software development.

Acknowledgement. This effort is sponsored by the National Key Research and Development Program of China under Grant No. 2023YFF0616901.

References

1. Novak, J.D., Cañas, A.J.: The theory underlying concept maps and how to construct them. Florida Institute for Human and Machine Cognition, p. 1 (2006)
2. Kang, Y.: An analysis on SPOC: post-MOOC era of online education. Res. Educ. Tsinghua Univ. **35**(1), 85–93 (2014)
3. Wang, S., Ororbia, A., Wu, Z., et al.: Using prerequisites to extract concept maps from textbooks. In: Proceedings of the 25th ACM International on Conference on Information and Knowledge Management, pp. 317–326 (2016)
4. Liang, C., Wu, Z., Huang, W., et al.: Measuring prerequisite relations among concepts. In: Proceedings of the 2015 Conference on Empirical Methods in Natural Language Processing, pp. 1668–1674 (2015)
5. Wang, Z., Li, J., Wang, Z., et al.: XLore: a large-scale English-Chinese bilingual knowledge graph. In: International Semantic Web Conference (Posters & Demos), vol. 1035, pp. 121–124 (2013)
6. Huang, X., Liu, Q., Wang, C., et al.: Constructing educational concept maps with multiple relationships from multi-source data. In: 2019 IEEE International Conference on Data Mining (ICDM), pp. 1108–1113. IEEE (2019)
7. Yin, H., Zheng, Y., Sun, Y., et al.: An API learning service for inexperienced developers based on API knowledge graph. In: 2021 IEEE International Conference on Web Services (ICWS), pp. 251–261. IEEE (2021)

8. Yin, H., Sun, Z., Sun, Y., et al.: Automatic learning path recommendation for open source projects using deep learning on knowledge graphs. In: Proceedings of 2021 IEEE 45th Annual Computers, Software, and Applications Conference (COMPSAC). IEEE (2021)
9. Freira, M., Caetano, J., Oliveira, J., et al.: Analyzing the impact of feedback in GitHub on the software developer's mood. In: 2018 International Conference on Software Engineering & Knowledge Engineering (2018)
10. Rastogi, A., Nagappan, N., Gousios, G., van der Hoek, A.: Relationship between geographical location and evaluation of developer contributions in github. In: Proceedings of the 12th ACM/IEEE International Symposium on Empirical Software Engineering and Measurement, ESEM 2018, pp. 22:1–22:8. ACM, New York (2018)
11. Kikas, R., Dumas, M., Pfahl, D.: Using dynamic and contextual features to predict issue lifetime in GitHub projects. In: Mining Software Repositories. ACM (2016)
12. Liao, Z., Dayu, H., Chen, Z., et al.: Exploring the characteristics of issue- related behaviors in GitHub using visualization techniques. IEEE Access **6**, 24003–24015 (2018)
13. Sinha, V., Lazar, A., Sharif, B.: Analyzing developer sentiment in commit logs. In: Proceedings of MSR 2016 (2016)
14. Guzman, E., Azócar, D., Li, Y.: Sentiment analysis of commit comments in GitHub: an empirical study. In: Mining Software Repositories (2014)
15. Vasilescu, B., Filkov, V., Serebrenik, A.: StackOverflow and GitHub: associations between software development and crowdsourced knowledge. In: International Conference on Social Computing. IEEE (2013)
16. Ma, W., Lin, C., Zhang, X., et al.: How do developers fix cross-project correlated bugs? A case study on the GitHub scientific python ecosystem. In: 2017 IEEE/ACM 39th International Conference on Software Engineering (ICSE). ACM (2017)
17. Kalliamvakou, E., et al.: The promises and perils of mining GitHub. In: MSR. ACM (2014)
18. Tsay, J.T., Dabbish, L., Herbsleb, J.: Social media and success in open source projects. In: Proceedings of Computer Supported Cooperative Work Companion, pp. 223–226 (2012)
19. Mcmillan, C., Grechanik, M., Poshyvanyk, D.: Detecting similar software applications. In: Proceedings - International Conference on Software Engineering (2012)
20. Santos, A., Souza, M., Oliveira, J., Figueiredo, E.: Mining software repositories to identify library experts. In: Proceedings of the VII Brazilian Symposium on Software Components, Architectures, and Reuse, SBCARS 2018, pp. 83–91. ACM, New York (2018)
21. Yun, Z., Lo, D., Kochhar, P.S., et al.: Detecting similar repositories on GitHub. In: IEEE International Conference on Software Analysis. IEEE (2017)
22. Prana, G., Treude, C., Thung, F., et al.: Categorizing the content of GitHub README files. Empirical Softw. Eng. **24**, 1296–1327 (2018)
23. Soll, M., Vosgerau, M.: ClassifyHub: an algorithm to classify GitHub repositories. In: Joint German/Austrian Conference on Artificial Intelligence (Künstliche Intelligenz) (2017)
24. Sas, C., Capiluppi, A.: Multi-granular software annotation using file-level weak labelling. Empir. Softw. Eng. **29**(1), 12 (2024)
25. Anvik, J., Hiew, L., Murphy, G.C.: Who should fix this bug? In: 28th International Conference on Software Engineering (ICSE 2006), Shanghai, China, 20–28 May 2006 (2006)
26. Linares-Vasquez, M., Hossen, K., Dang, H., et al.: Triaging incoming change requests: bug or commit history, or code authorship?. IEEE Computer Society, pp. 451–460 (2012)
27. Xia, X., Lo, D., Wang, X., et al.: Accurate developer recommendation for bug resolution. In: 2013 20th Working Conference on Reverse Engineering (WCRE). IEEE (2013)
28. Yue, Y.: Reviewer recommender of pull-requests in GitHub. In: IEEE International Conference on Software Maintenance & Evolution. IEEE (2014)
29. Rahman, M.M., Roy, C.K., Collins, J.A.: CORRECT: code reviewer recommendation in GitHub based on cross-project and technology experience. In: 38th International Conference on Software Engineering (ICSE). IEEE (2016)

30. Nalini, N., Rishabh, S., Bhat, B.D., et al.: Github recommendation system and user analytics. In: 2023 9th International Conference on Smart Computing and Communications (ICSCC), pp. 582–587. IEEE (2023)
31. Sharma, S., Mahajan, A.: A Collaborative Filtering Recommender System for Github (2017)
32. Liu, C., Yang, D., Zhang, X., et al.: Recommending GitHub projects for developer onboarding. IEEE Access **6**, 52082–52094 (2018)
33. Xu, W.Y., Sun, X.B., Xia, X., et al.: Scalable relevant project recommendation on GitHub. In: Proceedings of the 9th Asia-Pacific Symposium on Internetware, Shanghai (2017)
34. Zhou, Y., Wu, J., Sun, Y.: GHTRec: a personalized service to recommend GitHub trending repositories for developers. In: 2021 IEEE International Conference on Web Services (ICWS), pp. 314–323. IEEE (2021)
35. Xiao, W., He, H., Xu, W., et al.: Recommending good first issues in github OSS projects. In: Proceedings of the 44th International Conference on Software Engineering, pp. 1830–1842 (2022)

Author Index

B
Bao, Yubing   188

C
Chen, Jia   3, 46
Chen, Pengyang   14
Cui, Huihui   73

D
Deng, Ruijun   188
Deng, Yuan   136
Ding, Ming   122
Duan, Qiang   136, 188

G
Gao, Deyun   46
Gao, Shuai   3
Gu, Mingyu   136, 188
Guan, Qiao   174
Guo, Hengqi   136
Guo, Zhiwei   14

H
He, Ting   63
Hu, Shijing   136
Huang, Gang   203
Huang, Xu   3, 46

K
Kang, Guosheng   88

L
Li, Weiping   107
Li, Wen   88
Li, Ziyu   107
Liang, Zhihao   73

Liao
Liao, Chenxi   3, 46
Liao, Yongxin   63
Lin, Junxiong   188
Liu, Jiadi   14
Liu, Jianxun   88
Liu, Jing   136, 188
Liu, Jingjing   46
Liu, Jinlan   174
Liu, Lincong   153
Liu, Shang   3, 46
Liu, Shijun   153
Liu, Zihao   88
Lu, Jixiang   30
Lu, Zhihui   136, 188
Lyu, Yiming   73

M
Ma, Chuan   122
Mao, Sheng   188
Mao, Yingzhe   63
Mo, Tong   107

N
Nie, Yamei   88

P
Pan, Li   153
Peng, Zhenlian   88

Q
Qian, Dongsheng   3, 46
Qian, Yuwen   122

R
Ren, Hongshuai 88

S
Song, Bingyu 73
Sun, Hongliang 174
Sun, Yanchun 203

T
Tu, Zhiying 73, 107

W
Wang, Feifei 174
Wang, Meng 174
Wang, Quyuan 14
Wang, Shuang 30
Wang, Ying 14
Wei, Kang 122

Wu, Jiawei 203
Wu, Shuchi 122

X
Xing, Yongchao 73
Xiong, Yifeng 63

Y
Yang, Jirui 136
Yang, Jiyun 122
Yang, Weipan 73

Z
Zhang, He 30
Zhang, Jiaqi 203
Zhang, Yueyou 30
Zhou, Yuqi 203
Zhu, Wenlong 63

Made in the USA
Monee, IL
03 May 2026

49453299R00131